Reviving Citizen Engagement

Policies to Renew National Community

Books by Larry N. Gerston

Reviving Citizen Engagement: Policies to Renew National Community, 2015

Not So Golden After All: The Rise and Fall of California, 2012

Confronting Reality, 2009

American Federalism: A Concise Introduction, 2007

Recall: California's Political Earthquake (with Terry Christensen), 2004

Public Policy Making in a Democratic Society: A Guide to Civic Engagement, 2002

Public Policy Making: Process and Principles, 1997

American Government: Politics, Process, and Policies, 1993

California Politics and Government: A Practical Approach (with Terry Christensen), 1991

The Deregulated Society (with Cynthia Fraleigh and Robert Schwab), 1987

The California Connection: Politics in the Golden State (with Terry Christensen), 1984

Making Public Policy: From Conflict to Resolution, 1983

Reviving Citizen Engagement

Policies to Renew National Community

Larry N. Gerston

CRC Press
Taylor & Francis Group
Boca Raton London New York

CRC Press is an imprint of the
Taylor & Francis Group, an **informa** business

CRC Press
Taylor & Francis Group
6000 Broken Sound Parkway NW, Suite 300
Boca Raton, FL 33487-2742

© 2015 by Taylor & Francis Group, LLC
CRC Press is an imprint of Taylor & Francis Group, an Informa business

No claim to original U.S. Government works

Printed on acid-free paper
Version Date: 20141020

International Standard Book Number-13: 978-1-4822-3176-2 (Hardback)

Visit the Taylor & Francis Web site at
http://www.taylorandfrancis.com

and the CRC Press Web site at
http://www.crcpress.com

For Lee Daniel Gerston and Rachel Sarah Gerston:

Each building community in your own

way and making the world a better place

Contents

SECTION I   Detached Spirit

SECTION III   A Tale of Two Economies

Preface

Democracies function on terms far different from societies ruled by arbitrary force. Instead of outright physical domination by authoritarian regimes, democracies depend on the consent, cooperation, and commitment of the citizens for their existence. Over the past 240 years, the United States has differed from most nations because of a democratic framework dependent upon citizen allegiance and belief that public officials consider articulated needs.

This efficaciousness linchpin stands as a critical component to American life. In a democracy, the role of citizens is as important as the conditions under which leaders govern, for through their participation, citizens confer legitimacy on the government and its leaders. We rarely agree on everything government does, but we champion the process under which it operates. That's how democracies succeed.

But what happens if "the system" breaks down? What occurs if citizens no longer feel connected to the political system and the rules under which it operates? When the linkage between citizens and their government weakens, the democracy in which they live is threatened, no matter how strong its original foundation, no matter how sacred the rules, no matter how it outwardly appears to the rest of the world. This weakened relationship is the subject of *Reviving Citizen Engagement: Policies to Renew National Community.*

You see, American society is on the verge of uncoupling the sacred linkage between the governed and the governors, and the causes are as worrisome as the possible severance. It's not because of a foreign attack or devious domestic revolutionary plot. Nor is it due to a particular election, sudden political movement, or changing global landscape. Rather, our potential unraveling stems from Americans losing faith in their country and its promise.

Large numbers no longer believe that this society is a just society, where everyone has a fair shot at achieving success. They no longer concern themselves with the collective good because they don't feel part of it. Instead, many Americans increasingly believe that the system has been commandeered by powerful individuals and organizations that care only about their personal power and accumulation of resources. These disaffected citizens feel removed from government, the supposedly neutral institution that was designed to protect individuals from inequities and mistreatment. Just like the troubling cracks in a building's cement foundation extend in a spiderweb-like fashion, the cracks in American society are spreading throughout the nation's political underpinning. And the more unstable our society becomes, the less that its citizens want to be part of it. They're fed up.

But how is this happening? The causes of our unraveling are complex and not always easy to see. Opportunities are availed to some groups more than others, conferring incredible advantages for them. Segregated communities provide superior educations for the affluent members of society, leaving minorities without the same opportunities. In the workplace, women, minorities, and other groups lack the same upward mobility as white males, despite similar training and skill sets. The gaps between the "haves" and "have-nots" grow every day; those who succeed are too busy to look back, while those at the bottom are discouraged from looking ahead.

Corporations, the once-prized cornerstone of the nation's capitalist economy, have abandoned their loyalty to country—at least *this* country. Sure, they are "American" in terms of tax breaks, protection of intellectual property, and security from terrorist threats to corporate installations and factories abroad. But when it comes to employment opportunities and pension benefits, they have different values, shifting labor where the deal is best for their bottom line—often anywhere but the United States. And most of their vast resources abroad, upwards of $2 trillion, remain offshore, protected from American taxes. For so many of the largest corporate interests, there is no relationship between what they get and what they are obligated to give. They are loyal only to their bottom lines.

Government institutions, once viewed as guarantors of a strong political and economic foundation, have either abandoned or watered down core responsibilities, such as public education, care for the poor and elderly, and attention to infrastructure. Rhetoric notwithstanding, elected officials these days tend to be much more reactive than proactive, coddling the privileged, minimizing attention for the neediest, and responding to private pressures that frame the conditions for public policies. "Equality of opportunity," historically a prized American value, has been pushed aside for private gains at the expense of those lacking the resources to succeed.

These are among the many elements that have damaged American society, elements that have carved out the nation's core and left the exterior with few protective political girders. People may discuss the value of the body politic in an intellectual sense, but in the end, growing numbers are concerned more with what they can get out of the system than what they might give to it. With so many examples of desertion, no wonder that Americans feel detached from their country. And as this collective malaise becomes the new status quo, the United States is fast losing its place as a global leader. This is our condition as we slowly, yet consistently, disengage as citizens.

Is America doomed to implode? Not necessarily. There are opportunities for repair, if enough people are willing to make the necessary sacrifices. We must return to the values that once propelled us to the top. Commitment to the best education system that provides the tools for all to succeed would be a good place to start. But beyond the learning that comes with education, we need to teach our young that citizenship rights are accompanied by a host of obligations, and that the collective good sometimes is more important than individual gains.

We need to think about enabling every citizen to connect with the country through the contribution of time and skills. Such commitments would provide an abundance of talent while building a sense of individuals attaching to the political community. In return, we need to protect the rights of all citizens to participate freely in the political process, particularly with respect to the franchise.

And we ought to seriously examine ways of reducing the huge gaps between the haves and have-nots in our society. The one-sided tax system conferring so many benefits to the wealthy at the expense of the rest of us must undergo substantive overhaul. Resources shifted abroad by the wealthy should count as income and be taxed here. Corporations must account for shady international finances as well as their many ways to increase profits at the expense of their workers, whether through offshoring, temporary hires, or weakened pension plans.

With respect to our increasingly ineffective institutions, our leaders must look beyond their immediate political opportunities and parochial interests for the collective good, even if it competes with their personal desires. Of course, there should be room for differences, but on major, long-standing collective values our leaders must come together much more than they have in recent years.

Yes, American society is at a crossroads. We can choose as individuals to take care of ourselves as we ignore the systemic problems of those around us, or we can rediscover the importance and advantages of national unity and public good. The choice is ours, but we need to act while we still have a choice, before our growing abandonment of American values renders our nation permanent harm.

It's time to recommit to citizenship in the manner described by Abraham Lincoln in his famous Gettysburg Address—a working partnership with government that is "of the people, by the people, and for the people." Lincoln's goal was to make the nation whole again; that goal needs to be ours today.

Acknowledgments

A book is composed under an author's name, but rarely written without a good deal of support from others. To that end, several people offered their wisdom, guidance, and research assistance for this project. At San Jose State University, Lawrence Quill read the first chapter and insisted that the story of flagging citizenship must be told. Ian Gallmeister provided masterful research on tricky topics, always coming up with appropriate materials. Lee Gerston read every word along the way and offered valuable criticism and editing recommendations. Last but not least, Joel Heimlich provided constant tech support to a writer much more comfortable with words than computers.

At Taylor & Francis, my gratitude is extended to the many people participating in the editing and production processes. Special thanks go to Lara Zoble, editor, who not only signed the project but also worked with me at every step along the way to fulfill its objectives. I also offer thanks to Jessica Vakili, project coordinator; Elise Weinger, cover designer; Tara Nieuwesteeg, project editor; Stephany Wilken, copywriter; Datapage, typesetter; and Rebecca Rothschild, marketing manager. Considering the many potential obstacles along the road to publication, this team minimized the burden.

Finally, my deepest appreciation goes to Elisa Gerston, for putting up with those many moments in conversation when her husband just drifted away, hopelessly seized by the project. Her patience is endless.

About the Author

Larry N. Gerston, PhD, is professor emeritus of political science at San Jose State University. A specialist in public policy, he has written 11 other books in addition to *Reviving Citizen Engagement: Policies to Renew National Community*. His policy books include *Making Public Policy: From Conflict to Resolution* (1983), *Public Policy Making: Process and Principles* (1997), *Public Policy Making in a Democratic Society: A Guide to Civic Engagement* (2002), and *Confronting Reality: Ten Issues Threatening to Implode American Society* (2009). Dr. Gerston's *Not So Golden After All: The Rise and Fall of California* was published by Taylor & Francis in 2012.

Along with his larger works, Dr. Gerston has written numerous journal articles and penned more than 125 op-ed pieces in leading newspapers. He appears weekly as the political analyst at NBC Bay Area (the NBC-owned television station in the San Francisco Bay Area), and has also been interviewed for his political insight on NBC *Nightly News*, CBS *Evening News*, BBC, NPR, and CNN's *Inside Politics*.

1

A Turning Point for America

Ask not what your country can do for you; ask what you can do for your country.

Those often quoted words of President John F. Kennedy were exclaimed at the end of his inaugural address on January 20, 1961. They reflected his hope that Americans would rise to meet the challenges of the day. Prior to that exhortation, Kennedy focused almost entirely on the precarious condition of world peace. It was, after all, a time defined by the Cold War between the United States and the then-Soviet Union, later described by another president, Ronald Reagan, as the "evil empire." But Kennedy's words emphasized the value of freedom, and the need to protect it at all costs. Then, as closure came, he urged his fellow Americans to be a part of the solution, rather than remain on the sidelines as idle bystanders. It was a powerful conclusion to what many presidential historians consider one of the most compelling inaugural speeches in American history.

Kennedy's address set the tone for an incredibly active decade of government-driven programmatic initiatives, beginning with establishment of the Peace Corps and ending with the historic landing of an American astronaut on the moon, a feat that has never been duplicated. In between, the nation witnessed an explosion of domestic policy breakthroughs, including the passage of powerful civil rights legislation, the enactment of Medicare, and the start of affirmative action. Political commotion was almost as frenetic on the foreign policy side of the activism ledger. Between the Cuban missile crisis, the Vietnam War, and the persistent global chess game between the United States and the Soviet Union, Americans had more than their share of collective character tests. All this and more in a single decade.

There were passionate disagreements on many of these fronts during the 1960s, but challenges were met and hurdles were overcome. The United States was on the move, not just the government, but also the people. Taxes were high by today's standards, but it didn't seem to matter; unemployment averaged 4.9 percent, which meant that just about anyone who wanted a job had one.[1] For the most part, times were good. Yes, there were ugly moments during the Vietnam War and the civil rights revolution, but at the nation's core there existed a common bond and sense that the country had direction. People felt efficacious and that they made a difference.[2] Compared with other nations, Americans felt good about their country and its institutions. They were politically engaged, and stood out as an example for the rest of the world to envy and respect.[3]

Whatever our disagreements on policy issues—and there were many then as now—for the most part the public coalesced behind elected leaders, showing that the many facets of American society could congeal with regularity. For example, during Kennedy's truncated presidency, his public approval averaged 70.1 percent. The unpopular Vietnam War hurt Johnson's standing somewhat, although he still commanded an average of 55.1 percent public approval,[4] well above the support levels we've seen in recent years. Congress also benefited from public support, garnering approbation from 47 percent of the public in 1975, the second year that the Gallup Poll asked the question.[5] Compare these levels of approval with recent years, where the president often fails to get above 50 percent and congressional approval hovers in the low double digits.[6] In fact, in 2013 an NBC/*Wall Street Journal* national survey found Americans so disgusted that 60 percent wanted to dump the entire Congress and start from scratch![7]

AMERICA ADRIFT

The transformation of the public's attitudes toward their government and their place in society from those days to the present has been a journey harmful to both their collective psyche and the nation. Underlying it all has been a loss of faith in the system and its leaders, a sense that America has lost its way—at least for many. Voting percentages have drifted downward over the past 50 years, loosening the linkage between the governed and our governors. Respect for legitimate authority has diminished, with increasing distrust about the value and merit of government.[8] A Pew Research Center poll in 2011 found that 55 percent of the respondents believed that "government is wasteful and inefficient,"[9] while 53 percent of those interviewed in a 2013 Rasmussen Survey believed that the U.S. economy is unfair.[10] Clearly, there exists a state of disaffection, if not outright alienation, among many Americans.

Beyond the growing disillusionment with the system, great schisms have emerged among different sectors of society. Those at the bottom of the economic ladder have soured because of the growing chasm between the wealthy and the poor. Many expressed their sense of injustice in 2011 when hundreds of thousands across the nation participated in "Occupy America" protests. Meanwhile, corporations and individuals of affluence have pulled up stakes and withdrawn from American society, through moving to another country, sheltering resources in safe havens abroad, or shipping well-paying jobs to foreign locations with little concern for the well-being of their homeland. Young people have drifted away because of uncertain futures on the economic and social fronts.[11] Countless others maintain a physical presence with little emotional attachment to their country or its values. Increasingly, notes one assessment, Americans have fallen into "civic disengagement," a condition where few are willing to invest their time in the political process.[12]

Growing numbers of people—commonly a majority—believe that the United States is headed in the wrong direction.[13] One national poll conducted in 2011 asked whether "the past decade has been one of progress or decline for the U.S. as a country." Only 24 percent answered yes, while 68 percent said no.[14] Yet the future looks even more daunting than the past. When asked in a McClatchy–Marist 2014 national survey "how much effort will it take for the next generation to get ahead?" 78 percent replied it would take more effort, compared with 5 percent who said it would take less.[15]

Public opinion has soured on investing in infrastructure, choosing instead to let the next generation deal with pressing fundamental needs that have been deferred for decades. Meanwhile, political parties, historically moderating sources of aggregation, have become increasingly splintered, ineffective, and accountable much more to narrow constituencies than their broad memberships. Polarization has replaced civility.

Combined, these attitudes help to provide a glimpse into the deteriorated connection between the American public and its policy makers from those relatively heady days. More pointedly, they are snippets of a far greater problem, mainly the detachment of Americans from the political process and the social framework under which we grew and thrived for the past 240 years, to the point of becoming the world's superpower with one of the best standards of living. They are precursors to the sense of malaise and resignation that has overpowered large swaths of American society.

What has gone wrong? Has the country really gone adrift, and if so, why? The United States may still stand proud as a nation, but its citizens aren't so sure. The "we can do anything" attitude that once prevailed has given way to a hyperindividualistic "I've got mine, go get yours" mentality. Of course, not all Americans have abandoned the nation's political bosom, and not all have given up on the American dream. But the numbers of the disengaged are sufficiently large enough to cause concern for the current direction as well as the future of our society. If, as Thomas Dye and Brigid Harrison write, "legitimate governments derive their power from … consent of the governed,"[16] we need to give pause as to how few Americans are bothering to give that consent, and why. The United States may still remain the world's most powerful nation, but the glue holding together the nation's polity has lost a good deal of its adhesive quality.

This chapter explores the missing spark in America's once dynamic political engine, with respect to both causes and effects. Beginning with the drift away from collective commitment to the nation's values, we identify the foundations of the disenchantment and the high costs to American society. The America of today is moving in a different direction from the America we have known in the past. Our inattention to the nation's pressing needs has resulted in a troubled handoff from the "greatest generation" to the "disengaged generation." As a result, Americans today stand at an unfamiliar juncture, with long-term uncertainties that few of us ever anticipated.

WEAKENED CITIZENSHIP: THE CATALYST FOR DISAFFECTION

The proposition is simple, if troubling: many Americans no longer connect with their country, or each other, for that matter.[17] Citizenship, that special collection of rights, responsibilities, and obligations that fuses people in a given geographical locality to a foundation of shared basic values, has lost its attraction as a treasured attribute for Americans. Oh sure, we possess passports, driver's licenses, and other forms of personal identification that prove our physical status as Americans. And millions of American citizens dutifully raise flags on important holidays, sing the national anthem at ball games, and write checks to their favorite charitable organizations. But on a deeper level, the true emotional sense of belonging among Americans has dissipated greatly, leaving our membership a superficial, one-dimensional experience.

In 21st-century America, larger numbers of people no longer feel emotionally attached to the nation, nor do they embrace the basic attributes that have shaped our collective values over the past few centuries. That absence presents a serious problem. Without the basic commitment of society to citizenship, America has no whole. Imagine a wheel with strong spokes but no hub, and you get the sense of the importance of citizenship as the political glue that binds society.

From Inclusion to Isolation

To be a citizen is to be connected with something beyond one's self, family, or friends. That "something" is much more an emotional bond than anything else; it is a feeling of inclusion in a welcome, supportive, and nurturing sociopolitical environment. Citizenship is about being part of a larger organization in which members choose to subordinate themselves to the decisions of others for the good of the community, even when they disagree with those decisions. The subordination takes place because an individual agrees to be part of the basic collection of values that define a nation and what it stands for. This doesn't mean that people have to check every box the same way or that robust differences of opinion cannot exist. But being a citizen conveys a willingness to accept and honor differences as healthy parts of the nation's whole, for that tolerance in itself is an essential ingredient of healthy citizenship.

In a democracy, citizenship comes with a particularly unique set of conditions. Democracies do not compel citizens to belong; rather, they include opportunities for citizens to be part of an experience dedicated to the greater good as well as individual happiness. The relationship is designed to be mutually beneficial for citizens and the government that serves them. Unlike most authoritarian societies where the terms of existence are dictated by those in power, democracies are settings where citizens participate in defining the terms of association and the roles of those who belong. Such a setting, drawn from voluntary membership, is what the political philosopher John Locke described as a "political society," where people freely and willingly "enter into society to make one people, one body politic, under one supreme government."[18]

Citizenship, in other words, is based upon a close, consensual relationship between people and their governing system. Furthermore, a democracy is dependent upon persistent, ongoing interaction between the governors and the governed. The people have an integral role in the political process by approving or disapproving the actions of their leaders through the peaceful expression of public opinion and, more definitively, through elections. Ideally, there is no free ride in a democracy. Participation matters. Citizens and their governments have responsibilities to each other.

Shared Attributes

How is it that people with separate hopes and dreams agree to congregate as citizens under the same political roof? They are bonded by shared values. In American democracy, two shared attributes stand out as fundamental components of citizenship: rights and obligations. These attributes comprise the political bookends that guide our relationship with government and our roles as members of the polity.

Rights

In exchange for subordinating ourselves to the legitimate authority of government, Americans are endowed with a series of basic individual rights. These rights protect certain freedoms that can't be arbitrarily denied or changed by those in power. They also protect us from illegitimate government intrusion into our lives. The most fundamental of our rights have been hammered out in the Bill of Rights, guarantees that were added and approved by the states shortly after the creation of the U.S. Constitution. Other everyday rights are all around us—the right to pursue a vocation, the right to be safe from physical harm, the right to live in peace with our neighbors, and the right to own property, to name a few. Our rights are part of the "social contract" we seal with government in exchange for our loyalty and support of government.[19]

Rights don't always work the same way for everyone. When a police officer stops a well-dressed person in a fancy new car for a minor infraction, she may send the person on his way with a mild warning. When the same police officer stops an unkempt person of color in an old pollution-emitting car, the officer may well check to see if the person is wanted by authorities for a crime, and perhaps arrest that person on a questionable charge. Such racial profiling is hard to fathom in a society with a philosophy committed to equality under the laws, yet it occurs more than we'd like to admit.[20] It's one of many examples that show the system is far from perfect.

The issue goes beyond treatment by public authorities. In 21st-century America, some people feel that their rights have not always lived up to expectations. Despite their efforts to work hard in pursuit of the American dream, they are falling farther and farther behind the privileged few. Rights may exist "on paper," but for those at the bottom, rights never seem to provide the same opportunities for them the way they do for others. Poverty, racial discrimination, and educational disparities seem to transfer from one generation to the next, conferring a sense of despair, with upward mobility seemingly out of reach. Rights don't have much meaning for these citizens.

Simply put, the system is a work in progress; flaws must be addressed. Nevertheless, at least on paper, the concept of rights provides us with a constitutional shield against others as well as government interfering in our lives. Americans treasure their rights because in addition to the protection they provide us, we see them as the bases of our freedoms.

Obligations

While Americans consider rights part of the basic contract with government, obligations are another matter. Obligations refer to the loyalties we provide for society in exchange for our membership. Some elements are clear enough. For example, we are obligated to honor speed limits and the assortment of laws, pay taxes, place stamps on envelopes, and obey the demands of police officers who are the only legitimate holders of coercion. We're also obligated to serve on juries in judgment of those accused of crimes. At one time, Americans (at least, most males) were obligated to serve in the armed forces to defend the well-being of the nation, but that requirement has been replaced by voluntary participation. These requisites are fairly clear and generate little disagreement.

Obligation is intended to ensure that we consider the well-being of the greater good as much or more than we think of ourselves, for it is acceptance of the greater good that helps to promote the general health of society, and by extension the security of its individual members. Obligation comes in all shapes and sizes. Sometimes it's as simple as helping an elderly person cross the street; other times it may be notifying authorities when we witness a crime. To ignore our obligations threatens the public good and our long-term survival as a society. It's reminiscent of the saying "a chain is only as strong as its weakest link."

Yet, we are often slow to appreciate what we must do as citizens to ensure a congealed community. Those who fail to carry out their share of the burden effectively harm those who do. As Derek Heater notes, "A society of selfish individuals is, at its extreme, no society at all, nor does it have citizens properly speaking—it is nothing more than an agglomeration of competitive units" that deny the sense of community and collective health.[21]

But increasingly, obligations call for sacrifices some citizens are unwilling to undertake for the collective good. For these individuals, the cost is too high or doesn't fit in with their individual values. Some don't accept the outcomes of elections as legitimate because their candidates failed to prevail; others refuse to pay their share of taxes per the laws enacted by policy makers because they feel they have paid enough or that the revenues aren't put to use in ways they approve. Then there are those who simply balk at the redistribution of public resources that are intended to help some members of society who are less fortunate than others. These naysayers have had enough of society's rules. They no longer see the advantages of membership even though they probably have attained their successes by benefiting from those rules.

Likewise, those who can't seem to succeed have also had enough. The only standard of living they know is one with a downward direction that offers little indication of ever pointing in the other direction. Why, they ask, should they commit to the greater good when all they experience are roadblocks to success by those who have already achieved it? For these people, citizenship—that special sense of belonging—is more illusory than reality, and that absence of hope takes a toll.

When Rights Clash with Obligations

Not surprisingly, Americans, like most people, are more at ease with rights than obligations. The reasoning is simple enough: we get things from rights, whereas we contribute through obligations. Yet for society to thrive, rights and obligations must coexist. As Joseph Tussman has written, an individual with rights can still believe in public obligation as long as he or she sees such as promoting the public interest.[22]

Citizenship depends on individuals viewing their relationship with the government as valuable and worthwhile for their own good as well as the public good.

The Lost Nation

And that's the point. Increasingly, elements of American society are opting out of citizenship. Some who opt out want to preserve precious rights at the same time they would abandon their obligations. The rules they abhor are for everyone else but them. They find ways to avoid taxes as individuals and move jobs elsewhere to maximize corporate profits, even if such movements mean fewer jobs at home. They opt out of political participation because they are dissatisfied with the country's direction or are required to pay taxes that come with their success. They are no longer drawn to American society and the political process, and despite the benefits conferred upon them, feel little need to pay back. Amazingly, they see no contradiction in their behavior.

Others opt out because they've never felt part of society regardless of their official standing as citizens. They view society as an arrangement consisting of entitled and unentitled people; they feel betrayed by a political system that never gave them a chance. We may all be citizens on paper, but for many the lack of opportunity to succeed renders them second-class citizen status.

Whether disaffection occurs from those at the bottom or the top, whether individually inspired or corporately conspired, this is the crisis that confronts us in the 21st century—a crisis of abandoned citizenship. The more these feelings grow, the more threatened is the future of America as we know it.

CHARACTERISTICS OF THE HOLLOWED-OUT SOCIETY

Citizenship includes commitment to the political system. This does not mean that every citizen must run for office, vote in every election, or accept an active position in government. It does convey the basic value, however, that the citizen supports the system. Support may vary from passively accepting the rules to actively participating through campaigning and other political acts associated with membership in society. There's a benefit from this sense of belonging. Sidney Verba and Norman H. Nie write that involvement produces positive outcomes from government for society "even if citizens bring their narrow and selfish interests into politics."[23] The point is, everyone can and should have a say if they choose.

Government has a huge role in providing a solicitous environment for its citizens, but that outreach effort is not always well demonstrated or successful. Some policies have conferred excessive benefits for narrow groups, while leaving others at a disadvantage. Over time, they lead to alienation. When disgusted citizens refrain from involvement, trouble brews, particularly if their numbers are high and their disaffection is substantial. In less democratic societies, disgust with the system can lead to revolution. And it can be contagious, as we've witnessed with the Arab Spring that has impacted nations along the geographical arc extending from North Africa to the Middle East.

In a democracy like the United States, however, the outcome is detachment. Individuals move to the political periphery and, no longer involved, leave it to others still committed to the system to make government work—or not. As the number of participating citizens shrinks, fewer people make decisions for the public good. Our disinterest in participation relates to a growing lack of trust. A national study in 2013 found that only one-third of Americans believe that most people can be trusted. In 1972, half of the respondents felt that people could be trusted.[24] No wonder we look askance at leaders. To the extent that decision makers become less connected with the rest of society, democracy is jeopardized. Such are the risks associated with citizens opting out of the process, whether by choice, from neglect, or worse yet, from discouragement and disfranchisement by those in power.

Several factors have led segments of American society to move to the periphery of politics, if not physically outside altogether. They include lack of the nation's commitment to investment, manipulation of the rules of the game, the perpetuation of inequality, and disregard for the world around us. Some are caused by individual selfishness; others are the result of failed government policies. Combined, these factors help to account for an increasingly hollowed-out society where individuals have abandoned their interest in the greater good for a narrow life of self-preservation.

Lack of Investment

Investment refers to the commitments of society to long-term economic and social health. With investment, citizens look beyond the present to provide for forthcoming generations. Some might view investment as an act of unselfishness. Yet, if one is truly interested in preserving the legacy of past and present successes, investment is a somewhat natural activity. That said, Americans have shown little interest in investing in the future. We'd rather have reduced tax obligations than set aside resources to preserve a more secure future. Below, we examine infrastructure, public education, and research as indicators of public investment. The data show that the United States is falling behind other nations.

Infrastructure

The physical composition of society is underscored by its infrastructure. Roads, bridges, power grids, dams, rail networks, airports, and seaports are among the myriad elements that facilitate safe movement of people and goods. They are also a statement about the extent to which society invests in itself and its future. With a per capita income of $48,112 (as of 2012), the United States ranked seventh among the world's richest nations.[25] Nevertheless, the United States is far from the top in key areas of public investment. According to the Global Competitiveness Report 2011–2012 produced by the World Economic Forum, out of 142 nations, the U.S. ranks 24th overall in infrastructure outlay.[26] More troubling, the U.S. commitment to infrastructure has slowed precipitously from 3.1 percent of the gross domestic product (GDP) in the early 1960s to 2.4 percent today.[27] Rather than invest in the future, we're content to leave the issue to someone else, namely, the next generation, or maybe the generation after that. Meanwhile, countries like China are spending as much as 9 percent of their GDP on infrastructure—nearly four times the U.S. rate. The lack of commitment to a first-class infrastructure translates to a less competitive nation, and a less competitive nation means a population with fewer good jobs.

Public Education

The nation's commitment to an educated population has been slipping for years. As of 2009, the United States ranked 15th when comparing public spending on education as a percentage of total public expenditures; the United States ranked 6th as recently as 2000. The same research shows that the United States ranked 11th in 2010 in high school graduates.[28] With respect to college graduates, the U.S. ranked 14th among the world's industrialized nations. Among college graduates, the United States ranked 74th in the percentages studying science and engineering.[29] Combined, these data are hardly an indication of a nation preparing a competitive 21st-century workforce. Moreover, the American deficiency begins in the earliest grades. A 2010 Organization for Economic Cooperation and Development (OECD) study of 15-year-old students placed the United States at 14th in reading, 14th in science, and 25th in math. American students simply aren't getting the tools they need. With performances this low at early stages in life, it's no wonder that Americans have a tough time catching up and competing on the international marketplace. The less that Americans compete, the more they are left behind. The more they are left behind, the more that the standard of living declines, with a frustrated workforce as a result. A workforce without meaningful, well-paid jobs leads to disenchanted and disengaged citizens.

Research

Societies advance because of research and development, some much more than others. A key indicator lies in the extent that a government supports university research as well as research in the private sector. The United States has long languished behind others in government-funded research support, but even that second-tier standing has slipped in recent years. Between 2000 and 2008, the United States slipped in government research support from 18th to 22nd place out of the 30 leading industrialized nations. Here's a big part of the reason why: during the same period, the United States increased research support by 17 percent; meanwhile, Korea increased support by 85 percent, China by 40 percent, and Russia by 43 percent.[30] Research leads to innovation and new products. Here again, the United States has slipped in recent years, and rather quickly. According to an independent study, in 2012 the United States ranked 10th in innovation, down from 7th in 2011. Switzerland, Sweden, and Singapore held the top three positions. Once again, the lack of government support has helped to create an uncompetitive environment and fewer quality jobs for American workers. Once again, we're falling behind.

The Takeaway

Americans aren't investing in the future, which leaves open the opportunity for other nations to take their place as the centers of innovation, well-paid jobs, and an educated population. The irony is that corporate America doesn't really care where the jobs are as long as they can get products to market at the lowest possible costs. So, while businesses flourish with huge profits (and low tax obligations in friendlier foreign environments), American workers are left behind.

Manipulation of the Rules of the Game

While respect for basic rights has been a staple of American democracy, many citizens no longer feel the need to honor that fundamental guarantee. From elected officials to individuals, there have been increasing incidents of ignoring, and in some cases abusing, the rules of the land. Simply put, they reject the nation's rules in favor of conditions that are more acceptable to their individual preferences. Two examples lie with voter suppression and opting out of tax obligations, whether as individuals or corporations. It's part of the game where we preach one set of values and live by another.

Voter Suppression

Historically, large swaths of Americans have suffered the stigma of voter suppression. Too often the denial of the vote and other political activities has been enforced by government authorities, raising serious questions about the legitimacy of government institutions in the process. The most obvious transgression occurred with African Americans in the south for decades until national legislation, presidential executive orders, and U.S. Supreme Court decisions clearly indicated that such efforts were illegal and would be punished.

That landscape was rearranged in 2013 when the U.S. Supreme Court struck down the heart of the 1965 Voting Rights Act, which had required states with histories of discrimination to obtain federal government approval before changing voter laws.[31] Before the year expired, following the court's edict, 10 states passed laws that tightened the voting process. The rearranged rules focused on a variety of impediments, including rigorous voter identification requirements such as birth certificates, a shortened time period for voters to cast their ballots in advance of the election, limitations on voter registration drives, and inadequate numbers of voting booths for the election day events.[32] The effort has had the chilling effect of raising the comfort bar for a large swath of Americans.

Opting Out of Financial Obligation

It began as a trickle, but in recent years, growing numbers of Americans have decided that they would rather live elsewhere than the United States. The reason: less taxes. Ironically, many of those choosing to leave have done so after making a financial killing here. In 2011, 1,781 people renounced their American citizenship, up 16 percent from 2010. Moreover, the 2011 figure was eight times the number that exited the United States in 2008, according to the U.S. Treasury.[33] In 2013, 2,999 Americans gave up their citizenship.

Some ex-Americans are more candid than others about their exits. For example, when Facebook co-founder billionaire Eduardo Saverin left the United States for Singapore a week before his company went public, he claimed he did so because he would be doing most of his work there. Nevertheless, in Singapore, most of his capital gains were taxed at 0 percent, rather than the 20 percent rate in the United States. Another expat billionaire was more direct when he said, "The U.S. government creates conflict and abuses me. I feel under duress to understand and comply with laws that have nothing to do with me and are constantly changing—almost never in my favor."[34] And what was the conflict about? Obligation. A U.S. tax expert attributed the surge of departures to increased awareness of the laws requiring tax returns and beefed enforcement by U.S. officials.[35] Ironically, moneyed expats don't think twice about the fact that they earned their wealth under the same American laws they now resent; somehow paying their fair share seems to be a separate matter from earning their fair share.

Perpetuation of Inequality

Equality may be part of the American dream, but some have achieved success easier than others. That's because the road to accomplishment can be filled with obstacles, depending upon who is on it. The fact is that even though the Declaration of Independence declares that all men should be treated equal, they are not, and women even less so. The most egregious examples of inequality in America center on race and gender. These conditions have persisted since the days prior to the American Revolution, with little change other than on the periphery of human relations.

Race

Few mistreatments in American society plague the nation as much as the differences in opportunities because of race and ethnicity. Whites consistently enjoy better educations and less unemployment than non-whites; at the same time, whites have considerably higher incomes than non-whites, especially African Americans and Latinos. Predictably, non-whites find themselves with poverty rates nearly three times as high as those of whites, yet another sign that they have been left behind,[36] largely because of fewer education opportunities to gain good skill sets. But it's not only simply a question of economics; it's also about social standing and the persistence of racism in the 21st century. When asked during the 2012 presidential election whether "racism in the United States is by and large a thing of the past," 58 percent of the African American respondents strongly disagreed, compared with 32 percent of whites who strongly disagreed.[37] Nevertheless, studies show people of color are treated differently than whites. Law enforcement officials are much more likely to stop non-whites for questioning than whites, yet another sign of inconsistent application of the laws.[38]

With respect to incarceration, people of color comprise about 30 percent of the national population, yet they account for about 60 percent of those imprisoned. Specifically, 1 out of every 15 African Americans and 1 out of every 36 Latino men are locked up, compared with 1 out of every 106 white men.[39] These data weigh heavily on non-white citizens. African Americans and Latinos feel unfairly treated by police and judicial authorities, which contributes to a sense of reduced loyalty and commitments to the rules of the game.[40] In effect, they ask: Why be part of a system that leaves us with fewer opportunities than others? The answer is that many are not.

Gender

Along with ethnic minorities, women have been left behind on the road to equality. Here the issue centers less on criminality and more on economic parity. True, women have closed the gap somewhat on the issue of economic compensation, but they remain a long way from parity. In 1963, President John F. Kennedy signed into law the Equal Pay Act, which requires women to be paid equal pay for the same work carried out by men. At the time, women were paid 59 cents of every dollar men earned; as of 2013, women were paid 77 cents of every dollar earned by men. Improvement, yes, but hardly parity. Even university training does not end the disparity. A study by the American Association of University Women (AAUW) found that female university graduates are compensated 7 percent less than men "even when they work in the same job, major in the same field, and work the same number of hours per week," projecting economic losses of up to $1 million dollars over a 40-year career.[41] In the 21st century, the "glass ceiling" still impacts women at all levels of employment.

From a global perspective, the United States has much work to do. The 2012 Global Gender Gap Report issued by World Economic Forum ranked the U.S. 22nd in terms of gender equality, trailing countries such as Germany and England. Even the Philippines, Nicaragua, and South Africa were ahead of the United States on the equality scale.[42]

The economic plight suffered by women in America translates into a sense of political malaise and exclusion from opportunities available to men. In their study of voters in the 2012 election, Celinda Lake and her colleagues found that women were less convinced than men that they or their children could succeed. They also were less likely than men to agree that "people get what they deserve."[43] These data are powerful reminders that women perceive themselves as second-class citizens in American society. And given the numbers cited above, it's difficult to conclude otherwise.

Support for Other Nations

Even with the world's largest economy, the United States shares the planet with others. As an early industrialized nation, we have benefited greatly from the raw materials and inexpensive labor in other, less developed nations. Many of these countries have become strategic allies over time, while others are still in the early stages of realizing their economic and political potential. It all points to a rather uneven world in terms of economic success, which leads to the question of foreign aid—a topic that leaves most Americans with little compassion or concern.

Retreat from Economic Assistance

The United States is among the wealthiest nations able to help those in need of economic support, yet our foreign aid stands near the bottom when compared to the efforts of less wealthy nations. Data compiled by the Organization for Economic Cooperation and Development shows two persistent trends: (1) the United States is the largest contributor to foreign aid (about $36 billion in 2011), and (2) when viewed as a percentage of national income, American foreign aid ranks 19th.[44] Critics might argue that the data are skewed because of the generosity of some small countries such as Sweden, Norway, and Luxembourg, which rank first, second, and third. Yet, countries such as France and Germany are also well ahead of the United States. The fact is that Americans aren't nearly as involved in the well-being of poor nations, especially since about one-third of all U.S. aid is dedicated to military assistance. Thus, the United States is not a major player in world assistance, and when it is, it does so largely for military purposes. In fact, many Americans are as isolated from foreign involvement as they are from their own country. A public opinion poll in 2010 found that Americans believed about 27 percent of the U.S. budget is going for foreign aid.[45] With a budget of $3.6 trillion, that would amount to $972 billion. In fact, the U.S. allocated $36.4 billion in foreign aid for the 2010–2011 fiscal year.[46] Clearly, Americans are as out of touch on foreign relations as they are with their own country.

Disregard for International Law

American disdain for the views of other nations and international law extends to dissenting positions on international treaties, many of which receive overwhelming support. Some of the issues are basic and straight-forward fundamental rights. For example, the United States has refused to ratify the Treaty for the Rights of Women, an accord designed to guar-antee basic rights and prevent discrimination. Only 6 other nations have opposed the agreement that has been approved by 186 nations. The United States has also not approved the Laws of the Seas Treaty, approved by 165 nations and not acted upon by 19. With respect to the UN Convention Rights of the Child, 193 nations ratified the agreement; only 3 have failed to sign—the United States, Somalia, and Sudan. In perhaps the greatest rejection of international opinion, the United States was one of two coun-tries (along with Kazakhstan) that refused to sign the Kyoto Protocol, the agreement designed to reduce greenhouse gas emissions.

And the list goes on. In a recent example of our isolation, the United States lost its voting rights at the United Nations Educational, Scientific, and Cultural Organization (UNESCO), an international body formed to promote and respect justice and human rights. The loss of membership occurred because of American nonpayment stemming from policy differ-ences over Palestinian rights in the Middle East. As a result, experts close to the program fretted that the United States had lost a valuable platform to extend American influence.[47] These and many other decisions to reject international consensus have left the United States very isolated, yet few Americans are troubled by this standing.

What Good Is a Bus if the Wheels Come Off?

The characteristics cited above have become mainstays of American society. Some have roots extending back to America's birth; others have emerged over the past few decades. The point is that in the 21st century, Americans are anything but united about the nation's purpose and their place in it. Many have lost faith in the system, and others no longer have any need for it. Worse yet, the numbers of the disaffected are growing, leaving the core of society on shaky political ground and a government very confused over how to respond to this dilemma. None of this bodes well for the future of the American people or the prowess of the United States as a world leader.

What to do? We must look into the soul of American society to appreciate its underlying political and social problems. This great nation cannot move forward if too many feel left behind or decide it's no longer worth being part of it. Such an examination is bound to be painful and sobering, but it's the only way to ferret out our issues and solve them if America is to avoid becoming a second-class nation filled with alienated citizens. To be sure, it's a daunting journey, yet it's the course we chart from this point forward.

PLAN OF THE BOOK

We will begin with an assessment of the extent to which America has become a fractured society and the residual damage from the social implosion. Next, we will turn to the fragile condition of the 21st-century electorate and a political system where private power too often has overcome values intended to protect the public good. Some of the transformation has occurred with the triumph of greed over equality, leaving the concepts of fairness and opportunity—cherished components of the American dream—far behind.

But America's misfortune stems from more than selfishness and greed. Our political institutions and policy-making bodies have withered to the point of dysfunction. With weak government oversight of society's problems, corporations have increasingly adopted positions that tend to their needs, and their needs alone, abandoning any responsibilities to society or government in the process. Meanwhile, government policies have failed to perpetuate hope and real opportunity for our citizens.

In addition, everyday Americans deserve blame for dropping the ball when it comes to appreciating the wisdom of engagement with their country and fellow citizens. Many see only the costs to themselves, while ignoring the benefits of membership in the nation. As far as they're concerned, these issues are not theirs to resolve. Put these three strands together, and the combination is anything but helpful to the future of the nation.

Sound depressing? It should, because it is. But the costly American mistakes of the past and present are not necessarily condemned to continue along this path in the future. There are steps we can—and must—take to repair, rebuild, and renew American society, and such recommendations are offered in the final chapter of the book. They are within our reach if we are willing to make the sacrifices long overdue in what historically has been recognized as the world's most powerful and successful nation. Time is of the essence, however, if the United States is to reassemble its national purpose. And that time is now.

ENDNOTES

1. These figures were actually for the period 1960–1973, according to the U.S. Department of Labor, Bureau of Labor Statistics. See http://www.bls.gov/opub/ted/2002/sept/wk1/art03.htm.
2. See M. Kent Jennings and Richard Niemi, *Generations and Politics*, Princeton, NJ: Princeton University Press, 1981, p. 37.
3. See Gabriel A. Almond and Sidney Verba, *The Civic Culture*, Boston: Little, Brown and Company, 1963, p. 64.
4. These aggregate data are found in Lori Cox Han and Diane J. Heith, *Presidents and the American Presidency*, New York: Oxford University Press, 2013, p. 176.
5. "Congress Approval Ties All-Time Low at 10%," August 14, 2012, http://www.gallup.com/poll/156662/Congress-Approval-Ties-Time-Low.aspx?version=print.
6. Ibid.
7. "NBC/WSJ Poll: 60 Percent Say Fire Every Member of Congress," December 23, 3013, http://firstread.nbcnews.com/_news/2013/10/10/20903531-nbcwsj-poll-60-percent-say-fire-every-member-of-congress?lite.
8. Lawrence R. Jacobs and Desmond King are among many who make this point in their "The Political Crisis of the American State," in Lawrence R. Jacobs and Desmond King, eds., *The Unsustainable American State*, New York: Oxford University Press, 2009, p. 24.

9. "Beyond Red and Blue: The Political Typology," Pew Research Center for the People and the Press, Washington, DC, May 4, 2011, http://www.people-press.org/2011/05/04/section-5-views-of-government-constitution-american-exceptionalism/.
10. "Only 41 Percent View Economy Fair to Those Who Work Hard," Rasmussen Reports, February 27, 2013, http://www.rasmussenreports.com/public_content/business/general_business/february_2013/only_41_view_economy_as_fair_to_those_willing_to_work_hard.
11. See Cliff Zukin, Scott Keeter, Molly Andolina, Krista Jenkins, and Michael X. Delli Carpini, *A New Engagement?* New York: 2006, p. 1932.
12. William E. Hudson, *American Democracy in Peril*, 7th ed., Thousand Oaks, CA: CQ Press, 2013, p. 157.
13. NBC News/*Wall Street Journal* poll conducted by the polling organizations of Peter Hart (D) and Bill McInturff (R), February 21–24, 2013.
14. Mark J. Penn, "The Pessimism Index," *Time*, July 11, 2011, pp. 36–37.
15. "McClatchy-Marist Poll: American Dream Seen as Out of Reach," February 13, 2014, http://www.mcclatchydc.com/2014/02/13/218026/mcclatchy-marist-poll-american.html.
16. Thomas R. Dye and Brigid C. Harrison, *Power and Society*, 10th ed., Belmont, CA: Thomson Wadsworth, 2005, p. 239.
17. Robert D. Putnam makes this point clearly in his *Bowling Alone*, New York: Simon & Schuster, 2000.
18. John Locke, *Second Treatise of Government*, edited by C.B. Macpherson, Indianapolis: Hackett Publishing Company, 1980, pp. 47–48, first published in 1690.
19. Jean-Jacques Rousseau elegantly makes this argument in his *On the Social Contract*, New York: Classic Books International, 2010, p. 10, first published in 1762.
20. For example, see Nadra Kareem Nittle, "Do Stop-and-Frisks in New York City Amount to Racial Profiling?" http://racerelations.about.com/od/thelegalsystem/a/Do-Stop-And-Frisks-In-New-York-City-Amount-To-Racial-Profiling.htm?p=1.
21. Derek Heater, *What Is Citizenship?* Maldon, MA: Polity Press, 1999, p. 73.
22. Joseph Tussman, *Obligation and the Body Politic*, New York: Oxford University Press, 1960, pp. 20–21.
23. Sidney Verba and Norman H. Nie, *Participation in America: Political Democracy and Social Equality*, New York, Harper & Row, 1972, p. 11.
24. "Americans Losing Trust in Each Other," *San Jose Mercury News*, December 1, 2013, p. A6.
25. "The World's Richest Countries," *Forbes*, February 22, 2012, http://www.forbes.com/sites/bethgreenfield/2012/02/22/the-worlds-richest-countries/.
26. "The Global Competitiveness Report 2011–2012," World Economic Forum, Geneva, Switzerland, 2012, pp. 33–378.
27. "Infrastructure 2011: A Strategic Priority," prepared for the Urban Land Institute by Ernst & Young, 2011, p. 24.
28. "Education at a Glance," Organization for Economic and Cooperative Development, Paris, France, 2012, pp. 13, 49.
29. "The Global Innovation Index 2012," edited by Soumitra Dutta, World Intellectual Property Organization, Geneva, Switzerland.
30. Robert D. Atkinson and Luke A. Stewart, "University Research Funding: The United States Is Behind and Falling," Information Technology and Information Foundation, May 2011.
31. The case was *Shelby County v. Holder*, 570 U.S. 193, decided in 2013.

32. "Voting Rights Roundup 2013," Brennan Center for Justice, November 4, 2013, http://www.brennancenter.org/analysis/election-2013-voting-laws-roundup.
33. "Special Report: Tax Time Pushes Some Americans to Take a Hike," www.reuters.com/article/2012/04/16/us-usa-citizen-renounce-idUSBRE83F0UF20120416.
34. "Rich Americans Voting with Their Feet to Escape Obama Tax Oppression," *Forbes*, July 18, 2010, http://www.forbes.com/sites/beltway/2010/07/18/rich-americans-voting-with-their-feet-to-escape-obama-tax-oppression/.
35. "Expatriations Rose to Record Last Year," *Wall Street Journal*, February 7, 2014, p. C2.
36. These data come from Christian E. Weller, Jaryn Fields, and Folayemi Agbede, "The State of Communities of Color in the U.S.," Center for American Progress, January 11, 2011, http://www.sacbee.com/2013/03/24/v-print/5285812/just-say-no-to-rate-hikes.html.
37. Celinda Lake, Michael Adams, and David Mermin, "New Voters, New Values," *American Prospect*, February 12, 2013, http://prospect.org/article/new-voters-new-values.
38. Yuen J. Huo and Tom R. Tyler, "How Different Ethnic Groups React to Legal Authority," Public Policy Institute of California, San Francisco, 2000, p. 29.
39. Sophia Kerby, "The Top 10 Most Startling Facts about People of Color and Criminal Justice in the United States," March 13, 2012, Center for American Progress," www.americanprogress.org/issues/race/news/2012/03/13/11351/the-top-10-most-startling-facts-about-people-of-color-and-criminal-justice-in-the-united-states/.
40. Hou and Tyler, op. cit., pp. viii–ix.
41. Beth Pearsall, "50 Years after the Equal Pay Act, Parity Eludes Us," AAUW, March 18, 2013, http://www.aauw.org/article/50-years-after-the-equal-pay-act-parity-eludes-us/.
42. "Global Gender Gap Report 2012: The Best and Worst Countries for Women," *Huffington Post*, October 24, 2012, http://www.huffingtonpost.com/2012/10/24/global-gender-gap-report-2012-best-worst-countries-women_n_2006395.html#slide=1677862.
43. Lake et al., op. cit.
44. OECD, December 2012, http://www.oecd.org/investment/stats/50060310.pdf.
45. "American Public Opinion on Foreign Aid," WorldPublicOpinion.org, November 10, 2013, http://www.worldpublicopinion.org/pipa/pdf/nov10/ForeignAid_Nov10_quaire.pdf.
46. "Executive Budget Summary, Fiscal Year, 2011," Department of State, http://www.state.gov/documents/organization/135888.pdf.
47. "U.S. Loses Voting Rights at Unesco," *New York Times*, November 9, 3023, p. A4.

Section I

Detached Spirit

2

Cracks in the Pavement

Americans have lost interest in each other, as well as their nation. Maybe we never really liked one another that much to begin with, given the stark divisions by race, gender, and class that have permeated our society since day 1. Still, cleavages notwithstanding, historically, most Americans have cherished the value of being part of this nation. But whatever bond that held us together in the past is no more—at least for many of us. Our great "melting pot," as sociologists Nathan Glazer and Daniel P. Moynihan once put it,[1] may have been much more a wishful fairy tale than political reality. Instead, these days it seems that the melting pot has boiled over, leaving many Americans scalded as a result.

In recent years, some researchers have determined that America is an increasingly fractured nation,[2] concluding that there are many more differences than similarities among us in a variety of ways, such as income, race, religion, and education. Some differences are natural extensions of our own personalities and ambitions; others, however, stem from institutional barriers or a skewed economic system that favors some over others. Our separation patterns have actually escalated over time, revealing an underlying—and occasionally pronounced—tension, particularly among those who feel left out of America's potential. Such concerns have led many to withdraw from a sense of belonging to the nation. If true, our lack of cohesion may speak volumes about the growing fragmentation of American society in the 21st century.

How has this come to pass? Of course, there is no single answer or cause for such a dramatic redirection. Nevertheless, polls show an increasing polarization of American society on key issues and values.

People are divided about the roles of the citizen, corporate America, and the government, as well as their responsibilities to each other. Some see the nation constructed on blocks of individualism; others worry that individualism overpowers the collective good. Some fret that corporations have abandoned loyalty to the country where they began and under whose laws they have flourished; others submit that corporations are the backbone of American success and are best left alone. Some think government should stay out of our lives; yet others still believe that government should provide a basic economic safety net for our lives, and does a poor job in the process.

Out of this cacophony has emerged a splintered society where many people have become very good at caring for themselves and little more. They ask why trust law enforcement if the only way we can be protected is with our own guns, private security companies, or gated communities? Why support public education if the system is so dreadful that students must spend extra time with expensive tutors? Why agree to pay more taxes if large swaths of public money go to those who contribute so little to society or the government in the first place? For these doubters, the "public good" is "no good," and the least government equals the best government. They would rather be in charge of their own destiny with their own resources on their own terms than depend upon dysfunctional institutions and disappointing policy makers.

Meanwhile, with economic and social fissures growing every day, society has taken on the appearance of a lopsided barbell. Yes, the dwindling few at the top are doing just fine, thank you, experiencing more affluence than at any time in American history, even during the Great Recession. But the growing number at the bottom see themselves with a reduced standard of living and a government that has retreated from its responsibilities to the public welfare at the same time that employers have laid them off in the name of productivity or jobs transferred abroad. Those at the top no longer need the country; those at the bottom no longer feel part of the country.

This chapter examines the dispirited America of the 21st century. It begins with the growing gap between the "haves and have-nots," which has placed Americans in two different worlds within the same nation. It ends with the growing tendency of Americans to live isolated lives in an increasingly complex, interdependent society. This social disarray has become the fractured framework of a nation with an increasingly splintered political foundation.

THE STAGNANT SOCIETY

Few want to talk about it and fewer understand it, but on a gut level most people get it: the standard of living for most Americans is eroding and has been deteriorating for more than two decades. Wages haven't kept up with inflation, which has left most people forced to do with less or work more for the same pay. Economists call the phenomenon productivity. The rest of us call it eroded purchasing power. This trend simply doesn't compute for a nation that became the world's economic juggernaut after World War II. Still, it's true—some have actually thrived despite the nation's general downward drift, widening the gap that seems so hard to understand. But most people find themselves living a human version of the mouse racing on a running wheel—no matter how fast it trots, the mouse gets nowhere. And so it is with most of us on the running wheel of life. No matter how hard we work, most of us fall behind the cost of living. All this takes place against a backdrop of an affluent society, at least in aggregate numbers. The nation may be wealthy, but the distribution of its wealth is more uneven today than any time in memory. Somehow, equal opportunity seems more equal for some than others.

Lost Purchasing Power

Too often we gauge the nation's (as well as our individual) economic well-being through the lens of quarterly or annual economic reports. To be sure, these markers tell us something in terms of real-time circumstances, that is, what's happening to the nation overall *now*. But the more serious numbers about the economic condition of Americans lie in trend data, which account for temporary surges and declines as moments in a longer time horizon.

On this front, the news is not good for most Americans. Long-term assessments reveal what many of us have suspected for years but have not been able to quantify: the standard of living of most Americans is in decline and has been contracting for more than a quarter century. This means that whatever our incomes, most of us have less purchasing power for the same goods today that we might have bought decades ago.

The evidence is eminently clear, if terribly discouraging. In 2010, a Rockefeller Foundation study defined economic insecurity as a condition when household incomes drop by 25 percent from one year to the next. Examining the incomes of all Americans between 1985 and 2007, the study concluded that the percentage of Americans at risk during the period jumped from 12.2 percent to 20.4 percent of the population.[3] A Gallup Poll conducted in June 2008 found 43 percent of the respondents agreeing that their standard of living was worse than 5 years ago.[4] Another survey taken by the Pew Research Center in early 2008 found 31 percent of the respondents saying their economic conditions were worse than in the past; in 1964, only 16 percent said that their economic conditions were worse than in the past.[5] The time periods of these statistics are important, for they illustrate trends in place long *before* the Great Recession of 2008–2009, which might have otherwise distorted the data. As for the Great Recession, the typical family's net worth fell a whopping 39 percent between 2007 and 2010, according to the Federal Reserve Board,[6] adding more pressure to the downward trend.

Most economists declared an end to the Great Recession in 2010, when the gross domestic product began to climb. But for most Americans, the Great Recession continues. As of 2013, the median household income was still more than 6 percent below 2007, when the economic downward spiral began.[7] Meanwhile, the top 1 percent of all wage earners recovered almost all Great Recession losses by the end of 2012, taking home one-fifth of all the money earned by all Americans.[8]

The loss of purchasing power is bleakest for those earning the federal minimum wage, for its value has plummeted over the past half century. Last increased by Congress in 2009, the minimum wage stands at $7.25 per hour. More than 4 million full-time American workers paid on an hourly basis earn this much or less. But when adjusted for inflation, the federal minimum wage in 2011 had actually lost 12 percent of its value since 1967, according to the nonpartisan Economic Policy Institute.[9] Financially speaking, those at the bottom have seen their fortunes slip away day by day, year by year.

Even if Americans manage to recover most of their purchasing power from Great Recession losses, there is little expectation that the long-term decline will trend upward. Many Americans feel that way, anyway. Independent polling data gathered in 2013 found that only 31 percent of the respondents believed that the economy would improve over the next 12 months.[10] From before the Great Recession, through the Great Recession, and after the Great Recession, Americans have been plagued by one constant: an economy that for most people has left them behind.

Lost Jobs, Lost Futures

Not so long ago, the United States was the world's economic behemoth with unparalleled wealth. While allies and adversaries alike struggled to regain their footing at the end of World War II, the United States just kicked its economic engine into a higher gear. Yes, there would be recessions now and again, but the country was on the move. Jobs were plentiful—the defense industry, automobile manufacturing, mining, and an incredible agriculture sector were among the many areas where the United States towered over other nations.

Then globalization set in. Other countries began producing goods—and in some cases services—at prices less than charged by U.S. manufacturers, and with that change, the U.S. standard of living began to decline. It wasn't the first time that the world economy shifted,[11] but it was the first time that the United States would be so heavily impacted by global economic restructuring. As a result, the entire country wobbled with a new sense of fallibility and uncertainty.

U.S. manufacturing was hit particularly hard by globalization. From the post-World War II period on through the 1970s, manufacturing had been the source of well-paying jobs with incredible economic security. Yet, between 1970 and 2001, American manufacturing declined from 28 percent of all jobs to 12 percent. Some of the losses stemmed from new technology such as automation and robotics, but most came from countries where the same products could be made by considerably cheaper labor, often under the direction of American corporations.[12]

Over time, some manufacturing jobs have returned to the United States, albeit in fewer numbers and less money for the same work. The automobile industry represents an excellent case in point. From the 1980s on, the industry increasingly felt the threat of foreign competition. The bottom fell out with the Great Recession, however. Between March 2008 and March 2009, the industry lost a whopping 410,000 jobs.[13] The industry slowly recovered with the help of the Troubled Assets Relief Program, the federal government's response to the Great Recession, which provided loan guarantees to General Motors and Chrysler.

The industry may have recovered, but the workers haven't—at least many, anyway. About 75 percent of 1.1 million jobs lost since 2005 returned by 2013, yet with a stunning caveat: new hires went to work for about $16 per hour, about half the pay of longtime workers. Moreover, instead of a defined retirement pension, the new hires receive less stable 401(k) plans. And unlike longtime workers, new hires don't get health-care insurance support after their retirement.[14] The auto industry is not alone in these changes.

Other industries have experienced similar reductions, leaving the American worker to perform the same or more work for considerably less money. In 2013, when U.S. Steel expanded and remodeled an aging plant in Ohio, it did so with nonunion employees who now earn less money and are required to pay more for healthcare insurance. In addition, they participate in a 401(k) retirement plan rather than a defined benefit. And the plant operates with a new technology that requires fewer workers.[15] Likewise, Hostess Brands (the baker of beloved Twinkies) declared bank-ruptcy in 2012, after unions refused to accept an 8 percent pay cut; as a result, 19,000 employees lost their jobs. When a restructured Hostess Brands company emerged in its place a few months later, management hired 1,800 nonunion employees in automated plants at drastically reduced salaries. The new company also outsourced delivery drivers to third-party providers at considerably reduced salaries.[16]

Retirement benefits make up a sizable portion of employee compensation, and as such have become a target for companies seeking to cut costs and increase profits. Between 1979 and 2011, the number of workers partici-pating in defined pension programs with guaranteed retirement incomes from their years of service dropped from 62 percent to 7 percent.[17] The precipitous drop began long before the Great Recession and continued after recovery, yet another sign of a declining standard of living for mil-lions of Americans.

The jobs that emerged after the Great Recession were much different from those that were lost. A 2012 study by the National Employment Law Project found that lower-wage jobs ($7.69 to $13.83 per hour) accounted for 21 percent of the jobs lost before the Great Recession. Yet, as the recov-ery grew, lower-wage jobs comprised 58 percent of the new positions in the workplace.[18]

And why? Because of automation and increased productivity, as well as the shift by employers of many jobs offshore. In addition, an evolving cor-porate sector mentality changed the view of employee pensions from long-term employer-employee relationships to minimal short-term investment imperatives so that funds could be used for other needs.[19] Combined, these structural alterations have had a disproportionate impact on the American workforce.

Leaving the Future Behind

It's hard to feel part of something when one's role is marginalized, yet that is the status of many American workers today. For those near the bottom of the economic ladder, purchasing power buys less every year as their wages and benefits erode. No wonder so many Americans feel left out. For all intents and purposes, they are.

DIVISIONS OVER BASIC VALUES

Societies thrive when their populations coalesce around basic values, core beliefs that unite most members most of the time.[20] Conversely, societies suffer when people are unable or unwilling to come together over those guiding principles. Americans have reached the point where consensus of basic themes is no longer a part of the political landscape. That missing ingredient has placed the nation in jeopardy, for a divided nation is vulnerable to implosion from within.

Modernization is a challenge for any nation. From the most primitive to the most advanced societies, modernization brings change, and change disrupts the status quo. The disruption can be sweeping, from different methods of production to new habits of consumption. Along with all of the economic and social changes generated by modernization, government changes, too. Some adjustments are clearly observable, such as governments building modern transportation networks to move large numbers of people. Others aren't so obvious, even though they serve important needs. Making sure our food is safe to eat and monitoring the quality of our water supplies are two modern services of government, yet most of us rarely think about these efforts and their results.

Most Americans agree on the need for government, but for what? Sure, some areas produce near unanimity of opinion; the defense of the homeland and Social Security come to mind as areas of widespread agreement for government involvement. But what about what some observers call the social safety net, the panoply of jigsawed programs dedicated to the poor, the infirm, the mentally ill, and others who are unable to cope in society? What about people who have suffered because of a changing economy or industries that have relocated abroad and left them unemployed at home? What about veterans who return from military conflict abroad addicted to drugs or left permanently without the use of limbs? Should these individuals be left without any help or should government step in with assistance? These questions are more difficult to address, especially when large dollar amounts are part of the answer. All of which leads to discussions of taxing and spending and rights and liberties.

Taxing and Spending

Nobody likes paying taxes. Still, as U.S. Supreme Court Justice Oliver Wendell Holmes once said, "Taxes are the price we pay for civilized society." But what kind of society do we want? Increasingly, America has become divided over how much government should collect taxes, and from whom. Americans are also split on how much money government should spend, and on whom. We know this much: Americans—and especially high-income earners—pay fewer national taxes today than they have in the past. And while the wealthy have benefited the most, 85 percent of Americans keep more of their incomes today than they did in 1980, according to one study.[21]

Even though Americans pay relatively low taxes compared with other industrialized nations,[22] a lopsided plurality nevertheless believes that their tax bills are too high. One recent survey finds 48 percent saying their taxes are excessive, compared with only 3 percent who claim they are too low; 45 percent say their taxes are "about right."[23] Moreover, by better than a two-to-one margin, Americans believe that government should be smaller, specifically, offer fewer services.[24] Yet, at the same time, solid majorities believe that the federal government should spend more money on assistance for the poor, Social Security, and national health, among domestic areas—programs that amount to about three-fourths of the budget. Only reduction in foreign aid secures a majority of public support, and this category amounts to less than 1 percent of the national budget.[25]

One growing group of Americans, known as the sovereign citizens movement, believes that individuals are entitled to decide for themselves which, if any, laws to obey—including taxes. Many sovereigns contend that U.S. currency is a sham, and as such worthless.[26] Some might consider such an idea as far-fetched, or even outrageous, but more than a few people actually subscribe to this philosophy. The Southern Poverty Law Center notes that the loosely organized movement has grown substantially since the turn of the 21st century to as many as 300,000 adherents.[27] These individuals often resort to violence to protect their "rights" and have been classified by the FBI as domestic terrorists. Other secessionist movements have called the U.S. government an illegal institution with abusive powers, particularly with the way that government raises and spends tax dollars. Many are race obsessed, claiming that "White America" is under siege by non-whites, and that the only way to survive is for whites to break away.[28] To be sure, secessionist movements are on the fringes of American society, but their claims go on, particularly when the economy suffers troubled times.

What do we make of these conflicting values? It's America's version of the "you can't have your cake and eat it" argument, except that's exactly what we want—to pay few taxes to the government, but have government spend freely on costly programs that are important to us. There's nothing wrong with a society tending to those who need or who are struggling to get by. There's something very wrong with a society that won't own up to its obligations because its members don't want to pay to fund that need. It's yet another way that Americans have become disengaged from their membership in society.

Protecting Individualism over the Public Good

Americans value freedom as a guarantee of our independence and autonomy. At its root, freedom is an individual-based right that forms the basis of more complex sociopolitical arrangements. In fact, while some view government as the logical extension of individuals banding together for the common good, that extension is predicated upon individuals seeking to maximize their self-interest.[29] In other words, society is built upon individual blocks.

Fair enough. Yet, at its extreme, individualism can be tricky stuff and tear the heart out of the body politic. For example, if someone decides to withhold payment of taxes because of opposition to a particular government policy, the very ability of government to protect all of society suffers as a consequence. That's actually happened, or been attempted, anyway, by protesters who have rejected their income tax obligations for reasons such as desegregation implementation, the funding of unpopular wars, or welfare spending.

More commonly, those who view individualism as sacred do so in opposition to government programs or proposed programs they don't like or approve. The firearms control issue is a case in point. Individuals opposing government constraints point to the right to bear firearms provision in the Second Amendment as absolute and inviolable, even though the federal courts repeatedly have ruled that Congress has the power to regulate ownership and operations of weapons under certain conditions.[30] These efforts at protecting individual rights are powerful impediments. In 2013, some public opinion polls showed more than 90 percent of Americans favoring universal background checks on would-be owners of firearms,[31] yet the National Rifle Association and other pro-gun owner groups unleashed their massive influence on Congress, which refused to consider even the mildest changes. More significantly, in the aftermath of several mass tragedies, 25 states passed legislation weakening gun laws, while only 8 sought to strengthen them.[32]

When so many people feel committed to an idea and it fails to take root, something is amiss. In the case of gun owner background registration checks, the individual claims of the few overpowered the wishes of the many. What does that say for the government's commitment to protect the public safety of its citizens? And at what point do such protests threaten the very legitimacy of our institutions?

To be sure, there are instances where the collective good prevails over individual dissent. Consider local governments that fluoridate their water supplies, state requirements that school-age children receive inoculations against serious diseases, or the federal government mandating seatbelts for individuals who ride in motor vehicles. Yet, even commonsense requirements such as these find dissenters willing to ignore, even defy, the rules because their values trump anything else.

At a minimum, resisting the rule of law is, as Lawrence Quill contends, "to exercise a form of uncommon sense,"[33] in the eyes of the dissenters, but that uncommon sense taken to its extreme can be harmful to the public good. More to the point, excessive individualism is yet another rupture in the governance of the United States. Such rebelliousness tests the durability of society's political fabric.

Immigration and the Growing Dislike for One Another

More than ever, America is a collage of different people from different cultures, ethnicities, and backgrounds. In fact, over its rich history, the United States has accepted more immigrants than any other nation.[34] In the earliest years, hundreds of thousands were forced to come here as slaves. Aside from that tragic stain, the United States has drawn an endless stream of people who have come here willingly to make better lives with more opportunities.

Still, many Americans see immigration as a distasteful and alienating experience, as well as a threat to the nation. That's because the sources of immigration have changed over the years. Other than slaves, immigration to the United States began as an exodus from Europe. That is, the people who came here were similar in appearances to most of those already here, language and modest cultural differences notwithstanding. Translation: They were white. Congress endorsed this selectivity as early as 1790 with the Naturalization Act by welcoming to the United States only those who were free whites. Later, during the late 1800s and early 1900s, Congress passed several other acts to severely restrict the entry of Asians, and later Latinos, to the United States.[35] Simply put, national policy was intentionally designed to keep the United States as white as possible. Until recently.

With open borders to the north and especially the south, non-whites easily found their way into the United States, at first in spite of American laws, and later after new policies eased the conditions for admission of people other than Europeans. Add to that the large numbers of immigrants who came illegally over the past century, and we see a United States today that has a much more complex look and feel than even 50 years ago. The multiplicity of languages and cultures, along with assorted skin tones and religions, has changed the texture of 21st-century America, so much so that between immigration and birth patterns, the Census Bureau predicts that whites will lose their majority in the United States by 2042.[36]

Many have embraced the recent waves of immigrants as hardworking people who have made valuable contributions to the nation in myriad areas ranging from menial jobs to technological innovation and entrepreneurship.[37] Others haven't been so accepting. One recent negative assessment describes immigration as responsible for "transporting ethnic conflict to communities and regions where nothing of the sort even existed in the 1960s."[38] Lost in this account are the facts that illegal immigrants often perform jobs Americans won't do, and that skilled immigrants perform jobs Americans can't do because of a lack of education or specialized training.

It may not be pleasant to acknowledge, but much of the resistance toward these new arrivals stems from mass xenophobia, the fear of strangers. Research shows that Americans don't like immigrants who don't look like them.[39] Immigration—legal or otherwise—simply reinforces the introduction of more people of different backgrounds than those already here, even if they or their predecessors arrived here as immigrants in earlier generations—as is the case for almost all of us. It's an oxymoron to be sure, but one that plagues and divides American society.

Little Knowledge, Less Interest

Part of the disconnect of Americans from their country lies with their low levels of political knowledge. Studies show that Americans are generally not well informed about the political process, basic constitutional rights and guarantees, political offices, and major political issues of the day. There's more. Comparatively speaking, Americans tend to be conceptually less knowledgeable about political life than citizens in other developed countries. This information gap starts early in life. According to the results from an international study of 28 advanced democracies, young Americans score well on facts but lack an abstract or theoretical understanding of democracy and citizenship.[40] And so it is with adults. A Pew survey of adults in 2007 found that half of the sample failed to correctly answer 60 percent of the questions on a political knowledge quiz.[41] This unfortunate condition has framed American politics for more than half a century.[42] To be sure, not all Americans are uninformed about the process, but sizable numbers remain unaware of how things work and the values behind them.[43] Who are these people? They tend to be those who are the most disadvantaged economically and socially.[44] They are the ones on the outside looking in.

There are consequences from the lack of knowledge and insight about the American political system. To begin with, without a basic understanding of the way things work, it's difficult for people to evaluate the impact of issues and events on their lives and the well-being of a society. Moreover, the less people know about their political circumstances, the more likely they are to wash their hands of any thoughts of participating. In other words, they choose to opt out from a system and policy makers they distrust. The result is a smaller group of people participating in a process that impacts the entire society,[45] a condition that can't be helpful in promoting and protecting democracy.

There's No *There* There

In his well-received book *Collapse*, political geographer Jared Diamond attempts to determine why some societies succeed and others fail. He writes, "Perhaps a crux of success or failure of a society is to know which core values to hold on to, and which ones to discard and replace with new values, when times change."[46] That seems logical enough. But what if a society no longer has a core? What if fundamental values are so splintered that members move in different directions, so much so that sufficient numbers lose interest in the whole because there is so little left to attract them? That's when the political foundation begins to implode, not because of collective decisions to move in one direction or another, but because there is little agreement on any direction, and even less reason for many to be part of it.

THE FRACTURED SOCIETY—THE GREATER GOOD NO MORE

At the heart of our struggle over values lies a society whose members are very much removed from one another, sometimes by choice, other times by illegitimate coercion tacitly or overtly sanctioned by government. Consider our residential patterns. It's hard to believe, but the United States is more segregated today than at any time since the collection of civil rights laws and court decisions dedicated to eradicate the government-endorsed separation of people because of race or ethnicity. Some of it is elective, but much of it is driven by past, and even current, government practices.

Self-Selected Separation

There is an element of truth that some people seek to live and associate with others like themselves. They have a sense of comfort being with those of similar race, religion, vocations, education, or economic status. Bill Bishop refers to this trait as the clustering of like-minded individuals who live and work in small, narrow communities with people of similar values and traits.

While we may find a certain security in embracing people like ourselves, at the same time such arrangements leave us isolated from others and removed from different people and their values. As a result, we know little about others and remain disconnected from the rest of society. We exist unaware of and often disinterested in diverse ideas and life experiences, whether they are political or otherwise. Bishop concludes that in 21st-century America there is tremendous solidarity within individual communities because of the similarities appreciated by the residents, but the price comes in the incredible differences across the nation that are little understood by anyone outside of our self-contained networks. Bishop writes, "We have replaced a belief in a nation with a trust in ourselves and our carefully chosen surroundings."[47] Thus, the contradiction: many Americans build tight communities within their own small spheres, yet remain apart from others in their own spheres.

This self-selected isolation is widespread, occurring among whites and non-whites alike. A good deal of misinformation and distrust emerges in the process, and not just between whites and non-whites. In fact, public opinion data find that each of America's largest ethnic minorities (Latinos, blacks, and Asians) view the other ethnic minorities as harmful and disrespectful.[48] It's pretty hard to find a country's core when so many of its people want little to do with one another.

What does this self-sorting have to do with the loss of loyalty to America? More than you might imagine. To the extent that we hunker down with others like us, we forego sensitivity to the rest of society. We lose sight of what works for us but does not work elsewhere. We relinquish understanding of others, especially those who may suffer or require special attention from government institutions. By tuning out the rest of society, we abandon our interest in the greater good. With that rejection comes the subtle, yet penetrating rejection of nationhood.

Government-Sponsored Segregation

Thought to be long gone (by many) are the endless examples of government-sponsored segregation. Surely, you say, such a claim must be erroneous more than half a century after the famous *Brown v. Board of Education* Supreme Court decision, followed by numerous civil rights acts, and the implementation of antidiscrimination and affirmative action throughout the land. Yet, that is not the case, especially with respect to public education.

Few concepts are more important to a nation dedicated to equality than universal public education. Education should deliver more than facts and basic know-how; it should inculcate the student with the tools for personal growth and efficacy, and development in the broader context of society. Much of this comes through the acquisition of "civic knowledge," a building process that helps the student "thoughtfully evaluate political choices and effectively contribute to political outcomes."[49] John Patrick correctly notes that without civic knowledge provided in the schools, "citizens are unable to act together to analyze public policy issues or problems, make cogent decisions about them, or participate intelligently about them."[50] Education is a gateway to promoting citizenship, and citizenship is cemented to the opportunity to participate, particularly in a democratic society. But what are we conveying to large swaths of society if their opportunities to participate are different from the opportunities of others? That gets to the essence of the many problems associated with school segregation.

Let's be clear: segregation is against the law, but laws and the enforcement of laws are two different matters. The best example of the enforcement dilemma is seen through the way that the U.S. Supreme Court has systematically backtracked on the racial equality issue since the original desegregation decision in 1954, when the justices ruled unanimously that "separate educational facilities are inherently unequal," and that public schools must desegregate "with all deliberate speed."[51] Since then, there has been a gradual judicial retreat. Initially, the court insisted on strict compliance of the desegregation order through several landmark decisions, but over time, as school districts and states complained about costs, commute issues, and other implementation difficulties, the U.S. Supreme Court pulled back. At first, the court accepted substantial compliance as sufficient desegregation change, and then accepted financial limits on the desegregation effort. Eventually, a majority actually concluded that race should not be the sole factor in addressing the issue of segregated schools.[52] As a result, "all deliberate speed" came to a very deliberate stop.

The watered-down judicial mandate has enabled local governments to return to segregated education patterns, as demonstrated repeatedly by reams of reports and data. According to a 2012 assessment, 80 percent of Latino students and 74 percent of African American students attend schools where majorities are non-white. More disturbingly, 43 percent of Latino students and 38 percent of African American students attend "intensely segregated" schools where more than 90 percent of the students are non-whites.[53] Further, these schools have disproportionately high poverty, poor curriculum, higher student-to-teacher ratios, and greater teacher turnover.[54] Predictably, these are also the areas with the highest student dropout rates.

Segregated housing patterns underscore educational segregation patterns. True, housing policies no longer support segregation. Still, studies show that modern neighborhoods remain segregated not because of economic disparities, but because of "the interaction of barriers, fears, and preferences."[55] Given such informal, yet powerful divides, what kinds of opportunities lie for citizens of segregated schools later in life? Not many for most of them.

Separation Is Separation, Period

As we see from the discussion above, whether by accident or by design, Americans are increasingly separated from one another. But not all see the significance of racial and ethnic separation the same way. What stands as comfort for some looms as an ugly discriminatory barrier for others, and that barrier lessens the commitment to being part of a society that is anything but just and brimming with unbridled prospects for success. The increasingly different roads to opportunity make it difficult for large numbers of citizens to embrace a sense of nationhood, leaving our nation's political fabric weakened and frayed.

I'VE GOT MINE ... GO GET YOURS

The fragmentation of American society manifests in many ways, some more subtle than others. Whether through outright separation or more subtle means of creating distance, some Americans go out of their way to remain apart from others, and they're quite willing to pay the sometimes hefty price for their protection and privacy.

At the same time, the perceptions of inept government institutions leave people less willing to support public investment in community services. Citizen reluctance forces governments to do more with less, but of course they can't. The outcome leaves those with the least resources having the greatest array of unmet needs, further exacerbating fundamental differences in society. Meanwhile, those with resources don't require—and therefore see no need to support—many traditional government services, whether they come in the form of public safety or public education. As a result of these trends, fewer and fewer Americans have "skin in the game," or interest in seeing society flourish. They see no reason to be part of the larger community.

Circling the Wagons

Increasingly, many Americans are trending inward. Some efforts seem innocent enough, yet they carry serious connotations. The more fortunate attempt to alleviate insecurities found in open society through various forms of collective self-protection. They sometimes turn to gated communities as their artificial Shangri-La, many of which contain the private counterparts of the outside world, including police and fire protection, parks and social facilities, banks, medical facilities, supermarkets, and restaurants.

Gated communities are hardly microcosms of society at large. Whites are much more likely than non-whites to pursue these revered and exclusive accommodations.[56] Shielded from the vagaries of the outside world by high walls, electronically operated gates, and intercepting security personnel, their isolation often legitimizes racism and other forms of segregation found in the less structured communities of everyday citizens.[57] In other words, gated community residents buy their way to safety via isolation and self-reliance, leaving others on the outside world to fend for themselves with the limited resources at their disposal.

Other forms of separation are more circumspect, yet effective in separating various segments of society. Consider something as seemingly wholesome as Neighborhood Watch programs. Over the past few decades, these groups have spawned in great numbers, especially in suburbia. There, many residents who relocated to escape the ills of city life find themselves with less separation from urban areas than they anticipated. That realization is disconcerting because of cities' many unattractive elements: centers of crime because of depressed economies, fewer opportunities, and higher unemployment, and the presence of ethnic minorities. Thus, Neighborhood Watch networks are formed, often in conjunction with local police who lack the resources to adequately protect the public.

A major goal of Neighborhood Watch groups is to reduce access to their neighborhoods by potential troublemakers. They often put up signs indicating regular patrols by their members. Sometimes they construct barriers that physically reduce the possibility of intrusion or comingling by "undesirables."[58] But fundamentally, Neighborhood Watch groups want to separate themselves from others by keeping them away.

Some Neighborhood Watch groups have gone so far as to hire private police patrols because of the fear that understaffed local governments are unable to ensure safe neighborhoods. In other cases, citizens in the community patrol in police officer-like uniforms, sometimes armed, in an effort to act as the "eyes and ears" of law enforcement. But these citizens often lack the training given to law enforcement, and that insufficient instruction can result in tragedy, such as accidental death of someone thought to be an intruder but who may not be.[59]

There is little doubt that Neighborhood Watch groups operate in the name of preserving law. Some even feel a sense of community from the "us versus them" bond that emerges from their association. Such noble attitudes may have merit on a superficial level. Yet, the very presence of these associations has the effect of using the law as a tool to keep others away, law abiding or otherwise. These preservationist groups may build some protection, but in the process they are also separating themselves from the rest of society. It's another sign of the fragmentation of America.

The Problems of Shrinking Government

Organizations like Neighborhood Watch groups form, in part, because residents are unsatisfied with the level of local government services. After all, if people felt secure enough about their surroundings, there would be no need to form private security associations or hire private patrol services. Yet, it's abundantly clear that 21st-century America has spawned an era of less government, with people fending for themselves as the consequence. Recent polls suggest the public wants government to retreat from public programs, leaving it to citizens to meet more needs or do without them.[60] It doesn't really matter because these groups have taken themselves out of the public equation. Still, the needs are there, although they are not always addressed successfully.

The concerns for less spending have trickled down to the states and local governments, where public safety and other socioeconomic issues receive considerably more attention than at the national level. The budgets of state and local governments collectively well exceed federal spending. Since 2009, between the Great Recession and the post-recession era of reduced federal spending commitments, state and local law enforcement agencies have consistently pared their personnel because of fewer resources at their disposal.

And so it is with community public safety issues. Smaller law enforcement departments have led local governments to increase reliance on volunteers, although their value and success vary by community. In fact, the outcomes are rather uneven. Predictably, high-income, homogenous white areas tend to experience few problems with community policing and Neighborhood Watch services. It's another story for low-income, racial, and ethnic minority areas, however, where community patrol success is much more fleeting. Moreover, the most problematic issues tend to be found in racially mixed areas where discrimination abounds.[61]

The takeaway is clear enough: whether with gated communities or volunteer community patrols, high-income areas are relatively unaffected by society's ills. In other words, those who have the means to protect themselves in the absence of well-functioning government public safety agencies do so. Those with less affluence and of different color live in another world altogether without adequate protection and security. Again, affluence and race tell much of the story: those with means are safely ensconced on the inside; those without are on the outside looking in. Either way, neither is buying into 21st-century America.

SUMMING UP

One of the most intriguing aspects of a performing symphony orchestra centers on the way that the conductor seamlessly coordinates the various instruments to blend from the many into a moving presentation. If executed well, every musician plays in a manner that complements the others, resulting in a full, vibrant outcome that mesmerizes the audience. Collective, disciplined dedication to the same objective, along with endless practice and rehearsals, produces a memorable moment for the performers and audience alike. Even dissonant notes have their place.

Democracies don't operate with the precision and synergy of a symphony orchestra. In fact, they deliver pretty sloppy performances, considering the many players, varying talent levels, and weak coordination. But the closer democracies get to that dedication and discipline, the healthier they are. Conversely, the more that their citizens feel denied or without place or purpose, the more likely that the democratic engine sputters for lack of fuel, otherwise known as loyalty and commitment. All of which brings us back to the allegory that opened the conclusion to this chapter: if the nation's collective voice were a symphony, it would be performed by isolated musicians playing with a host of sour notes too painful to watch and too dissonant to hear.

And that's the problem. For many years, American democracy hummed with a collective purpose. It wasn't perfect—no democracy is by definition. Over the course of our history, there have been terrible cases of discrimination, uneven opportunities, and occasional abuses by those in official positions of authority. Some people have always been wealthier than others, as is the nature of an open economy, but the differences haven't been nearly as large in the past as they are today. But in these instances and others, most people identified with the value of making this a place they could be proud of; they resolved to improve their lot and the lots of others rather than walk away physically or psychologically. Especially in the days after World War II, there was a collective purpose that unified most Americans, and there was healthy, constructive debate about unsettled issues. America was more a land of collective change agents than not. To borrow from a sports metaphor, most everyone had skin in the game.

That era has been replaced by one of profound extremes—extremes in the ways we treat each other and stay away from each other, extremes in widely differing opportunities for individuals to excel, extremes in terms of the way people find it easy to walk away from commitment and obligation, and extremes in attitudes about the value of the American political system. For too many, the American dream has become the "American nightmare." As a result, many no longer feel invested in American society because their investment is yielding poor returns. For all these reasons and more, our nation is at risk of irreparable political implosion.

ENDNOTES

1. Nathan Glazer and Daniel P. Moynihan, *Beyond the Melting Pot*, 2nd ed., Cambridge, MA: MIT Press, 1970.
2. For a recent discussion on the divisiveness within American society, see the discussion by Dante Chinni and James Gimpel, *Our Patchwork Nation*, New York: Gotham Books, 2010.
3. Jacob S. Hacker, Gregory A Huber, Philipp Rehm, Mark Schlesinger, and Rob Valletta, "Economic Security at Risk," Rockefeller Foundation, New York, July 2010, p. 3.

4. "Four in 10 Americans See Their Standard of Living Declining," *USA Today*/Gallup Poll, June 9, 2008, http://www.gallup.com/poll/107749/Four-Americans-See-Their-Standard-Living-Declining.aspx.

5. "Inside the Middle Class: Bad Times Hit the Good Life," Pew Research Center, Washington, DC, April 9, 2008, http://www.pewsocialtrends.org/2008/04/09/inside-the-middle-class-bad-times-hit-the-good-life/.

6. "Changes in U.S. Family Finances from 2007 to 2010: Evidence from the Survey of Consumer Finances," *Federal Reserve Bulletin*, 98(2), 1, 2012.

7. "Median Income Rises, but Is Still 6% below Level at Start of Recession in '07," *New York Times*, August 22, 2013, p. A13.

8. "Top 10% Took Home Half of U.S. Income in 2012," *New York Times*, September 11, 2013, pp. B1, B3.

9. Lawrence Mishel, Josh Bivens, Elise Gould, and Heidi Shierholz, *The State of Working America*, 12th ed., Ithaca, NY: Economic Policy Institute, Cornell University Press, 2012, p. 279.

10. http://ap-gfkpoll.com/main/wp-content/uploads/2013/04/AP-GfK-April-2013-Topline-Posted-FINAL_economy.pdf.

11. Jeffrey D. Sachs cites earlier examples of globalization where new ideas, products, and modes of production changed the order of nations. See his *Common Wealth: Economics for a Crowded Planet*, New York: Penguin Press, 2008, pp. 7–8.

12. David S. Mason, *The End of the American Century*, Lanham, MD: Rowman & Littlefield, 2009, p. 40.

13. "A Look Back at GM, Chrysler and the American Auto Industry," Executive Office of the President, Washington, DC, April 21, 2010.

14. "The American Automobile Industry about to Go on a Hiring Spree," Associated Press, June 9, 2013, http://bigstory.ap.org/article/american-auto-industry-about-go-hiring-spree.

15. "The Newest Face of U.S. Steel," *Wall Street Journal*, May 10, 2013, pp. A1, A2.

16. See "The Return of Hostess," *Wall Street Journal*, July 9, 2013, pp. B1, B2, and "Hostess Employees Unhappy with Wage Cuts," July 9, 2013, MSN, http://money.msn.com/now/post-hostess-employees-unhappy-with-wage-cuts.

17. "FAQs about Benefits—Retirement Issues," Employee Benefits Research Institute, Washington, DC, 2013, http://www.ebri.org/publications/benfaq/index.cfm?fa=retfaq14.

18. "Majority of Jobs Added in the Recovery Pay Low Wages, Study Finds," *New York Times*, August 31, 2012, pp. B1, B3.

19. See Keith P. Ambactsher, *Pension Revolution: A Solution to the Pensions Crisis*, New York: John Wiley & Sons, 2007, p. 114.

20. Gabriel A. Almond and Sidney Verba make this point in their *Civic Culture*, Boston: Little, Brown Publisher, 1963, p. 227.

21. "Complaints Aside, Most Face Lower Tax Burden Than in the Reagan '80s," *New York Times*, November 30, 2012, pp. A1, A20.

22. "The Numbers: How Do U.S. Taxes Compare Internationally?" Tax Policy Center, Washington, DC, September 13, 2011, www.taxpolicycenter.org/briefing-book/background/numbers/international.cfm.

23. AEI Online, Washington, DC, May 14, 2012, http://www.aei.org/papers/politics-and-public-opinion/polls/public-opinions-on-taxes-1937-to-today/.

24. "America's Best Days," Rasmussen Reports, January 26, 2013, http://www.rasmussenreports.com/public_content/politics/mood_of_america/america_s_best_days.

25. "Survey: Many Conflicted on Government-Spending Cuts, but Most Want Foreign Aid Cut," *Seattle Times*, March 6, 2013, http://seattletimes.com/html/nationworld/2020518965_govtspendingxml.html.
26. "By a Code of Their Own," *Los Angeles Times*, April 6, 2013, pp. A1, A11.
27. "Sovereign Citizens Movement," Southern Poverty Law Center, http://www.splcenter.org/get-informed/intelligence-files/ideology/sovereign-citizens-movement#.UXA56MpMhI0.
28. "New Secessionist Movement Is a Disturbing Throwback," *Progressive*, November 21, 2012, http://www.progressive.org/new-secessionist-movement-disturbing-throwback.
29. See Robert N. Bellah, Richard Madsen, William M. Sullivan, Ann Swidler, and Steven M. Tipton, *Habits of the Heart: Individualism and Commitment in American Life*, New York: Harper and Row, 1985, p. 143.
30. In *District of Columbia v. Heller*, no. 07-290 (2008), the Supreme Court overturned a District of Columbia law banning all handguns, but the justices went to state that, consistent with previous decisions, the Second Amendment is not absolute.
31. http://abcnews.go.com/blogs/politics/2013/03/some-gun-measures-broadly-backed-but-the-politics-show-an-even-split/, March 13, 2013.
32. "Pro-Gun Laws Gain Ground," *Wall Street Journal*, April 4, 2013, pp. A1, A4.
33. Lawrence Quill, *Civil Disobedience: (Un)Common Sense in Mass Democracies*, New York: Palgrave MacMillan, 2009, p. 21.
34. "Mexican Immigrants in the United States, 2008," Pew Hispanic Center, April 15, 2009, p. 1, http://www.pewhispanic.org/2009/04/15/mexican-immigrants-in-the-united-states-2008/.
35. For a history of anti-White immigration laws and court decisions, see Aviva Chomsky, *"They Take Our Jobs!" and 20 Other Myths about Immigration*, Boston: Beacon Press, 2007, pp. 77–90.
36. "Whites to Lose Majority Status in U.S. by 2042," *Wall Street Journal*, August 14, 2008, p. A3.
37. See "Embracing Illegals," *BusinessWeek*, July 18, 2005, pp. 56–64, and "Shortage of Skilled Workers Looms in U.S.," *Los Angeles Times*, April 21, 2008, pp. A1, A7.
38. Roy Beck, *The Case against Immigration*, New York: Norton, 1996, p. 29.
39. For some cutting-edge research on this topic, see Ted Brader, Nicholas Valentino, and Elizabeth Suhay, "What Triggers Opposition to Immigration? Anxiety, Group Cues and the Immigration Threat," *American Journal of Political Science*, 52(4), 959–979, 2008.
40. Judith Torney-Purta and Carolyn Henry Barber, "Strengths and Weaknesses in U.S. Students' Knowledge and Skills: Analysis from the IEA Civic Education Study," Center for Information and Research on Civic Learning and Engagement (CIRCLE), Medford, MA, June 2004.
41. "Public Knowledge of Current Affairs Little Changed by News and Information Revolutions," Pew Research Center for the People and the Press, Washington, DC, April 7, 2007, p. 2.
42. See Michael X. Delli Carpini, "An Overview of the State of Citizens' Knowledge about Politics," Departmental Papers, University of Pennsylvania, 2005, pp. 29–30.
43. Barbara A. Bardes and Robert W. Oldendick, *Public Opinion: Measuring the American Mind*, 4th ed., Lanham, MD: Rowman and Littlefield, 2012, p. 129.
44. Michael X. Delli Carpini and Scott Keeter, *What Americans Know about Politics and Why It Matters*, New Haven, CT: Yale University Press, 1996, p. 265.

45. William A. Galston makes this connection in his "Political Knowledge, Political Engagement, and Civic Education," *Annual Review of Political Science*, 4, 224 2001.
46. Jared Diamond, *Collapse: How Societies Choose to Fail or Succeed*, New York: Viking Press, 2005, p. 433.
47. Bill Bishop, with Robert G. Cushing, *The Big Sort*, Boston: Houghton Mifflin Company, 2008, p. 302.
48. "Poll Surveys Ethnic Views among Chief Minorities," *New York Times*, December 13, 2007, p. A24.
49. Anne Colby, Elizabeth Beaumont, Thomas Ehrlich, and Josh Corngold, *Educating for Democracy*, San Francisco: Jossey-Bass Publisher, 2007, p. 6.
50. John J. Patrick, "Introduction to Education for Civic Engagement in Democracy," *Education for Civic Engagement in Democracy*, edited by Sheilah Mann and John J. Patrick, Bloomington, IN: ERIC Clearing House for Social Studies, 2000, p. 3.
51. *Brown v. Board of Education*, 347 U.S. 483 (1954).
52. The two cases were *Parents Involved in Community Schools v. Seattle School District No. 1*, no. 05-908 and *Meredith v. Jefferson County Board of Education*, no. 05-915 (2005).
53. Gary Orfield, "E Pluribus ... Separation: Deepening Double Segregation for More Students," Executive Summary, Civil Rights Project, UCLA, September 20, 2012, p. 3.
54. Gary Orfield and Chunngmei Lee, "Why Segregation Matters: Poverty and Educational Inequality," Civil Rights Project, Harvard University, Cambridge, MA, 2005, p. 17.
55. Margery Austin Turner and Karina Fortuny, "Residential Segregation and Low-Income Working Families," Urban Institute, Washington, DC, February 2009, p. 2.
56. "Gated Communities More Popular, and Not Just for the Rich," *USA Today*, December 16, 2002, http://business.time.com/2012/06/20/our-net-worth-is-down-39-how-worried-should-we-be/.
57. Setha Low, *Behind the Gates: Life, Security, and the Pursuit of Happiness in Fortress America*, New York: Routledge, 2004, p. 11.
58. Carol F. Horowitz, "An Empowerment Strategy for Eliminating Neighborhood Crime," Heritage Foundation, *Backgrounder*, 814, 16, 1991.
59. For a much discussed recent example, see Charles M. Blow, "The Curious Case of Trayvon Martin," *New York Times*, March 12, 2012, http://www.nytimes.com/2012/03/17/opinion/blow-the-curious-case-of-trayvon-martin.html?_r=0.
60. "Majority in U.S. Still Say Government Doing Too Much," Gallup Poll, September 17, 2012, http://www.gallup.com/poll/157481/majority-say-government-doing.aspx.
61. For an interesting study on the successes and failures of community policing, see Wesley G. Skogan, Susan M. Hartnett, Jill DuBois, Jennifer T. Comey, Marianne Kaiser, and Justine H. Lovig, "Problem Solving in Practice: Implementing Community Policing in Chicago," Institute for Policy Research, Northwestern University, Evanston, IL, 2000.

3

An Uneven Electorate

American democracy depends upon free-flowing interaction between the governed and their leaders. The linkage is fostered through several conduits. With respect to the governed, people petition leaders through meetings, protests, letters to editors, and blogs, sometimes individually and on other occasions through the efforts of organized groups. For their part, leaders avail themselves to venues such as town hall meetings, formal addresses before interest groups, meetings with editorial boards, occasional one-on-one meetings with constituents, and other outreach mechanisms. The point is that without these connections, political walls separate these political forces, jeopardizing the well-being of both. Nevertheless, that chasm has become a regrettable mainstay in American politics.

More than ever, the polity has been pushed to the sidelines of the political process, particularly in terms of the linkage with political parties. These organizational agents have no official standing as government entities, yet political parties historically have served as valuable midwives between the voters and elected officials.

Much like an interpreter for two people speaking different languages, party organizations have received and delivered messages between those outside and inside of government, helping to legitimize the relationship between the governors and the governed. They have served as candidate recruitment instruments, political education agents, conduits for the exercise of the vote, platforms for candidates, and fund-raising machines. In addition to all these important characteristics, political parties as organizations have managed the elections of candidates to political office. Without any mention whatsoever in the U.S. Constitution, American political parties have become critical instruments in arranging the routine transfers of power in the nation's electoral system.

It wasn't always this way. Political parties emerged slowly as an organizational tool after the Constitutional Convention in 1787. At their earliest stage, parties were little more than the personal extensions of national leaders.[1] But by the mid-1800s, they had inserted themselves as vital linkages in American democracy. With the approach of the Civil War, party organizations grew beyond the personal political bases of elected officials and their allies outside of government. They appealed to larger numbers of voters as more states availed the franchise to greater numbers of citizens. Scholars began to view political parties much like a three-legged stool: the party as an organization, a full-time assortment of people who promote party values year-round; the party of the electorate, otherwise known as the voters; and the party in government, those who are elected to and serve in political office.[2]

At one time, all of these elements were interdependent and functioned fairly seamlessly. These days, however, large swaths of voters are estranged from party organizations and elected officials, leading many to question the very legitimacy of the transfer of power in the nation's political system. After all, if political parties no longer connect voters with elected officials through open elections, what's there to protect society from irresponsible or even tyrannical governance?

The linkage began to loosen in the early days of the 20th century innocently enough. Reformers associated with the Progressive movement questioned the undemocratic selection of state and local candidates by party bosses and powerful interests removed from the voters. Under the reform banner described as direct democracy, their quiet revolution pursued political party nominations through direct primaries. Many also adopted the initiative, referendum, and recall in various combinations as checks on elected leaders out of touch with the voters.[3] The unraveling of ties continued after World War II as the smoke-filled rooms filled with self-appointed party leaders gave way to national nominating conventions with increasing numbers of presidential delegates elected by voters to represent their choices. Recently, additional ruptures have undermined political party clout further through several U.S. Supreme Court decisions that have enabled campaign contributions to flow outside of political party channels and even circumvent candidate campaign organizations.

With the dawn of the 21st century, other agents have also reshaped the relationship between political parties and the voters, especially the flow of massive amounts of political campaign funds through television, direct mail, and others means of communication, as well as social media.

These tools have allowed candidates to approach voters directly with their messages, further breaking down the role of parties as conduits. Combined, the many developments of the past half century have reorganized the political landscape that once made political parties the center of the political universe.

To be sure, political parties have not gone the way of the dinosaur and other prehistoric animals, but they no longer play much of a role in linking candidates and voters. If anything, today's candidates run campaigns in ways that circumvent traditional party functions.[4] Party labels almost seem superfluous other than to give those with historical connections a now-hazy standard they can lean on for guidance, no matter how removed that standard is from the voter.

Our principal concern centers on the evolving organizational capacities of political parties and their consequences. The waning of political parties as accountable, participatory linkage channels has left a gaping hole between voters and the candidates. Grassroots politics and old-fashioned park rallies have given way to 30-second television hit pieces, untraceable independent campaign spending, and communication through social media. Those elected to serve quickly find themselves almost blocked off from voters by powerful interests, the perpetual quests for huge campaign war chests, and gerrymandered congressional districts that protect incumbents from the most worthy challengers.

It would be unfair to portray American elections these days as meaningless exercises, for they are not. Nevertheless, for those who feel intentionally separated from the political process, there is little reason to participate. And for those who have achieved all they have ever needed and more, their primary reason to participate in the political process is to protect their political or financial investments, rather than advance discussions connected with national concerns.

This chapter begins with a discussion of the deterioration of the American political party system from a strong political bridge to a poorly functioning conduit for voter participation. It continues with a focus on new competing power centers that are isolated from the body politic, the masses of voters who are on the outside of the process and looking in only from great distances. Even those who dare to climb the participation mountain are often overwhelmed by myriad elections, confusing rules, and erratic voting systems. The chapter ends with the consequences of a public uncoupled from political power centers historically in the hands of political parties.

BLURRED WINDOWS OF OPPORTUNITY

The famous humorist Will Rogers is well known for his poignant observation about American political parties. Said Rogers, "I am not a member of any organized political party; I'm a Democrat." Rogers was referring to the fact that the modern Democratic Party has a history of a rather diverse and sometimes conflicted base, which makes its core a bit disheveled and something of a mystery at times—think of a soft-boiled egg where the yolk is not quite congealed. It's almost as true today for both major political parties as when Rogers made his observation nearly 100 years ago. But complaints about dysfunctional political parties are commonplace in American politics. The issue here is the way poorly organized parties have discouraged participation of select groups of Americans, rejecting their interest and leaving these would-be voters with the distinct impression of second-class citizenship.

Disfranchised Voters

No issue in a democracy is more important than conferring to all the right to vote. Participation in elections assures representation of all who choose to be part of the process. Those on the winning side feel validated that their numbers have carried the day; those on the losing side take solace that they will have their opportunity in the next election. Simply put, the opportunity to vote is a fundamental element of citizenship. That unfettered opportunity also confers legitimacy on the process and the outcome.

The process works, assuming the system allows everyone eligible to participate. To the extent that people are excluded, the reputation of the system comes into question, which can foster feelings of political impotence and suspicion. Moreover, elected officials may not have an accurate picture of society's issues, or find it easier to ignore issues they would rather not see. As one observer notes, "Since voter turnout rates are skewed according to income, education, and race, the citizens who depend most on the government may have their concerns neglected.... This represents a serious flaw in our democracy and process for decision making."[5] That flaw is likely to discourage sizable swaths of society and weaken the legitimacy of our institutions.

Nevertheless, American history is riddled with examples of selected groups shut out of political involvement, particularly the right to vote,

through either the denial of the franchise or removal of otherwise con-
stitutionally eligible participants. Until the mid-20th century, unrepresentative state legislatures reinforced discriminatory practices by enacting
restrictive laws. Little wonder that large portions of American society felt
hopeless. That's history, but what about now? Of significance is the extent
to which the denial of the vote exists today, which augurs the question, if
you can't fully participate as a citizen, why remain committed to a system
of exclusion?

Institutional Denial

Early on, people of color, poor whites, and women were denied participation in American elections largely because of state laws. Many voter restrictions for males, non-whites or otherwise, were eliminated in the North
in the early 19th century. However, antiparticipation policies for African
Americans continued in the South after the Civil War, and passage of the
13th, 14th, and 15th Amendments to the Constitution, otherwise known
as the civil rights amendments. Women were not enfranchised until passage of the 19th Amendment in 1920.

Still, discrimination persisted most prominently (though not exclusively) in the South, largely through the actions of state legislatures that
were dominated by the Democratic Party. Denial of the vote occurred
through a variety of clever obstacles, such as poll taxes, literacy tests, or
exclusion of people of color from primary elections, the latter of which
restricted their candidate choices in general elections a few months later.
These sanctions, too, were eventually eliminated through either civil
rights laws or U.S. Supreme Court decisions during the 1950s and 1960s,
although informal intimidation by election officials remained largely in
rural counties.[6] Since the latter part of the 20th century, Republicans have
emerged as the most popular party in the South, to the extent that they
controlled every southern state legislature in 2013. Today, discriminatory
practices linger. The parties have changed positions of power, but voter
obstacles continue.

"Legal" Redistricting

These days, state and local election officials are much more subtle about
the management of voter turnout. After all, numerous national laws and
court decisions have guaranteed the franchise for all qualified citizens.

One of the most common approaches to limiting the effectiveness of the franchise comes in the organization of congressional districts and other legislative constituencies. At the conclusion of each federal census of the population that occurs at the beginning of a decade, states are required by law to create voter districts equal in population. With few exceptions, they can decide the physical boundaries of those districts.

That's where policy making can become questionable, if not duplicitous. About half the states employ independent commissions to carve out districts irrespective of political considerations. These entities are largely removed from politics. The rest of the states empower their legislatures to form legislative districts without preconceived rules or conditions, assuming new district populations are equal in population. When state bodies are controlled by a particular political party, the redistricting process can be manipulated to predetermine election outcomes by shaping the populations of district boundaries in ways that will include or exclude various groups. The practice is known as gerrymandering, named after a 19th-century Massachusetts governor, Albert Gerry, who was particularly adept at manipulating election outcomes through the use of this concept.

Gerrymandering tends to produce powerful and often one-sided political results to this day, especially if it occurs on a widespread basis. According to one study, after the 2010 Census state legislatures dominated by Democrats had authority to draw boundaries for 44 congressional seats; meanwhile, state legislatures dominated by Republicans had the ability to create boundaries for 210 seats,[7] nearly half of all the seats in the 435-member House of Representatives. The rest were organized in states with nonpartisan independent commissions that were largely removed from political tints.

The outcomes of gerrymandering can produce outcomes irrespective of the voters' wishes. Consider the redistricted results in the state of Florida after the 2012 election. There, Republican congressional candidates gained 55 percent of the seats to the U.S. House of Representatives, yet when totaled statewide, Democratic candidates collected more than half a million more votes than Republicans. A similar outcome occurred in Ohio, where even though Democratic presidential candidate Barack Obama won the state by 2 points, Republicans garnered 12 of the 16 congressional seats. In Pennsylvania, Obama won reelection by a comfortable 5 points; nevertheless, congressional Republican candidates scored 13 of the 18 seats.

Gerrymandering has produced some potent outcomes in the form of "safe" seats, contests with uncompetitive congressional races, particularly for Republicans. Since 1998, the number of safe Republican seats in the House of Representatives has swelled to 186 from 148; the number of safe Democratic seats has also increased, to 159 from 123. Meanwhile, the number of "swing districts" where elections could go either way has dropped precipitously to 90 from 164.[8] This kind of rigidity preordains election outcomes, hardly the objective of a truly representative democracy, and certainly discouraging to change advocates. Fundamentally, it has the effect of compacting minorities into fewer districts, thereby reducing their political influence in elections, thereby reducing their potential influences in other districts.[9] The bottom line is that when carried out on a widespread basis, gerrymandering can be a huge force in creating a House of Representatives majority anything but representative of the national voter turnout.

Republicans had the same post-2010 Census political advantages in organizing state legislative districts, which all but assured similarly skewed election outcomes in 2012, and helped to produce one-sided legislatures for years to come. The result? Outcomes that bend the representation process in ways that artificially give more clout to some groups than others.

Loaded State and Local Election Rules

Emboldened by state legislative victories in 2010, Republican Party leaderships in many states moved to change the participation rules for the 2012 national election. Some changes focused on early registration, while others centered on early voting. In Florida, a swing state, the Republican legislature and Republican governor reduced early voting to 1 week in 2012 from 2 weeks in 2008. In Ohio, another swing state, the Republican-led legislature and Republican Governor John Kasich eliminated voting on the Sunday before election day, a change that reduced participation abilities particularly for people who didn't have the opportunity to vote during the week. Altogether, more than 30 states enacted laws that shortened the voting schedule or tightened the registration process through requiring multiple pieces of identification.

Some defenders of the changes claimed they were necessary to prevent voter fraud; others said they were only trying to control the cost of elections. But there's another side: critics charged that the changes were closeted as an effort to reduce the number of participants who might sway the outcomes toward Democratic candidates. To continue with the Florida case, an independent study found 173 cases of double voting out of 8.4 million ballots cast, almost all of which resulted from individuals voting in two different states.[10] Such data hardly smack of massive fraud.

Regardless of the motives, the potential changes were anything but inconsequential. As various state suppression efforts unfolded, the Brennan Center for Justice, a nonpartisan, nonprofit organization concerned with voter rights, estimated that as many as 5 million voters could be denied the franchise in the 2012 elections, representing, according to executive director Michael Waldman, "the most significant rollback of voting rights in decades."[11]

Winners and Losers

Clearly, election systems in numerous states produce outcomes that benefit some and harm others. And the outcomes are anything but random. According to several studies, those most discouraged tend to be racial minorities, students, and the elderly. Coincidentally, an examination of the 2012 voting patterns shows that racial minorities and students voted overwhelmingly for Democrat Obama, whereas seniors tilted slightly toward Republican presidential candidate Mitt Romney. These groups suffered the most in attempting to vote.

Examples of voter intimidation unfolded during the campaign. Although individuals from both political parties engaged in suppression efforts, the most serious attempts came from Republicans in swing states. In Florida, Virginia, and Indiana, targeted voter groups received phone calls telling them they could vote by phone instead of going to the polls. In Wisconsin and Ohio billboards advertised in minority, low-income areas that voter fraud was a felony; the billboards were put up without attribution. In Latino-heavy New Mexico, Republican officials circulated a video saying that voters would be required to show identification and couldn't use interpreters—neither of which was true.[12]

The purported bases for the slew of new state and local voting procedures centered on concerns about voter fraud. Time and time again, officials claimed that protecting the sanctity of the vote was their only concern. Yet, that simply has not been the case, other than an occasional isolated example. A national study of more than 2,000 voters funded by the Carnegie–Knight Foundation produced ten cases of voter fraud over a 12-year period.[13] But that didn't keep states from passing restrictive legislation. As the American Civil Liberties Union concluded, "Poll taxes and literacy tests [employed by states prior to the 1965 Voting Rights Act] have given way to more modern voter suppression tactics packaged as voter ID laws, restrictions to voter registration and cuts to early voting."[14]

These intimidation efforts continued throughout the 2012 national election campaign with some success. One post-election assessment showed that Latinos and African Americans waited longer to vote than whites. Likewise, twice as many Democrats reported long waits than Republicans.[15] Another examination of the turnout in Florida found that more than 200,000 voters gave up because of excessive waits, with most saying they would have voted for Democrat Barack Obama[16]—this, in what turned out to be the single most important swing state in the 2012 presidential race. In Ohio, the Republican Secretary of State allowed early voting in Republican-leaning counties, while denying it in Democratic counties until a public uproar forced him to capitulate and equalize the voting process.[17] In Virginia, another Republican-run state, thousands of voters waited hours to vote in precincts with inadequate numbers of voting machines; many left in disgust after hours. Those affected were disproportionately minorities and Democrats.[18] The pattern of political suppression for some and enhanced opportunities for others was inescapable.

Referring to a series of recently passed laws in Republican-controlled states that discouraged early registration and voting, political observer Ari Berman wrote that the election was a fiasco: "New voting restrictions and confusion over recent court decisions exacerbated problems lingering since 2000: broken voting machines, an antiquated voter registration system, ungodly lines, misinformed poll workers and partisan election officials."[19] Denials of state and local election officials notwithstanding, the motivations of those involved with tighter voting rules had a distinctly Republican hue.

In the end, efforts in 2012 to suppress the minority vote actually produced a higher participation rate than at any time in U.S. history. Overall, the share of the ethnic minority vote increased to 28 percent in 2012 from 26 percent in 2008. For the first time, a higher percentage of African Americans voted than whites.[20] The suppression efforts stimulated participation, much to the dismay of their architects. As one National Association for the Advancement of Colored People (NAACP) leader said, "We are accustomed to people trying to deny us things, and I think sometimes you wake the sleeping giant, and that's what happened here."[21] Yet, it augurs the question: Why should people have to fight so hard to exercise such a basic right? Because suppression of the franchise creates outrageously unrepresentative outcomes downstream. As Steven Rosenstone and John Mark Hansen conclude, inequalities in participation lead to inequalities in influence, which yields inequalities in policies, which generates unequal resources for those not allowed to participate in the first place.[22]

The vicious cycle continues to future elections, only now with a new wrinkle. In 2013, the U.S. Supreme Court weighed in on a challenge to the Voting Rights Act of 1965. Section 5, the most critical portion of this act, required officials in 15 mostly southern states with histories of voter discrimination to gain approval of the U.S. Department of Justice before enacting any legislation on district boundaries, voter registration rules, and anything that might reduce minority voter turnout. Although the law was last extended in 2006 by votes of 98–0 in the U.S. Senate and 390–33 in the U.S. House of Representatives, the court declared by a 5–4 majority that the rules were out of date, and thus effectively gutted the law.[23] State election officials glowed over the possibilities of creating new voter laws, but others worried that "the most powerful tool to realize the objectives of the Civil War Amendments is dead."[24] Absent new congressional legislation, a barrage of new state and local restrictive voting laws now have a clear path. With federal preapproval out of the way, many have begun the process yet again of passing restrictive legislation.[25]

COMPETING POWER CENTERS

Bit by bit, American political parties have lost their abilities to nominate candidates and run elections, but not without a fight. After the direct primary was introduced early in the 20th century, state political party organizations responded to this threat through a variety of tactics, ranging from preprimary endorsements to funding of preferred candidates. In many instances, such tools have helped to offset the lack of discipline and reinstate some cohesion. Still, over time, party functions have weakened. While party labels almost always remain attached to candidates, they have become little more than political symbols.

In the 21st century, political party organizations play second fiddle to two powerful entities: interest groups and super political action committees. Both of these speak for narrow constituencies, with numbers as large as a few million to as little as a few dozen. But more to the point, they have separated the voters from the parties by virtue of the financial clout they wield. If American political parties were designed as umbrella-like organizations to aggregate large swaths of society, they have lost too many spokes to fulfill that important function.

Interest Groups

Long a part of America's political fabric, interest groups gradually have assumed key functions formerly controlled by political parties. Like parties, interest groups are officially outside of the governmental process. But unlike political parties, their ability to control the political process has grown over time to the point that, in many respects, they have replaced the clout of party organizations.

Interest groups utilize many of the tools once used by parties, only they are accountable to much more defined constituencies with objectives usually limited to their specific interests. These private organizations seek to influence the policy makers mainly through campaign contributions. In addition, they provide resources such as phone banks, equipment, subject expertise, legal counsel, and technology for uses in campaign activities. Some interest groups represent broad-based economic concerns; the American Federation of Labor and Congress of Industrial Organizations (AFL-CIO) and U.S. Chamber of Commerce come to mind. Others, such as American Medical Association and American Farm Bureau, reflect the concerns of narrower groups. Still others, like the American Cancer Society or Sierra Club, operate with the public in mind more than any self-interest. Regardless, all interest groups seek to impress their stamp on the process. Their numbers have proliferated into the thousands, so much so, one study concludes, that they "have become increasingly powerful political actors in campaigns in support of political parties and their candidates."[26] As a result, those often with narrow political concerns have left others who are less organized and with few fewer resources far behind in the effort to influence what comes out of government.

Political concerns over the potentially excessive power of interest groups on policy makers can be traced as far back as the earliest days of the nation. James Madison fretted in the *Federalist Papers* No. 10 about the ability of factions—the earlier term for interest groups—to disrupt the overarching goals of representative government. Others have viewed interest groups as positive checks on narrow-minded governments that serve the needs of the majority at the expense of the minority.[27] This debate notwithstanding, one fact is clear: over time interest groups have multiplied in numbers and influence to the extent that they now seem almost intertwined with political parties, if not above them.

Periodically, elected officials have enacted legislation intended to tamp down excessive interest group influence on the political process. In an effort to limit interest group involvement in political campaigns, the McCain–Feingold Campaign Reform Act of 2002 banned interest group contributions to political parties and candidates. Nevertheless, interest groups circumvented the ban by forming 527 groups. Named for the Internal Revenue Service (IRS) section of the tax code that regulates their status, these tax-exempt political organizations are allowed to advocate political issues and take out ads *opposing* candidates without the constraints of any financial limits. As a matter of law, 527 groups may not endorse candidates, although it doesn't take much imagination to understand their preferences. As a result, interest groups have further ingratiated themselves with candidates for office through spending unregulated funds known as soft money.[28]

Another set of issue groups base their political activity on the promotion of social issues. Classified by the IRS as 501(c)4 nonprofits, these organizations may contribute to political campaigns and candidates as long their primary purpose is the advocacy of social welfare issues. As with 527 groups, there are no spending limits for 501(c)4 groups. Moreover, they are not required to publicly disclose their donors, which allows money to flow freely and without attribution. Planned Parenthood, the National Rifle Association, the Environmental Defense Fund, and America's Families First are among the hundreds of purportedly social welfare issues that have established separate 501(c)4 groups to advocate on behalf of their issues, pointing out their friends and enemies in the process.

PACs and Super PACs

For many years, national legislation has limited the amount of money any single individual can contribute to a campaign for federal elective office. For example, in 2012 an individual was permitted to contribute up to $2,600 to a primary election and up to another $2,600 for the general election campaigns of a candidate for Congress or the presidency.[29] Of course, those relatively low limits don't mesh well with the realities of modern campaigns. Similarly, individuals were limited to contributing no more than $30,800 to the national political parties for the 2012 presidential year.[30] While those amounts might seem substantial, they pale in comparison to the totals raised for election campaigns. In fact, the tab for the 2012 presidential election alone was estimated at $2.6 billion, with another $1.8 billion spent on congressional races. So, where does the rest of the money come from? The answer lies with new revenue streams that have been developed for modern-day fund-raising activity.

In an effort to circumvent federal election limits, individuals and interest groups have created political action committees (PACs). These organizations emerged after the Federal Election Campaign Act (1971), which established a mechanism that allowed corporations or unions to create campaign funds. With PACs, contributions go to the committees, which in turn donate to various campaigns. In other words, there is separation between the donors and recipients.

PACs changed the nature of campaign fund-raising. In effect, they replaced political parties as the fund-raising arms for candidates. Combined, PACs raised a total of $6 million the following year for the 1972 presidential candidates. Although PACs were limited to $5,000 per campaign, they could contribute to as many candidates and candidate committees as they wanted. The influence of big money continued to grow.

Recent developments have further increased the role of money in political campaigns. In the process, they have all but severed the connection between political parties and the voters. In 2010, the U.S. Supreme Court ruled by a 5–4 majority in the *Citizens United* case that independent expenditures of any amounts did not necessarily threaten democracy or provide undue influence over candidates for office.[31] Thus, corporations, unions, and any other bodies are now free to spend unlimited amounts of money to support or oppose candidates for office. The names of the donors must be disclosed, contrary to more opaque 501(c)4 committees, but candidate campaign messages can be more direct and to the point. The new rules led to the development that became known as Super PACs because of their ability to spend more money with fewer guidelines. Once again, the role of independent contributions became even more pronounced in the presidential campaign as well as other national and state contests.

The Fallout

What do we make of the changes in campaign finance regulations with respect to the potential participation of the average voter? Big money in election politics has emerged as a dominant force in American politics. Moreover, the contributions are coming from fewer and fewer people in larger and larger amounts. Super PACs accounted for more than one-fourth of all the money spent in the 2012 presidential campaign; worse yet, about 18 percent came from just four organizations.[32] Of the ten largest Super PACs, Republican presidential candidate Mitt Romney received 71 percent of the funds,[33] helping to make it the first time in memory that a challenger for the presidency outspent the sitting incumbent. A single individual, Sheldon Adelson, contributed more than $150 million to Republican candidates and related political groups, according to one report.[34]

But Obama prevailed in 2012, due in large part to a massive, unprecedented online campaign effort directed to small contributors. Fifty-seven percent of Obama's donors contributed $200 or less to his presidential campaign, compared with 24 percent of the Republican donors who fell underneath the $200 threshold.[35] In all, more than 4 million donors contributed to the Obama election effort, another record. For the moment, big money did not buy the 2012 presidential election, but what about future contests? To what extent will the Super PAC floodgates open even more?

Still, it's hard to imagine that the huge contribution numbers are not discouraging to regular people. In fact, they are. A national Rasmussen Poll of likely voters in 2012 found that 69 percent of the respondents believed "most politicians break the rules to help people who give them a lot of money."[36] An even more telling recent national survey by the Pew Research Center found that 77 percent agreed that "there is too much power in the hands of a few rich people and corporations."[37] Finally, when asked by an AP/Roper Poll during the 2012 presidential race about campaign donations by corporations, unions, and individuals, a lopsided 83 percent agreed that there should be limits on the amounts of monetary contributions.[38] Such data can't help but point to a discouraged electorate that has been left behind with the lack of mobilization by the political parties for their votes.

ELECTION IMPEDIMENTS

Pick almost any month of any year and it's almost certain that there will be an election somewhere in the United States. Our federal system of governance ensures a plethora of contests from coast to coast because states and their local governments are allowed to schedule their elections whenever they wish. Added to that is the nature of what's become the "permanent presidential campaign," an election process that seems to morph from one race to the next with little interruption. The result: airwaves, telephones, mailboxes, and social media sites saturated with information and demands for your vote. This mode may be wonderful for political junkies, the media, and consultants, but it has a deleterious impact on the American public.

There are other troubling elements of the voting process. Voters are viewed as almost afterthoughts to the election; few are prepared for the important decisions they must make. Turnouts tend to be small, sometimes even dismal, because of unusually parochial candidates and issues that, while important, don't play to the major issues of the day. Outcomes can be skewed by the order of contests on the ballot; in addition, different types of voting equipment can affect who votes. Combined, these factors can skew voting patterns, leaving some people with more advantageous conditions than others. It's just another example of how stewards of the political system make it easy for some voters to participate, while presenting painful obstacles to others.

Frequency

If the frequency of elections alone qualified as the measuring stick for the quality of a nation's democracy, the United States would be in a category without comparison. American election campaigns are endless in number, although not necessarily robust with voter participation. Turnout is greatest at the national level, particularly during years with the presidency at stake, but even this race attracts less participation in the United States than the voting patterns in other democracies.[39] From there, the downward participatory trend escalates. Fewer voters turn out during even-numbered, nonpresidential years, and fewer still during odd-numbered years.

The turnout differences are substantial. In 2012, 59 percent of all registered voters cast ballots. In 2010, an election year highlighted by 34 gubernatorial contests, 42 percent of all registered voters cast ballots. Yet in 2011, a year with no congressional or presidential races, four states held gubernatorial elections. The turnouts? Kentucky, 28 percent; Louisiana, 31 percent; Mississippi, 36 percent; and West Virginia, 23 percent. Only the 42 percent turnout in Virginia's odd off-year gubernatorial election in 2009 approached the 2010 turnout rate, and that was no doubt due to the proximity of so many voters to the political hotbed otherwise known as Washington, DC. Clearly, state elections not connected with the federal races during presidential years suffer reduced rates of voter turnout.

Voter participation is least present in local elections that occur independently of state and national elections during odd-numbered years. Consider Los Angeles, California, the second largest city in the United States, with a population of 3.8 million. In the open race for mayor in 2013, the March primary drew 21 percent of the vote. Two months later, the May runoff drew 19 percent of the electorate in what had been billed as a competitive race. Translation: 1 out of 10 eligible voters selected the winner, Eric Garcetti.

It's important to remember that registered voters represent only a portion of the potential electorate. In 2012, for example, while 126 million Americans cast votes, another 90 million eligible Americans were not registered, and therefore did not vote. Thus, in terms of the potential voter universe, all of the above-mentioned turnout statistics would be substantially lower, suggesting incredibly small portions of American society making monumental decisions about governance.

Large numbers of elections on different dates and times of the year scatter public focus and have a deleterious impact on the voter universe. As they become more parochial and less connected with other races, would-be voters have diminished interest in participation. In the end, incredibly small numbers can determine the winner, with everyone else on the sidelines. That's harmful to the nature of representative democracy, which depends on the intersection of voter, candidates, and elective offices. As one study concludes, "the greater the number of participants in political activity, the greater the equality in political participation."[40] Conversely, the smaller the number of participants, the less likely that the few who vote will represent the others. The biases that favor the rich and powerful voters—people who regularly participate in all contests—are reduced substantially by larger voter turnouts, yet the nature of American elections discourages voters from participating in elections other than national contests.[41]

Preparation

Because voting administration is assigned to the states, patterns vary wildly with respect to the actual voter experience. Only a handful of states provide sample ballots to help the voters consider the various contests before them. Even fewer states conduct voter education programs for high school students who will soon be eligible to vote and participate in other political matters as adults.[42] It's as if we expect that during the summer between high school graduation and the upcoming election students will have taken a magic pill that prepares them for the myriad functions of citizenship. But there is no pill, and most of those students-turned-adults are woefully unprepared for political participation. More than one-third of all potential first-time voters failed to do so because they were disgusted with politics or found politics befuddling, according to one study.[43] And if they don't vote in their earliest opportunities, chances are good that they will be lost for a lifetime. One-third of the nonvoters in 2012 were also nonvoters in 2008.[44]

The lack of voter investment is particularly troublesome among the young, where studies show the extent to which members of this age group are unprepared to assume responsibilities connected with the franchise. According to the 2010 results of the "National Assessment of Educational Progress" report, less than one-fourth of 12th grade students are proficient in civics.[45] The term *civics* refers to the knowledge, assessment, and evaluation of politics, the structure of government, and an understanding of the American constitutional system, as well as the citizen's grasp of his or her political roles in society.

It should not be surprising that the lack of preparation and political investment in young people results in disengagement. Typically, young adults have the lowest turnout among voters. Such behavior occurred in 2012, when 41 percent of voters between the ages of 18 and 24 cast ballots, compared with 62 percent of the rest of the electorate. This is a disturbing statistic, given that young people have more at stake with respect to the nation's future than anyone else. Clearly, they are among the least connected elements of American society, despite the voter outreach efforts of political parties.

Ballot Order

Some instances of reduced voting occur simply because of the number of races on the ballot as well as the order in which they appear. Evidence shows that increased numbers of races on the same ballot can discourage voters from deciding issues found toward the end of the election document. The difficulty, and perhaps even reluctance, of the voter to deliberate these races is known as ballot fatigue. The individual voter may not think about the ramifications of what some political scientists refer to as the roll-off, but the lack of participation can affect the outcome, particularly in a closely contested election, because of the changed composition of the electorate.

Moreover, the decision not to vote is hardly random. Those with the greatest knowledge, investment, and commitment will be more likely to stay the course; those with fewer ties to the process will be less likely to go through the entire ballot, if they vote at all. In many cases, these differences are typically accented in socioeconomic demographic differences such as income, education, and civic knowledge.[46]

This information is hardly trivial. For example, in states where issues are placed on the ballot by the order in which they qualify, strategists may work hard to collect the necessary signatures so that their proposals appear at more advantageous positions on the ballot. In other cases, such as school bond elections, campaign strategists may decide to qualify their proposals at elections where few or no other issues are on the ballot. The thinking goes that in these campaigns, only the most motivated voters—parents of school-age children with something at stake—would have interest in participating. Simply put, those with the resources and knowledge of the process have the capability to organize campaigns in advance of the election in ways that will benefit some more than others.[47] Still, given the institutional limitations directed toward selected segments of the electorate, it's easy to understand how the voter participation deck can be stacked.

Equipment

Last, we take a moment to consider voting equipment as a cause for erratic election balloting opportunities and outcomes. Inasmuch as states bear responsibility for providing voting machines, the types of equipment vary not only between states but also sometimes within states. Some equipment is modern and reliable; other equipment is plagued by unpredictability in terms of both operational performance and voter confusion.

While voting equipment has always been a concern for those worried about free exercise of the franchise, the issue garnered unprecedented interest since the 2000 presidential election. With Florida's votes deciding the outcome of the extraordinarily tight Electoral College battle between Republican George W. Bush and Democrat Al Gore, the voting process was stained in large part in claims of voter fraud and suppression. It was further troubled by a combination of poorly designed ballots, flawed machines, inconsistent behavior of election personnel, and an equally disturbing ballot recounting process.[48]

The Florida embarrassment was an ugly capstone to decades of widespread concerns about voting machines throughout the United States. And the issues were hardly random. An independent study for Congress immediately after the 2000 election found that voters in low-income, high-minority congressional districts throughout the nation were more than three times as likely as whites to have their votes rejected, largely because of faulty equipment.[49]

In an attempt to put the voter equipment issue to rest, Congress passed the Help America Vote Act (HAVA) in 2002. The act established requirements for voter registration and accessibility, and provided more than $3 billion to states for purchases of up-to-date, reliable voting machines. But the act turned out to be far more symbolic than substantive. With respect to voting machines, the heart of the participation issue, HAVA devised only voluntary guidelines for voter computer hardware and software, with implementation left to the discretion of the individual states.[50] In other words, the national objectives were without enforcement provisions.

A System at Risk

A decade later, in the 2012 presidential election, the *Christian Science Monitor* reported: "Electronic voting-machine jams, and glitches were strewn across the Election Night landscape, creating long lines when machines broke down."[51] Prior to the election, the Brennan Center for Justice estimated that because of discriminatory laws, intimidation, poor personnel training, and faulty equipment, as many as 25 million voters would be at risk from a "broad-based attempt to suppress voter turnout."[52] As in the past, problems were most prevalent in "battleground states," where local officials were left to accept or reject voter machine irregularities, while thousands of lawyers determined whether to take their objections to court. So much for the voting process in what has been commonly described as the world's greatest democracy. So much for the idea that voting rights take place on a level playing field.

COPING WITH A DISJOINTED PARTICIPATORY NETWORK

It would be an overstatement to dismiss the modern American political party system as irrelevant to 21st-century politics and elections. Clearly, political parties play major roles in organizing issues before the voters and promoting election turnout. Some observers go so far as to argue that political parties are more vibrant today than they have been over the past 50 years, and that more than ever they help voters understand the issues that separate the candidates who also have become more partisan in recent years.[53] Others say that bipartisanship, once viewed as essential to consensus politics and compromise, is a thing of the past, again emphasizing the critical position of political parties in American elections.[54]

American political parties may still move politics and the political process, but are they taking the voters with them or bypassing Americans for everything except for their votes? Even if citizens understand what parties stand for, that doesn't mean that they feel included in the party organization or relate to the candidates much beyond the R or D behind their names. In fact, many don't identify with the process or the products that emerge from it. In a September 2012 national survey by the Pew Research Center, barely half of those interviewed were satisfied with the choice of presidential candidates.[55] Simply put, the connection between candidates and voters is not playing well in 21st-century America for many voters.

The disconnect underscores the fact that while political parties have not exited from the American stage as political actors, their audiences and supporters have changed markedly. More than ever, parties and their respective candidates are not as beholding to voters as much as they are to the powerful financial resources that support their efforts. These influence agents have huge impacts on the issues addressed and the nominees selected for office. As such, in some ways elections become false choices between big money-backed candidate A and big money-backed candidate B. And increasingly, we don't even know the sources of those funds. Of course,

American elections were never dependent upon a bottom-up system where the masses moved the process. But clearly, dramatic changes in funding coupled with manipulation of the electoral system have left many wondering about the value of their votes when it comes to questions of deciding who shall be elected to office. Many are not tuned in to the changing election environment, but for those who are, the new arrangements stand out as a threat to their representation.

As for those motivated to vote, their intentions are met with numerous obstacles. In some cases, the voting deck is stacked with institutional obstacles like gerrymandering, which minimize the value of the vote by artificially squeezing minorities into fewer districts. Off-year elections also dampen turnout, leading to unrepresentative outcomes. In other instances, state and local officials discourage turnout of racial minorities, students, and the poor through overbearing identification requirements, reduced voting times, and inadequate numbers of polling stations. Add to these obstacles questionable reliability of voting machines and the process of exercise, the franchise is challenging at best, and downright discouraging at worst. For many, the 21st-century voting environment is anything but a joy.

In 2012, as in previous years, thousands of lawyers battled to turn back legislation designed to intimidate voters or suppress exercise of the franchise. That these efforts were made, more times successfully than not, shows that the system can work, even if under trying circumstances. Nevertheless, there is permanent enforcement of opportunities to participate, large numbers of citizens will be at risk, and many will be unwilling to test an unwelcome political environment.

ENDNOTES

1. See John Kenneth White and Daniel M. Shea, *New Party Politics: From Jefferson and Hamilton to the Information Age*, Boston: Bedford/St. Martin's, 2009, pp. 37–40.
2. See Marjorie Randon Hershey, *Party Politics in America*, 12th ed., New York: Pearson Longman, 2007, for a comprehensive breakdown of these elements.
3. For a discussion of the evolution of the Progressive movement in state and national politics, see V.O. Key Jr., *Politics, Parties and Pressure Groups*, 5th ed., New York: Thomas Y. Crowell Co., Alfred A Knopf, 1964, pp. 175–180.
4. John Kenneth White and Matthew R. Kerbel, *Party On!* Boulder, CO: Paradigm Publishers, 2012, p. 72.
5. Tova Andrea Wang, *Voter Suppression: Defending and Expanding Americans' Right to Vote*, Ithaca, NY: Cornel University Press, 2012, p. 8.

6. For an account of the various restrictions and outcomes during this period, see Angus Campbell, Philip E. Converse, Warren E. Miller, and Donald E. Stokes, *The American Voter*, New York: John Wiley & Sons, 1960, pp. 276–282.
7. "It's Appalling That Gerrymandering Is Legal," *Slate*, November 9, 2012, http://www.slate.com/articles/news_and_politics/jurisprudence/2012/11/the_supreme_court_may_gut_the_voting_rights_act_and_make_gerrymandering.html.
8. Charlie Cook, "The Republican Advantage," *National Journal*, April 11, 2013, http://www.nationaljournal.com/columns/cook-report/the-republican-advantage-20130411?print=true.
9. See Roger H. Davison, Walter J. Oleszek, and Frances Lee, *Congress and Its Members*, 13th ed., Washington, DC: CQ Press, 2012, pp. 53–57.
10. "Election Watchdog Hands Florida 173 Cases of Election Fraud," Election Watchdog, August 14, 2013, http://watchdog.org/101150/election-watchdog-hands-florida-officials-173-alleged-cases-of-voter-fraud/.
11. Quoted in "New State Rules Raising Hurdles at Voting Booth," *New York Times*, October 3, 2011, pp. A1, A14.
12. "As Election Nears, Efforts Intensify to Misinform, Pressure Voters," Reuters, November 5, 2012, http://www.reuters.com/article/2012/10/24/us-usa-campaign-voters-idUSBRE89N07M20121024.
13. "Cases of Voter ID-Election Fraud Found 'Virtually Non-Existent,'" News 21, August 13, 2012, http://www.minnpost.com/politics-policy/2012/08/cases-voter-id-election-fraud-found-virtually-non-existent.
14. "Voter Fraud or Voter Suppression: What Are New State Laws Trying to Do?" *Consumer Affairs*, September 20, 2012, http://www.consumeraffairs.com/news04/2012/09/voter-fraud-or-voter-supression-what-are-new-state-laws-really-trying-to-do.html.
15. "Waiting Times at Ballot Boxes Draw Scrutiny," *New York Times*, February 4, 2013, http://www.nytimes.com/2013/02/05/us/politics/waiting-times-to-vote-at-polls-draw-scrutiny.html?_r=0.
16. "Analysis: 201,000 in Florida Didn't Vote Because of Long Lines," *Orlando Sentinel*, January 29, 2013, http://articles.orlandosentinel.com/2013-01-29/business/os-voter-lines-statewide-20130118_1_long-lines-sentinel-analysis-state-ken-detzner.
17. Roland Martin, "Voter Suppression Fueled Back Turnout," CNN, November 10, 2012, http://www.cnn.com/2012/11/09/opinion/martin-black-vote/.
18. "In Battleground Virginia, Long Waits at the Polls," November 6, 2012, http://www.washingtonpost.com/local/virginia-politics/in-battleground-virginia-all-eyes-will-be-on-races-for-president-senate/2012/11/05/69eb061a-2770-11e2-b2a0-ae18d6159439_ story. html?
19. Ari Berman, "The GOP's Voter Suppression Strategy," *The Nation*, December 2012, http://www.thenation.com/article/171404/gops-voter-suppression-strategy#.
20. "For First Time on Record, Black Voting Outpaced Rate for Whites in 2012," *New York Times*, May 9, 2013, p. A16.
21. Ibid.
22. Steven J. Rosenstone and John Mark Hansen, *Mobilization, Participation, and Democracy in America*, New York: Macmillan Publishing Company, 1993, p. 245.
23. The case was *Shelby County v. Holder*, 570 U.S. __ (2013).
24. Thomas Mann and Raffaela Wakeman, "Voting Rights after *Shelby County v. Holder*," *Clear Politics*, June 26, 2013, http://www.realclearpolitics.com/articles/2013/06/26/voting_rights_after_shelby_county_v_holder_118983.html.

25. "Equality, Debated," *The Economist*, June 29, 2013, p. 28.
26. Mathew J. Burbank, Ronald J. Hrebenar, and Robert C. Benedict, *Parties, Interest Groups, and Political Campaigns*, 2nd ed., Boulder, CO: Paradigm Publishers, 2012, p. 180.
27. Robert A. Dahl is among those group theorists who view interest groups as essential guarantors of American democracy. See his *Pluralist Democracy in the United States: Conflict and Consent*, Chicago: Rand McNally & Company, 1967.
28. Nolan McCarthy, Keith T. Poole, and Howard Rosenthal, *Polarized America: The Dance of Ideology and Unequal Riches*, Cambridge, MA: MIT Press, 2006, pp. 139–140.
29. See the Federal Election Commission, *Citizens' Guide*, http://www.fec.gov/pages/brochures/citizens.shtml.
30. "Campaign Contribution Limits for 2012 Election Cycle," http://www.opensecrets.org/news/2011/02/campaign-contribution-limits-increa.html.
31. The case was *Citizens United v. Federal Election Commission*, 558 U.S. 310.
32. http://www.opensecrets.org/pacs/superpacs.php.
33. "Super PACs," http://www.opensecrets.org/news/2011/02/campaign-contribution-limits-increa.html.
34. Peter H. Stone, "Sheldon Adelson Spent Far More on Campaign Than Previously Known," *Huffington Post*, December 3, 2012, http://www.huffingtonpost.com/2012/12/03/sheldon-adelson-2012-election_n_2223589.html.
35. "The 2012 Money Race: Compare the Candidates," *New York Times*, http://elections.nytimes.com/2012/campaign-finance.
36. "69% Think Most Politicians Break the Rules for Big Contributors," Rasmussen Reports, August 23, 2012, http://www.rasmussenreports.com/public_content/politics/general_politics/august_2012/69_think_most_politicians_break_the_rules_for_big_contributors.
37. "Frustration with Congress Could Hurt Republican Incumbents," Pew Research Center for the People and the Press, December 15, 2011, http://www.people-press.org/2011/12/15/section-2-occupy-wall-street-and-inequality/.
38. http://ap-gfkpoll.com/main/wp-content/uploads/2012/09/AP-NCC-Poll-August-GfK-2012-Topline-FINAL_1st-release.pdf.
39. David Lee Hill, *American Voter Turnout: An Institutional Perspective*, Boulder, CO: Westview Press, 2006, p. 2.
40. Rosenstone and Hansen, op. cit, p. 238.
41. Hill, op. cit., p. 13.
42. Robert A. Pastor, "The State of Elections in the Fifty States: Evaluating the Process Where It Counts," Center for Democracy and Election Management, American University, July 15, 2009, p. 23, http://www.american.edu/spa/cdem/upload/CDEM-Final-Rpt-of-the-States-July-15-09.pdf.
43. "New Survey: First-Time Voters Propelled to Vote by Personal Contact," Harvard Kennedy School, Cambridge, MA, November 11, 2004, http://www.hks.harvard.edu/news-events/news/press-releases/new-survey-first-time-voters-propelled-to-polls-by-personal-contact.
44. "Why 90 Million Americans Won't Vote in November," *USA Today*, August 15, 2012, http://usatoday30.usatoday.com/news/politics/story/2012-08-15/non-voters-obama-romney/57055184/1.
45. "National Assessment of Educational Progress," National Center for Education Statistics, Washington, DC, 2010, http://nces.ed.gov/nationsreportcard/civics/whatmeasure.aspx.

46. Ibid., p. 12.

47. Ned Augenblick and Scott Nicholson, "Ballot Position, Choice Fatigue, and Voter Behavior," unpublished paper, December 18, 2012, p. 22.

48. For a moment-by-moment review of the 2000 presidential election, see *Deadlock: The Inside Story of America's Closest Election*, New York: Public Affairs Press, 2001.

49. Minority Staff, Committee on Government Reform, U.S. House of Representatives, "Income and Racial Disparities in the Undercount in the 2000 Presidential Election," Washington, DC, July 9, 2001, p. i.

50. Kevin. J. Coleman and Eric A Fischer, "The Help America Vote Act and Elections Reform: Overview and Issues," Congressional Research Service, Washington, DC, June 27, 2011, p. 3.

51. "Voting-Machine Glitches: How Bad Was It on Election Day around the Country?" *Christian Science Monitor*, November 7, 2012, http://www.csmonitor.com/layout/set/print/USA/Elections/2012/1107/Voting-machine-glitches-How-bad-was-it-on-Election-Day-around-the-country.

52. "The 2012 Election Protection Report: Our Broken Voting System and How to Repair It," Lawyers Committee for Civil Rights under Law, Washington, DC, 2013, p. 10.

53. See Jeffrey M. Stonecash, *Political Parties Matter: Realignment and the Return of Partisan Voting*, Boulder, CO: Lynne Rienner Publishers, 2006.

54. This is the theme of Nolan McCarthy, Keith T. Poole, and Howard Rosenthal in their *Polarized America*, Cambridge, MA: MIT Press, 2009.

55. "Fewer Satisfied with Candidates than in Any Campaign Since 1992," Pew Research Center for the People and the Press, Washington, DC, September 24, 2012, http://www.people-press.org/2012/09/24/fewer-satisfied-with-candidates-than-in-any-campaign-since-1992.

4

The Opportunity Conundrum

Few values are trumpeted in American society as much as the notion of equal opportunity, a principle prized as a cornerstone of American political culture. Yet, discussion of the topic often generates heated and passionate opinions among participants, revealing a polarized society. That's because different interpretations of the term touch not only on the essence of human nature but also on the appropriate role of government in managing the well-being of its citizens.

The political gulf is deep and wide. One school of thought views equal opportunity as the vehicle for anyone to make good irrespective of the challenges associated with their backgrounds, while unencumbered by arbitrary government rules that stack the deck more for some than others. According to this approach, the individual has sole control over his or her destiny and will benefit or suffer dependent upon his or her independent actions. In their *Free to Choose*, Milton and Rose Friedman write, "The system under which people make their own choices—and bear most of the consequences of their decisions—is the system that has prevailed for most of our history."[1] In other words, society functions best when an individual exercises his or her own life options as they relate to personal values, needs, and objectives, rather than living within an artificial set of values constructed and promoted by government that may well harm the individual's ability to live up to his or her potential.

A second school of thought views "equal opportunity" as a carefully calculated political response by government to the unequal standing of individuals created by past and present social and economic discrimination. Left without redress to oppressive treatment, some groups begin their journey through life far behind others—and rarely catch up without government practices that level the playing field with targeted policies of accommodation. John J. Harrigan makes the case that "the average lower-status person needs a great many things that can be achieved only by a strong and dynamic government…. How these social goals can be achieved is open to debate…. What should not be open to debate among lower-status people, however, is the principle that the federal government has a strong and vital role to play on achieving these goals."[2] For advocates of the poor and the disenfranchised who fail to succeed because of intentional discriminatory barriers, antiseptic opportunity in and of itself is insufficient without government making up for past or present unfair practices. Under these circumstances, government is obligated to step in to compensate the discriminated for their denied life chances. Many of these efforts have fallen under the umbrella of affirmative action, a federal government policy designed to ensure representation of underrepresented minorities and women in the private and public sectors.[3]

In some respects, advocates of the first school can look with pride to changes that have taken place in American society. Women now attend universities in greater percentages than men, paving the way for better opportunities down the employment highway. Large numbers of racial and ethnic minorities have reached middle-class status; some have even climbed to the top of their fields as corporate CEOs or elected officials in high offices, such as African American Barack Obama's election to the U.S. presidency. No doubt, these accomplishments in recent years helped the U.S. Supreme Court to narrow the concept of affirmative action in 2013, when a majority declared by an unusually lopsided 7–1 vote that university affirmative action admissions programs had to demonstrate the need for such admissions procedures only as a last resort for dealing with racial and gender inequities.[4] The topic contributed to an ever-narrowing definition of affirmative action first initiated by the court in 1978.[5] In 2014, the court took yet another step toward minimizing affirmative action by upholding a Michigan constitutional amendment that banned affirmative action outright as a tool for admissions to the state's universities, all but guaranteeing that there would be fewer admissions of African Americans and Latino students to prestigious universities.[6]

Concerns about processes and outcomes notwithstanding, the court's decisions have not reflected the political and economic realities of 21st-century America, which takes us to the second school of thought. Whatever the accomplishments of women and minorities, many successes have been due at least in part to affirmative action and related student outreach programs. This has left many believing that the disappearance of affirmative action will end recent gains.[7] Further, by just about whatever measuring stick one might choose—income, education levels, incarceration, or middle and upper management positions, to name a few—employment opportunities and earnings of women and minorities remain considerably below those of white males. Thus, the unfettered ability to excel in America remains tilted in favor of some groups much more than others.

This chapter examines the notion of opportunity in the United States. The discussion takes place along a variety of fault lines, including race, gender, age, military service, and sexual orientation. The information presented points to troubling circumstances in America, not only historically, but in the present day as well. The differences between the "haves" and "have-nots" have grown immeasurably in the past quarter century, with the middle class quickly becoming a footnote of U.S. economic history.

Uneven opportunities have showered relatively few Americans with wealth beyond description, while most of the rest of us are looking up, many increasingly from the lowest rungs of an economic ladder that seems to grow higher and more formidable every day. The financial chasm and inability to bridge it have rendered a sizable portion of American society powerless, generating an equally sizable reservoir of despair that only seems to grow and deepen over time. For many, the disconnection of hope from reality is too great to overcome and is the basis for feeling out of place in American society.

THE GROWING CHASM BETWEEN THE HAVES AND HAVE-NOTS

The United States is touted as a capitalism-based free market society where opportunity abounds for all. That precious value is a foundation for mainstream political thought. Setting aside for a moment the fact that the federal government subsidizes various categories of businesses and people ranging from technology research and development grants to food stamps and healthcare for the poor, our country operates on the premise that anyone who tries hard enough can succeed. Of course, ability and talent enter into the picture along with creativity and drive. Yet, this simple formula, while a mainstay of our political consciousness, is far from reality. It's an understatement to note that some Americans earn more income—in some cases, much more—than others. There's nothing wrong with these differences per se. Still, they have become part of the folklore that inaccurately explains success as the natural result of talent and hard work.

In fact, modern America exhibits wide differences between those at the top and the bottom of the economic ladder, with little likelihood that most of those who barely subsist with the smallest incomes will realistically ever have the opportunity or ability to catch up to those who have reached the top of the ladder. That's the modern-day American dilemma—a sizable segment of the population that has been left behind with virtually no chance to escape their condition, even though many don't want to believe that reality because it conflicts head on with the American dream.

Widening of the Gap

The simple, incontrovertible fact is that in 21st-century America, extreme wealth has become the privilege of the very few, leaving most of us far behind. Oddly enough, many Americans don't believe this divergence or understand the extent to which it impacts their lives. A recent national survey of American adults found widespread agreement that wealth is fairly evenly distributed in the United States, with a few rich at the top, a few poor at the bottom, and most everyone in between.[8] Yet, the economic data provide a much different picture. The middle class has been eroding for decades. Moreover, the inequality of wealth in the United States is one of the most unbalanced distributions of resources among the world's developed nations.[9]

Not only is the distribution of wealth highly uneven in the United States, but the distances between rich and poor have been increasing over time, with no sign of reversing the trend. A study by G. William Domhoff shows that in 1983, the wealthiest 1 percent of American society controlled 33.8 percent of the nation's wealth, while the bottom 80 percent had 18.7 percent. Fast-forward to 2010 and the top 1 percent controlled 35.8 percent of the total wealth, while the bottom 80 percent of Americans were left with only 11.1 percent. A wider view produces even more skewed results. In 1983, 20 percent of the population controlled 81.3 percent of the nation's wealth; by 2010, 20 percent of the population controlled 88.9 percent of the nation's wealth.[10] That leaves a sliver of wealth for the overwhelming majority of society. No matter how you look at it, the vast proportion of the nation has little wealth relative to the few at the top. All this in little more than a quarter century.

These discrepancies transcend economic cycles. They didn't change once the United States began to rebound from the Great Recession of 2008–2009; in fact they only widened. As the nation's recovery took hold, the wealthy gained at the expense of everyone else. On an aggregate level, the entire nation *seemed* to improve, but a closer look at the numbers revealed otherwise. According to data compiled by the Pew Research Center, between 2009 and 2011 the mean net wealth of the top 7 percent of Americans rose 28 percent, while the mean net worth of the bottom 93 percent of Americans dropped by 4 percent.[11] The chasm between the very wealthy and the rest of us is growing every day.

The differences between those at the top and bottom are graphically revealed in the workplace. According to the Social Security Administration, between 1979 and 2010, the wages of the bottom 90 percent of all workers grew by 15.2 percent. During the same period, the wages of the top 1 percent of all employees soared by 130.9 percent; and for the top 0.1 percent, the growth was an astronomical 278 percent.[12] Here's another way of looking at the disparity: depending on the valuation of compensation packages (e.g., bonuses, stock options, various allowances), the CEOs of major U.S. companies in 1965 earned between 18 and 20 times the salary of an average worker. As of 2011, the difference was between 209 and 321 times the typical worker salary[13]—and these estimates pale compared to other independent calculations, some of which assess the differential at as much as 475–1.[14] What's staggering is that these changes have occurred over a reasonably brief period.

Other industrialized countries don't get close to the economic divergence of C-level managers and ordinary workers in the United States. In 2010, the CEO-to-average worker ratio in Japan was 11–1; in Germany, 12–1; and in Great Britain, 22–1.[15] America may be the land of opportunity, but opportunity here is in the hands of the very few.

No doubt, other economic studies might show slightly different configurations between the wealthy and the poor, depending upon compensation assumptions connected with their revenue models. Nevertheless, the trend data clearly demonstrate that the ratio between CEOs and the average worker has exploded over the past few decades—a condition that leaves those at the bottom falling farther and farther behind, and that is indisputable.

For some observers, the acquisition of great wealth has implications for government and subsequent public policies. They see a direct political connection between wealth and power. Michael Parenti, a longtime critic of the distribution of wealth in America, asserts: "What we have in the United States is a plutocracy (political domination by the wealthy)," who in turn shape the economy and further their own well-being.[16] To the extent that the relatively few formidable forces among us limit the struggle for resources and power to a select few elites, even the larger battles leave most Americans on the outside looking in. Still, it's clear that some Americans have failed to escape the limited economic orbit that a few others have managed to break through with virtually unlimited success.

A Disappearing Middle Class

Meanwhile, what's happened to that great American economic bulwark of capitalism otherwise known as the middle class? In fact, the middle class is melting away before our very eyes. What many feel in an anecdotal sense is, in fact, reality. Using the same earnings criteria over a several-decade period, the Pew Research Center defined middle class as "all Adults whose annual income is two-thirds to double the annual median" of all annual incomes.[17] This approach allowed the center to control for inflation and other factors that may skew real dollar earnings over time. The center's findings? The middle class is not only in jeopardy, but in decline. The study found that the number of people in the middle class had declined from 61 percent of all adults in 1971 to 51 percent in 2011. In addition to fewer members, the actual real incomes of middle class members have fallen over time. According to one study, the middle class lost 4.8 percent of financial worth over the decade between 2001 and 2010, while the wealthy gained.[18] Another analysis of U.S. Census Bureau data goes so far as to conclude that the real wages of American factory workers are less today than they were in the 1970s.[19] To summarize, the middle class has dwindled in terms of both numbers and income. The economic losses suffered by this large group are not imaginary; they are real and painful.

Perhaps the most disconcerting fact about these data is the timeline over which they have been gathered. These problems are systemic and go well beyond any temporary fluctuations, including the miseries of the Great Recession years. In fact, a Rockefeller Foundation survey asked a national sample *before* the downward economic calamity in 2007 about financial security compared to 10 years earlier. Sixty-five percent expressed the sense of less economic security, compared with only 19 percent who believed there was more economic security.[20] Not only is the middle class in decline, but large numbers of Americans are living in a very insecure economic environment with no end in sight.

Shifting Assets by the Wealthy

While the middle class has struggled to keep its economic footing, many of America's wealthiest citizens have parked their fortunes offshore. In doing so, they have escaped much of their income tax responsibilities, leaving those at the bottom responsible for funding the U.S. Treasury. The offshoring of funds by wealthy Americans has become a massive enterprise. A 2010 study by the Internal Revenue Service estimated 516,000 Americans had offshore accounts, nearly double the number from 2007.[21] In total, it's believed that the amount exceeds more than $1 trillion.[22] Of course, the very rich benefit the most. One 2011 accounting found that individuals with assets of $30 million or more have at least one-third of their holdings invested overseas, where they can escape the otherwise long arm of the Internal Revenue Service (IRS).[23] The stakes are huge, almost beyond imagination. A 2008 report to the U.S. Senate estimated that the U.S. Treasury loses an estimated $100 billion in tax revenues each year because of hidden financial accounts offshore.[24] If collected as income taxes, those dollars could go a long way toward closing the annual federal debt.

In 2009, the Internal Revenue Service responded to the hidden revenue problem by creating the Offshore Voluntary Disclosure Program. Launched under the Obama administration, this initiative was designed to capture taxes from offshore accounts by reducing the possibilities of criminal prosecutions for those who cooperated with the IRS. The following year, Congress passed the Foreign Account Tax Compliance Act (FATCA), which required stricter reporting rules for individuals with offshore assets as well as disclosure of those assets by foreign banks.

The program has generated some results. Between 2009 and 2013, approximately 43,000 individuals participated in the program, whose self-reporting yielded nearly $6 billion in taxes.[25] That's a start, but clearly the lion's share of the taxable offshore funds has not been captured in the eyes of the General Accounting Office, which submitted its own independent report to Congress on the topic in 2013. During the same period, more than 80 Americans were charged by federal authorities with hiding taxable income after a Swiss bank admitted concealing $1.2 billion.[26] Still, given the potential $100 billion financial nut from a bounty of $1 trillion cited above, the U.S. government has only scratched the surface.

The avoidance of tax obligations by some of the wealthiest members of American society raises the question of their commitment to the country where they have fared so well. Even the quintessential capitalist Andrew Carnegie once said, "Men who continue hoarding great sums all their lives ... should be made to feel that the community, in the form of the state, cannot thus be deprived of its proper share," yet that call has been ignored by those who have gained the most from doing business. Yet, ironically, the sense of obligation alluded to in the Carnegie quote seems to have been missed by those in the best positions to strengthen our society and government.

In fact, among the wealthy there seems to be a trend away from participating as responsible U.S. citizens. It turns out that increasing numbers of American citizens of vast wealth have disowned their citizenship to better protect their assets that have come under closer U.S. government scrutiny. During 2013, 2,999 people renounced their citizenship ties with the United States, a number that was larger than the previous record of 1,781 Americans who abandoned their citizenship during 2011.[27] And the trend seems to be growing. In 2008, only 235 Americans gave up their American nationality. Bluntly put, such behavior pounds squarely on the issue of fairness. How fair is it for those who have benefited so much under American rules to dodge their U.S. tax responsibilities, while those with so little are scraping by as they meet their obligations? It isn't, yet it's true.

To be sure, much of the blame for the existence of offshore assets lies with the way the nation's public policy makers have ignored their responsibilities. Given that powerful interests in Washington are much more interested in protecting the status quo than surrendering any portions of their protected financial resources, it's easy to see why such influence would prevail. But there is a larger, more fundamental point here. That super-wealthy Americans no longer feel a connection with their country of origin speaks to the further fraying of the sociopolitical fabric that has bound the nation's citizens together over the past two centuries.

THE CHALLENGE OF EQUAL OPPORTUNITY

Despite all of the hope and promise connected with the concept of opportunity, increasing numbers of Americans have little of each. In fact, contrary to public values, inequality is a mainstay of society, giving those on the short end of the fairness stick good reason to wonder about their place in America.

Often, discrimination is associated with limitations on the ability of individuals to gain a quality education or earn an income commensurate with their formal training. In other instances, mistreatment takes place with employers who reject some groups because they just don't "fit in" with the values of what they perceive as the dominant culture. Either way, America is a lot less equal in opportunity than what meets the eye, and that sad reality leaves many with little upward social, economic, and psychological mobility.

True, the United States is becoming increasingly diverse in terms of demography, but changing percentages of various population groups shed little light on the distribution of resources. For many, the economic and social benefits of diversity have been left far behind, with the greatest disparities found in terms of race, gender, veteran status, age, and sexual orientation.

Race

The United States has two large racial and ethnic minorities: African Americans and Latinos. Each comprises about 15 percent of the nation's population. Smaller minority victims of discrimination also exist, with the oldest being Native Americans, but for our purposes here, we focus on the two largest minorities.

Although both African Americans and Latinos have long histories in the United States, they have traveled different paths. Most African Americans lived under the yoke of slavery for 300 years and, as such, were denied virtually all aspects of citizenship. Only after the passage of the 13th, 14th, and 15th Amendments were African Americans officially awarded citizenship, and even then commonly in a token sense and little else. Even then, for the next 75 years, African Americans lived lives separate from whites, an existence enforced by state and local laws that secured their second-class status.[28] Efforts to change the rules were consistently rejected. Eventually, along with some white activists, many in this group formed the front lines of the civil rights revolution during the 1950s and 1960s. Most of the national civil rights legislation and Supreme Court decisions during this period centered on mistreatment of African Americans, although other minorities benefited from the changes as well. Still, the odd feature of the African American struggle is that the group has a history of being part of American society, even if at an arm's length.

The plight of Latinos has drawn far less attention until recent times. Over the past 40 years, the numbers of Latinos have grown substantially through immigration, both legal and illegal, and high birth rates. For many decades, Latinos suffered marginalized lives in the Southwest. Some worked menial jobs as citizens or undocumented residents; others came from and returned to Mexico during the year in their capacities as farm workers. Collectively, this group is now the nation's largest demographic minority. Moreover, they no longer reside strictly in the swath of states extending from California to Texas. With pressing needs for low-paid food processing plant workers in agriculture centers in the farm belt and menial labor elsewhere, Latinos have migrated to the nation's Midwest and major urban centers.

Below we examine the experiences of racial and ethnic minorities in three categories: education, employment, and incarceration. These experiences have laid the foundation for feelings of rejection from the dominant white culture.

Education

Earlier we discussed the deleterious impact of segregated education in America (Chapter 2). Despite *Brown v. Board of Education* and the laudable efforts to end racial segregation, the outcomes have been incomplete. Today, the United States remains a nation with dramatically dissimilar opportunities for different groups, largely because of different educational tracks.

There are serious long-term consequences from this most unfortunate arrangement. At the beginning of the educational experience, knowledge and cognitive abilities among various races and ethnic groups show no significant differences.[29] Then changes occur over a relatively short period of time. By the fourth grade, stark distinctions are found among various groups, which set the stage for diverging paths and futures. A 2011 study by the U.S. Department of Education found that 68 percent of all fourth graders were not proficient in reading. When broken down by race and ethnicity, 84 percent of all African Americans and 82 percent of Latinos were not proficient. Non-Hispanic whites owned few bragging rights, given that 58 percent of all fourth grade students were not proficient in reading. Nevertheless, the gap existed and became the foundation for the public education experience.

By the eighth grade, 83 percent of all African Americans and 80 percent of all Latinos remained below proficiency, with the figure for whites at 57 percent.[30] Fast-forward a few more years to graduation, and the results are predictable enough. The graduation rates for African Americans and Latinos were 66 and 71 percent respectively, whereas the graduation rate for non-Hispanic whites was 83 percent.[31]

And so it goes up the education ladder, the portal that provides the best route to employment opportunities. According to the 2010 U.S. census, non-Hispanic whites constituted 63 percent of the nation's population, followed by Latinos with 16 percent and African Americans with 13 percent. Asian Americans, Pacific Islanders, and Native Americans made up most of the rest. Yet, an examination of university graduation statistics in 2010 found that 72.9 percent of all bachelor's degrees are awarded to whites, a percentage that far exceeds their population. Latinos received 8.8 percent of all bachelor's degrees, while African Americans garnered 10.3 percent of all bachelor's degrees. The gaps were even more significant for master's and PhD programs.[32] It's important to note that the differences have contracted a bit in recent years, thanks in large part to affirmative action programs—the very programs that have been weakened by the U.S. Supreme Court,[33] which leads one to wonder about minority higher education statistics in the coming decades.

Let's not ignore that public education occurs in largely segregated community environments. Those settings form the porous foundations for segregated school districts with poor income families, which in turn produce radically inadequate tax bases that form the foundation for poor education products. It all connects. Under such circumstances, how can we expect anything else but terribly unequal outcomes? The fact is, we can't; the deck is stacked from the get-go.

Employment

The general rule of thumb is that, all things considered, more education produces better economic opportunities in the workplace. As of 2012, the typical individual with a 4-year university degree earned 64 percent more than a high school graduate; a typical high school graduate earned 38 percent more than a high school dropout. It should not be surprising that unemployment rates parallel education and training data. During 2012, the unemployment rate for 4-year university graduates stood at 4.5 percent, compared with 8.3 percent for those with high school diplomas, and 12.4 percent for high school dropouts.[34] Bearing in mind the relationship between race and university degrees, we can expect that whites will earn considerably more than non-whites. And they do.

Income differentials accompany race and education. Using 2011 Census Bureau data, the median U.S. household income was $50,054. Among the largest ethnic groups, non-Hispanic whites generated median household incomes of $55,412. Latinos had produced household incomes of $38,624, and African Americans followed with $32,366. (Interestingly, Asian Americans were the highest, with median household incomes of $64,995.[35]) These data were reflected by the extent to which various groups suffered impoverishment. With 16 percent of the U.S. population, Latinos accounted for 30 percent of all families in poverty. African Americans, who comprised 13 percent of the population, accounted for 22 percent. Meanwhile, non-Hispanic whites comprised 42 percent of those in poverty, although they amounted to 72 percent of the population.[36]

Incarceration

The United States has the highest incarceration rate of any nation, something you wouldn't necessarily expect in the world's most admired democracy.[37] Approximately 2.3 million inmates reside in American prisons and jails. But these numbers, while surprising in their magnitude, only tell part of the story. Along with education and employment data, incarceration rates vary wildly among race and ethnic groups. More than 60 percent of all prisoners are people of color—a percentage that far exceeds their proportion of the U.S. adult population. Among white males, 1 of every 106 adults is in prison; among Latino males, the proportion is 1 of every 36 adults; and among African Americans, the proportion is 1 in every 15.[38] These data are neither random nor circumstantial; rather, they reflect purposive and persistent discrimination that extends from racial profiling to judicial remedies to incarceration.

An examination of the application of criminal justice in the United States shows a strong negative bias toward arrest, trial, and conviction of racial and ethnic minority groups. Routinely, police stop people of color much more often than whites because of racial profiling, a "tool" used by law enforcement that predetermines whether a person should be engaged in prearrest activities because of his or her race or ethnicity.[39] Race-related variations in the legal process move on from there. Minorities who commit the same crimes as whites are less likely to be denied pretrial release and more likely to receive longer sentences. One study finds that African Americans are 25 percent less likely to be granted bail; being Latino makes it 24 percent less likely to be granted bail for similar crimes committed by whites. Even when they are granted bail before trial, people of color are only about half as likely to be able to afford it as whites.[40]

The dramatic differences in treatment continue with prison sentences. A report by the U.S. Sentencing Commission in December 2012 found that prison sentences for African American men were nearly 20 percent longer than sentences for white men for similar crimes. Moreover, the differences have actually widened over time.[41] Simply put, on matters relating to criminal procedures from pretrial to post-conviction, America operates with a two-tiered system of justice.

To summarize, life chances for America's largest minorities are endangered almost from the beginning of their existence. From education to employment to incarceration, many experience little more than second-class citizenship that leaves them unable to pursue the opportunities available to their white counterparts. Of course, some surmount barriers and function successfully in a white-dominated American society in spite of the odds. Yet, too many are left behind early on and remain behind the rest of their lives.

Gender

If numbers alone accounted for success, then women would be on a par with men in American society, if not ahead. But numbers alone rarely tell the story about anything, including gender discrimination. In the United States today, women are more educated but still paid considerably less than their male counterparts. And they are underrepresented in just about every category, from C-level positions to elected political offices. More than anything else, this simple comparison underscores the position of women in America. The disconnect keeps women from achieving the successes they otherwise might achieve, a phenomenon that can be best explained by gender discrimination.

The place of women in American society is an evolving story, with many chapters yet to be written. Once American women were far less involved in the workplace than their male counterparts. In married households, most accepted roles as homemakers much more often than breadwinners. Rumbles for change began as far back as the women's suffrage movement from the late 1800s through the adoption of the 19th Amendment in 1920. The gender equality issue stalled during the Great Depression and World War II, only to resume anew during the 1950s. In 1961, President John F. Kennedy created the first Commission on the Status of Women, whose findings clearly documented the second-class status of women in the United States. In 1964, Congress passed the Civil Rights Act. Many view this legislation as a major step forward in promoting racial equality, but it was more. Unlike earlier civil rights acts, the 1964 Act specifically forbade workplace discrimination based on gender as well as on race, national origin, and ethnicity.

Subsequent legislative acts and executive orders have addressed gender inequality more directly. The most recent is the Lilly Ledbetter Fair Pay Act of 2009, which strengthened the 1964 Civil Rights Act by lengthening the period between employment and post-employment during which women may sue employers on matters relating to pay discrimination. Nevertheless, some of these gains may now be threatened because of recent actions by the U.S. Supreme Court on affirmative action, although the end of that chapter remains to be written.

Education

Unshackled from their historical roles, large numbers of women have responded to the new equality guarantees through pursuing more education. Their ascendance has been swift and demonstrable. In 1980, the percentages of men and women in post-secondary education were almost evenly split. By 2001, more women were earning bachelor's degrees than men. Fast-forward another decade, and we see that women's advances have altered the face of higher education as well as the composition of the workplace. As of 2010, women received 57 percent of all bachelor's degrees, 63 percent of all master's degrees, and 53 percent of all PhDs.[42]

Along with achieving parity in the university classroom, women have moved to roles once considered the exclusive domain of men. Early on, female students focused largely on the social sciences and humanities, with some opting for the nursing profession. But over time, women have moved into just about every education category imaginable. By 2006, more women than men received bachelor's degrees in engineering and science. Men still received more master's degrees and PhDs in these fields, but by 2012 women represented 43 percent of all graduate students in the engineering and science categories.[43] Thus, the facts are clear: American women today have more education than men and have become active participants of virtually every aspect of the nation's professional workforce.

Employment

Still, substantial inequities persist for women in American society. With respect to salaries, women lag behind men, modest gains notwithstanding. In 2000, women earned 69 percent of the salaries paid to their male counterparts with the same credentials and levels of experience.[44] By 2011, the difference had lessened, with women earning 82 percent of men in the same professions with the same training.[45] Yes, these data point to improvements, but true parity remains elusive. It's pretty amazing that nearly 100 years after being awarded the right to vote, women earn four-fifths the workplace compensation of their male counterparts, yet that is exactly the case.

Beyond income data, women still suffer from the effects of the glass ceiling, that invisible, yet almost impenetrable barrier on the management ladder beyond which is overwhelmingly dominated by men. A 2013 assessment of the S&P's largest 100 companies found that women held only 8 percent of the senior management positions and 19 percent of the board of directors seats. The same study determined that 56 percent of the top 100 companies had no women or people of color in the most compensated senior management positions.[46] Another independent examination found women serving in 17 percent of the board of director positions of S&P's largest 500 firms, with only 21 employed as CEOs. That's equivalent to women amounting to 4.2 percent of the nation's largest businesses.[47]

The disconnect is clear. Women are every bit as educated as men, if not more so. They are every bit as qualified as men, if not more so. Yet, women are denied positions of responsibility on the highest rungs of the corporate management ladder, despite their qualifications. This collective condition leaves women disadvantaged compared with men in a society whose values tout merit over position.

Veterans

Military veterans are among the most troubled and least understood members of American society. There are more than 23 million veterans of the armed forces in the United States alive today. That amounts to about 1 out of every 14 residents. Approximately 2.6 million veterans have served since the September 11, 2001, Al Qaeda terrorist attacks. About 1.6 million have been stationed in Iraq and Afghanistan, where many have completed three or more tours of duty. The transition from combat to domestic life has not always been easy. Some veterans have quickly assimilated into their families and society upon their return to the United States, but many have come back to a nation they no longer understand, and a nation in many instances that does not understand them. All this has taken a toll on countless numbers of veterans in the forms of joblessness, homelessness, and skyrocketing medical costs. Moreover, it's a toll that will cost American society for generations to come.

Joblessness

Historically, veterans have been welcomed back into the job market, where they have fared better than their nonservice counterparts. That axiom is true only in part these days. Although the unemployment rate for all veterans is below the national average, those who have served since the 9/11 attacks have much higher unemployment rates than the national workforce. For example, in December 2012 the U.S. unemployment rate was 7.8 percent. During the same period, the unemployment rate for veterans who served in Afghanistan or Iraq stood at 9.9 percent. Among male veterans 18–24 years of age, the unemployment rate was 20.0 percent, compared with 16.4 percent for their nonveteran peers.[48]

Employment for veterans is likely to become even more challenging in the next decade. Between reduced troop commitments abroad and reductions in military spending, as many as 1 million more young veterans will be reentering the job market, still struggling to find its feet in the aftermath of the Great Recession. Many returnees will not possess the university degrees or specialized training of their civilian counterparts, which in all likelihood will add to their disadvantaged positions in the workforce. Government-sponsored training programs could offset many of these problems, but whether the commitments and sufficient funds exist remain to be seen.

Homelessness

Veterans have suffered disproportionately with homelessness. As of 2011, there were about 634,000 homeless people in the United States, according to estimates from the U.S. Department of Housing and Urban Development (HUD). HUD determined that 163,000 were "chronically homeless," someone who is disabled, has been homeless for 1 year or more, or has been homeless at least three times over a 4-year period. Of this number, 38 percent, or 62,000, were veterans.[49] That said, some studies suggest that on any given night, as many as 300,000 veterans are likely to be homeless.[50]

There is some hope. Government statistics suggest that with the economy recovering from the Great Recession, the number of homeless veterans dwindled. In addition, in 2009 the Obama administration announced a 5-year plan to end veteran homelessness, but Congress has not followed through with the necessary funding—yet another casualty of the fiscal battles within the legislative branch.[51] With only patchwork quilt-like "solutions" in place, the numbers of homeless veterans in America remain sizable.

Medical Costs

Some of the joblessness for recent veterans centers on the high percentages that have developed service-connected disabilities. Indeed, the differences from the past are palpable and distressing. As of August 2012, about 14 percent of all veterans had a service-connected disability. But the most important distinction comes with different eras of military service. Among the military members who have served since 9/11, the federal government has accepted medical disability claims from 30 percent of the returnees.[52] Many more veterans await answers; in fact, nearly half of the 1.6 million who served in Iraq and Afghanistan have requested disability payments, compared with 21 percent of the veterans who returned from the first Gulf War in 1991.[53]

There's a no-win medical trade-off of sorts with today's veterans, compared with veterans of past military conflicts. During the Vietnam War, more than 58,000 Americans were killed in battle. During the recent wars in Iraq and Afghanistan, fewer than 7,000 American deaths occurred, thanks to modern medicine and superior equipment. However, more than 16,000 suffered serious physical injuries resulting in huge medical costs for the rest of their lives. Tens of thousands more have been left with post-traumatic stress disorder, brain injuries, and various forms of combat trauma that have caused permanent damage.[54] One Pentagon study estimates that as many as 360,000 returning veterans from Iraq and Afghanistan may have suffered permanent brain injuries.[55]

The battered conditions of military returnees have extracted a heavy price on both those who serve and the nation indebted to them for their service. As of 2011, 3.4 million veterans with service-connected disabilities received $35 billion in annual government payments.[56] One well-respected scholar estimates that over a 40-year span between 2014 and 2053, the total medical and disability costs for treating the veterans from Afghanistan and Iraq will amount to $970 billion.[57] Such outlays are bound to squeeze federal spending in other important public policy areas, which may cause additional rifts down the road. In the meantime, those who have sacrificed the most for their country in a military "no man's land" now find themselves in a medical "no man's land."

Age

Conventional wisdom suggests that people acquire a special sense of sagacity from their lifetime of experiences as they age. Novelist Madeleine L'Engle once wrote: "The great thing about getting older is that you don't lose all the ages you've been," hence the feeling that age confers upon someone a special view of the world and his or her unique place in it. That approach may leave older people feeling that they lead privileged lives in society, but the facts of life suggest otherwise.

Ageism, the pejorative attitude toward or mistreatment of someone because of his or her twilight years, exists in America, particularly in the workplace. Stereotypical anecdotal descriptions about older workers "losing it" or being "over the hill" often frame the employment setting, irrespective of their accuracy. Slower physical gaits are thought to parallel reduced mental capacities, yet no such linkage exists on a consistent basis. One study of 400 employers found older workers scoring higher than the average employee on performance, attitude, and turnover, yet the employers insisted that older employees were less flexible and less suitable for training without any evidence other than their bias.[58] Another study of 4,000 job applicants between ages 35 and 62 with similar work experiences for the same job found that the younger applicant was 40 percent more likely to get a job interview than an applicant 50 years of age or older.[59] Society may confer respect for the elderly, but employers operate within a different set of values.

Early Legislation

During the mid-20th century, policy makers began to address the age discrimination issue through legislative responses. In 1964, the U.S. Congress created the Equal Employment Opportunity Commission (EEOC) as part of the Civil Rights Act. The commission's mandate includes enforcing federal laws against age discrimination of persons 40 years or older. Three years later, Congress passed and President Lyndon Johnson signed the Age Discrimination and Employment Act. The legislation was written to prevent unfavorable treatment against people over 40 years of age, specifically in the workplace.

Like so many other elements of policy making, the new laws appeared to make a power statement "on paper." But as we know, what is intended and what is real are often very different. In fact, age discrimination in the workplace has persisted, even though the 1967 legislation has been amended twice to strengthen its enforcement. One study found that 20 percent of all cases filed before the EEOC during a 4-year period centered on age discrimination.[60]

Recent assessments show that older workers face challenges different from their younger peers. During the Great Recession, workers 55 or older represented 54 percent of the long-term unemployed (27 weeks or longer), even though they constituted 40 percent of the workforce.[61] They also stayed jobless longer than their younger colleagues. Even in the post-Great Recession era, when unemployed older workers attempt to find jobs, the search takes an average of 55 weeks, compared to 35 weeks for job seekers ages 25–34.[62] As if these obstacles aren't enough, when older workers find new jobs, they settle for less than younger workers.[63] Such conditions do not suggest age discrimination per se, yet they certainly point to a curious employment pattern for a select group of people.

Continuing Discrimination

In 2012, more than 22,000 age discrimination complaints were filed with the U.S. Equal Opportunity Commission, the federal agency responsible for enforcing national laws that forbid mistreatment because of race, gender, age, or religion. As with the past, the agency found reasons for taking action against the employers in about 30 percent of the age discrimination cases.[64] That doesn't count cases that settle to avoid federal action. For example, in 2009, Allstate Insurance settled a class action discrimination act for $4.5 million; in the same year, Massey Energy settled an age discrimination lawsuit for $8.75 million. In 2011, 3M Corporation paid $12 million to settle a class action age discrimination lawsuit by 7,000 employees; during the same year, AT&T agreed to rehire thousands of former employees who sued after retiring in a program that was misleading in benefits.

Uncertain Future

Antidiscrimination advocates might be pleased by such arrangements, but recent institutional policy changes may well slow down the efforts of ageism proponents. In 2009, the U.S. Supreme Court ruled by a 5–4 vote that plaintiffs suing for compensation had to prove that age was the sole reason for their misfortune, rather than one of several reasons, as it is in the civil rights lawsuits relating to gender or race.[65] Whereas business organizations applauded the decision, the AARP and other senior groups viewed it as holding older workers to a higher standard that is almost impossible to prove.[66]

Between unreported mistreatment, the fear of employer reprisal, ignorance of the process, and the lack of resources to pursue legal action, it's difficult to ascertain just how many people suffer from age discrimination. Despite the willingness of the federal authorities to proceed upon complaint, one EEOC commissioner acknowledged that "the number of formal complaints that come in to us understate the nature of the problem."[67] Thus, while we may not know how many victims suffer from age discrimination, the evidence is clear that the numbers are substantial.

Sexual Orientation

Historically, nonheterosexual orientation in America has drawn considerable discrimination.[68] Just how many gay Americans have suffered remains something of a mystery. Because of widespread prejudice and the unwillingness of victims to come forward, it has been difficult to calculate the numbers of lesbian, gay, bisexual, and transgender (LGBT) residents in America. A recent Gallup Poll of self-identified adults ascertained that LGBT adults comprise 3.5 percent of the U.S. population.[69] Harris Interactive calculates the LGBT percentage at 6.8 percent of the U.S. population.[70] Either way, the nonheterosexual community represents a sizable slice of the nation.

Until recently, mainstream American society has been slow to accept LGBT individuals as equal members of society. Some change is now occurring in the workplace and political life. For years, a few openly gay individuals have secured election to Congress. In 2012, Kyrsten Sinema became the first openly bisexual person elected to the U.S. House of Representatives, where she joined five openly gay men. In the same election, Tammy Baldwin became the first publicly known lesbian elected to the U.S. Senate. A smattering of nonheterosexual CEOs and professional athletes have also "gone public," but their numbers remain few. For members of the LGBT community, much more must be accomplished before they experience the same standing as other Americans.

Workplace

Within the workplace, members of the LGBT community have uneasy acceptance in some sectors, while continuing to suffer from outright discriminatory practices in others. Data gathered by the Williams Institute finds that over a recent 5-year period, 27 percent of LGBT individuals experienced discrimination on the job; 7 percent were terminated from their employment because of their sexual orientation.[71] Even if they are not fired, discriminated LGBT employees experience considerable psychological stress and depression because of their employment setting.

Some workplace environments are more accepting than others. For example, as of 2013, 90 percent of the largest federal contractors had policies in place that prohibited discrimination because of sexual orientation, courtesy of federal requirements for doing business.[72] There have been gains in other areas of the private sector as well. According to the Human Rights Campaign, as of 2013, 88 percent of the Fortune 500 corporations had antidiscrimination policies on sexual orientation, up from 61 percent in 2002. With respect to gender identification, 57 percent of the Fortune 500 companies had antidiscrimination policies in place, up from 3 percent in 2002.[73]

Still, public support for LGBT antidiscrimination policies remains weak. A 2013 national survey by the *Huffington Post* found that 52 percent of those interviewed endorse antidiscrimination laws for LGBT people, while 35 percent oppose such guarantees.[74] These data hardly reflect public consensus on the issue, even if it has been addressed in the workplace. In addition, according to the Human Rights Campaign, employees still can be terminated for their sexual identity in 29 states and gender identity in 23 states.[75]

There have been efforts to formalize protection for individuals irrespective of their sexual orientation. Chief among these has been proposed national legislation most recently known as the Employment Nondiscrimination Act (ENDA), which has been introduced in every Congress since 1994 except one. The proposed legislation would prohibit employers with 15 or more employees from discriminating against anyone because of his or her sexual orientation or identity. The bill passed in the House of Representatives only once, in 2007, but failed to secure passage in the Senate. An updated version of ENDA passed in the U.S. Senate in 2013, only to be set aside without a vote in the House of Representatives. Clearly, responding to gay discrimination in the workplace remains a divisive issue in the U.S. Congress.

Marriage Equality

The issue of marriage equality is in a state of flux. For years, the question went without attention at the national level, and had precious little consideration in the states. During the 1990s a few states enacted civil union legislation, which extended limited rights to same-sex partners without recognition of marriage. The watershed year came in 2003, when the U.S. Supreme Court overturned state legislation that banned sexual relations between consenting adults and the state of Massachusetts legalized same-sex marriage through the action of its Supreme Court.

With the gender equality issue pitting civil libertarians against evangelicals and other opponents, public policy makers struggled over possible legislation. In 1996, Congress passed and President Bill Clinton signed the Defense of Marriage Act (DOMA), which allowed states to refuse recognition of same-sex marriages performed in other states and denied federal benefits to same-sex married couples.

The same-sex marriage issue festered until 2013, when the U.S. Supreme Court handed down two decisions. The first case overturned DOMA, paving the way for same-sex married couples to enjoy federal guarantees, assuming they lived in states that allowed same-sex marriages. The second case upheld the decision of a U.S. District Court judge, who overturned a California voter-approved ban of same-sex marriage; here the Supreme Court didn't discuss the merits, but rather questioned the litigation process.[76] It's important to note that in neither case did the Supreme Court endorse same-sex marriage as a constitutional right; rather, the justices by 5–4 majorities in each instance decided rather narrow questions.

These two court decisions have altered the same-sex marriage environment. As of October 2014, 31 states now have same-sex marriage, 5 states are in appeal, and 61 percent of the U.S. population is covered by same sex marriage guarantees. Court challenges to same-sex marriages in a half dozen other states were awaiting resolutions. It's hard to imagine that this divergence will continue without further attention. Nevertheless, the blockbuster U.S. Supreme Court cases regarding same-sex marriage opportunities in 2013 suggest that although the issue has not been comprehensively addressed, major steps forward have been taken toward providing equal standing in this rapidly changing social policy area.

EQUALITY: SUBSTANCE VERSUS SYMBOLISM

Equality may be a cornerstone of American political values, but the foundation on which that cornerstone sits is prone to instability. The simple fact is that Americans are not equal. Economically, there is a huge gap between those at the top and those at the bottom, and the gap is growing. The much touted middle class is disappearing day by day, with most dropping below and few ascending in the other direction. Moreover, a sizable portion of American society is convinced that they will never be able to reach that middle class rung on the economic ladder. The rules may be the same for each end of the economic spectrum, but the few benefit from them much more than the rest.

The life chances of Americans are largely predetermined not only by initial wealth but also by other factors. African Americans and Latinos are denied opportunities largely because of racism. Women have economic hurdles much higher than their male counterparts, even when educations and work experiences are similar. Veterans are much less likely to succeed than nonveterans, even though they have sacrificed for their country. Older Americans have a much tougher time in the marketplace than younger Americans, largely because employers can hire young people at much lower salaries. And nonheterosexuals live in a world where their opportunities are threatened by bias and discrimination. These conditions do not speak to equality; rather, they speak to a fractured society.

Are there opportunities in America? Of course, but the qualities and the quantities of those opportunities vary substantially more with the circumstances surrounding an individual than his or her capabilities. Which leads us to ask, how long can the United States function successfully with uneven conditions for so many groups? At what point will there be a price to pay for discrimination and the denial of equal treatment, and by whom? For those who have explained away these discrimination circumstances, the day of reckoning is here. Yet, how long it will be before all Americans are incorporated under the big tent of true equality remains to be seen. Until that happens, America will remain a land more divided than not.

ENDNOTES

1. See Milton and Rose Friedman, *Free to Choose*, New York: Harcourt, Brace, Jovanovich, 1979, p. 129.
2. John J. Harrigan, *Empty Dreams, Empty Pockets: Class and Bias in American Politics*, New York: Macmillan Publishing Company, 1993, p. 301.
3. For a brief history of the evolution of affirmative action, see "Affirmative Actions: The Selective History of an American Idea," *New York Times*, June 29, 2003, p. 14.
4. The landmark case was *Fisher v. University of Texas*, 11-345, decided June 20, 2013.
5. The U.S. Supreme Court first narrowed the definition of affirmative action in 1978 when, in *University of California v. Bakke*, the justices held 5–4 that affirmative action programs could not contain specific quotas for racial minorities and women. Subsequent decisions have further narrowed the definition and its application. For a history of the affirmative action movement, see Terry H. Anderson, *The Pursuit of Fairness: The History of Affirmative Action*, New York: Oxford University Press, 2004.
6. "Justices Back Ban on Race as Factor in College Entry," *New York Times*, April 23, 2014, pp. A1, A12. The case was *Schuette v. Coalition to Defend Affirmative Action*.
7. "Affirmative-Action Ruling Could Complicate Diversity Efforts," *Education Week*, June 25, 2013, http://www.edweek.org/ew/articles/2013/06/25/36scotus.h32.html?tkn=WUVFPftSQrM2T7TbKFHHDUZANpZHBplQo5qp.
8. Michael I. Norton and Dan Ariely, "Building a Better America—One Wealth Quintile at a Time," *Perspectives on Psychological Science*, 6, 9, 2011, http//pps.sagepub.com/content/6/1/9.
9. Jordan Weissmann, "Yes, U.S. Wealth Inequality Is Terrible by Global Standards," *The Atlantic*, March 11, 2013, http://www.theatlantic.com/business/archive/2013/03/yes-us-wealth-inequality-is-terrible-by-global-standards/273908/.
10. G. William Domhoff, "Wealth, Income, and Power," http://www2.ucsc.edu/whorulesamerica/power/wealth.html, February 2013, pp. 2–3.

11. "A Rise in Wealth for the Wealthy; Declines for the Lower 93%," Pew Research Social and Demographic Trends, Pew Research Center, Washington, DC, February 2008, p. 1, http://www.pewsocialtrends.org/2013/04/23/a-rise-in-wealth-for-the-wealthydeclines-for-the-lower-93/.

12. Lawrence Mishel, Josh Bevins, Elise Gould, and Heidi Shierholz, *The State of Working America*, 12th ed., Ithaca, NY: Cornell University Press, 2012, pp. 197–198.

13. Ibid., pp. 290–291.

14. "CEO-to-Worker Pay Ratios around the World," 2012, http://www.aflcio.org/Corporate-Watch/CEO-Pay-and-You/CEO-to-Worker-Pay-Gap-in-the-United-States/Pay-Gaps-in-the-World.

15. Ibid.

16. Michael Parenti, *Democracy for the Few*, 9th ed., Boston: Wadsworth Publishing Company, 2011, p. 151.

17. "The Lost Decade of the Middle Class," Pew Research Social and Demographic Trends, Washington, DC, August 22, 2012, p. 1.

18. Ibid.

19. "America's Sinking Middle Class," *New York Times*, September 19, 2013, pp. B1, B4.

20. Jacob J. Hacker, Gregory A. Huber, Philipp Rehm, Mark Schlesinger, and Rob Valleta, "Economic Security at Risk," Rockefeller Foundation, New York, July 2010, p. 1.

21. "IRS May Be Missing Offshore Tax Evasion: Government Watchdog," Reuters, April 26, 2013, http://www.reuters.com/article/2013/04/26/us-usa-tax-offshore-idUSBRE93P12R20130426.

22. "Paradise of Untouchable Assets," *New York Times*, December 15, 2013, pp. BU1, BU6.

23. "The Rich Are Moving More Money Overseas," *Wall Street Journal*, May 18, 2011, http://blogs.wsj.com/wealth/2011/05/18/the-rich-are-moving-more-money-overseas/.

24. "Staff Report on Tax Haven Banks and U.S. Compliance," U.S. Senate Permanent Subcommittee on Investigations, July 17, 2008, p. 1.

25. See "Offshore Tax Evasion: IRS Has Collected Billions of Dollars, but May Be Missing Continued Evasion," General Accounting Office, March 2013, and "Senate Report Blasts Credit Suisse," *Wall Street Journal*, February 26, 2014, pp. C1, C2.

26. "'Bye' to Uncle Sam," *Wall Street Journal*, August 17–18, 2013, pp. B7, B10.

27. "2,999 Americans Renounced Citizenship in 2013," Tax Foundation, Washington, DC, February 7, 2014, http://taxfoundation.org/blog/2999-americans-renounced-us-citizenship-2013.

28. For an excellent account of the road to affirmative action, see Terry H. Anderson, *The Pursuit of Fairness: A History of Affirmative Action*, New York: Oxford University Press, 2004.

29. "A Dozen Economic Facts about K–12 Education," Hamilton Project, Brookings Institution, Washington, DC, September 2012, p. 10.

30. See *2013 KIDSCOUNT Data Book*, Anne E. Casey Foundation, Baltimore, MD, 2013, p. 26.

31. Ibid., p. 15.

32. "Fast Facts: Degrees Conferred by Sex and Race," National Center for Education Statistics, U.S. Department of Education, 2011, http://nces.ed.gov/fastfacts/display.asp?id=72.

33. For a comprehensive analysis on the benefits of affirmative action and the consequences of doing without it, see Richard D. Kallenberg, "A Better Affirmative Action," Century Foundation, Washington, DC, October 3, 2012, http://tcf.org/assets/downloads/tcf-abaa.pdf.

34. "Employment Projections: Earnings and Unemployment Rates by Educational Attainment," Bureau of Labor Statistics, U.S. Census Bureau, May 22, 2013, http://data.bls.gov/cgi-bin/print.pl/emp/ep_chart_001.htm.

35. "Household Income Sinks to '95 Level," *Wall Street Journal*, September 13, 2012, pp. A1, A6.

36. Margaret C. Simms, Karina Fortuny, and Everett Henderson, "Racial and Ethnic Disparities among Low-Income Families," Urban Institute, August 7, 2009, http://www.urban.org/publications/411936.html.

37. "New Incarceration Figures: Thirty-Three Consecutive Years of Growth," Sentencing Project, Washington, DC, December 2006.

38. "U.S. Incarceration Rates by Race and Sex," National Institute of Justice, U.S. Department of Justice, June 4, 2012, http://nij.gov/journals/270/criminal-records-figure2.htm.

39. See "The Persistence of Racial and Ethnic Profiling in the United States," American Civil Liberties Union, Washington, DC, June 30, 2009.

40. See Traci Schlesinger, "Racial and Ethnic Disparity in Pretrial Criminal Processing," *Justice Quarterly*, January 1, 2005, p. 11.

41. "Report on the Continuing Impact on *United States v. Booker* on Federal Sentencing," U.S. Sentencing Commission, Washington, DC, December 2012, p. E-2.

42. "Gender Equity in Education: A Data Snapshot," Office for Civil Rights, U.S. Department of Education, June 2012, http://www2.ed.gov/about/offices/list/ocr/docs/gender-equity-in-education.pdf.

43. National Science Foundation, National Center for Science and Engineering Statistics, Survey of Graduate Students and Postdoctorates in Science and Engineering, 2010 http://www.nsf.gov/statistics/wmpd/2013/pdf/tab3-1.pdf.

44. "The Wage Gap and Its Costs," in Paula S. Rothenberg, ed., *Race, Class, and Gender in the United States*, 8th ed., New York: Worth Publishers, 2010, p. 348.

45. "She Works Hard for the Money," Women's eNews, May 20, 2012, http://womensenews.org/story/economyeconomic-policy-labor/120526/wage-gap-womens-median-wages-compared-mens-in-the-same#.UdNg7pwgSik.

46. "Calvert Report: Few Women and Minorities Making It to S&P 100 Board Rooms, Executive Suites," May 13, 2013, http://www.calvert.com/newsArticle.html?article=20288.

47. "Women in Top Executive Positions Are Few," *San Francisco Chronicle*, March 13, 2013, http://www.sfgate.com/business/article/Women-in-top-executive-positions-are-few-4360451.php.

48. "Employment Situation of Veterans Summary," Bureau of Labor Statistics, U.S. Department of Labor, March 20, 2013, http://www.bls.gov/news.release/vet.nr0.htm.

49. "Number of Chronically Homeless, Including Veterans, Drops in U.S., *Los Angeles Times*, December 10, 2012, http://articles.latimes.com/2012/dec/10/nation/la-na-nn-number-chronically-homeless-veterans-drops-20121210.

50. "Statistics," Veterans, Inc., Worchester, MA: http://www.veteransinc.org/about-us/statistics/.

51. "Policy and Legislative Update: Is the Five-Year Plan to End Veteran Homelessness Working?" National Coalition for Homeless Veterans, Washington, DC, January 22, 2013, http://nchv.org/index.php/news/headline_article/policy_legislative_update_is_the_five-year_plan_to_end_veteran_homelessness/.

52. Ibid.

53. "The Waiting Wounded," *The Economist*, March 23, 2013, p. 13.

54. "Iraq, Afghanistan War Wounded Pass 50,000," *Huffington Post*, December 26, 2012, http://www.huffingtonpost.com/2012/10/25/iraq-afghanistan-war-wounded_n_2017338.html.
55. "360,000 Veterans May Have Brain Injuries," *USA Today*, March 5, 2009, http://usatoday30.usatoday.com/news/military/2009-03-04-braininjuries_N.htm.
56. "Trends in Veterans with a Service-Connected Disability, 1985–2011," U.S. Department of Veterans Affairs, May 2012, http://www.va.gov/vetdata/docs/QuickFacts/SCD_trends_FINAL.pdf.
57. Linda J. Bilmes, "The Financial Legacy of Iraq and Afghanistan: How Wartime Spending Decisions Will Constrain Future National Security Budgets," Cambridge, MA: Harvard Kennedy School Research Working Paper, March 2013, p. 10.
58. Robert McCann and Howard Giles, "Ageism in the Workplace: A Communication Perspective," in *Ageism: Stereotyping and Prejudice against Older People*, edited by Todd D. Nelson, Cambridge, MA: MIT Press, 1967, p. 171.
59. "Three Men, Three Ages, Which Do You Like," *New York Times*, July 22, 2013.
60. Ibid., p. 177.
61. "Record Unemployment among Older Workers Does Not Keep Them Out of the Job Market," U.S. Bureau of Labor Statistics, Washington, DC, March 2010, p. 1.
62. "Jobless Older Workers Struggle," *Los Angeles Times*, November 10, 2013, pp. B1, B8.
63. Charles A. Jeszeck, U.S. Government Accounting Office, testimony before the Special Committee on Aging, U.S. Senate, May 15, 2012.
64. "Age Discrimination and Employment Act," FHowaY 1997-FY 2012, http://www.eeoc.gov/eeoc/statistics/enforcement/adea.cfm.
65. The case was *Gross v. FLB Financial Services*.
66. "Supreme Court Makes Age Bias Suits Harder to Win," *Los Angeles Times*, June, 19, 2009, http://articles.latimes.com/2009/jun/19/nation/na-court-age-bias19.
67. EEOC Commissioner Stuart Ishimaru, quoted in "Age Discrimination Suits Jump, but Wins Are Elusive," NPR, February 12, 2012, http://www.npr.org/2012/02/16/146925208/age-discrimination-suits-jump-but-wins-are-elusive.
68. For a brief historical review of the stereotyping of gays in America, see Mark Snyder, "Self-Fulfilling Stereotypes," in Paula S. Rothenberg, ed., opt. cit., pp. 571–577, and Richard D. Mohr, "Anti-Gay Stereotypes," in Rothenberg, pp. 577–583.
69. "LGBT Percentage Highest in D.C., Lowest in North Dakota," Gallup Poll, Newport, RI, February 13, 2013.
70. "The Lesbian, Gay, Bisexual and Transgender (LGBT) Population At-a-Glance," Harris Interactive, 2010, http://www.harrisinteractive.com/vault/HI_LGBT_SHEET_WCC_AtAGlance.pdf.
71. Brad Sears and Christy Mallory, "Documented Evidence of Employment Discrimination and Its Effects on LGBT People," Williams Institute, University of California, Los Angeles, CA, July 2011, p. 1.
72. Brad Sears, Nan D. Hunter, and Christy Mallory, "Sexual Orientation and Gender Identity Non-Discrimination Policies of the Top 50 Fortune 500 Companies," Williams Institute, University of California, Los Angeles, CA, April 2013, p. 1.
73. "2013 Corporate Equality Index," Human Rights Campaign, Washington, DC, 2013, p. 6.
74. "Workplace Discrimination Poll Finds Most Favor Laws Protecting Gays, Lesbians," *Huffington Post*, June 22, 2013, http://www.huffingtonpost.com/2013/06/22/work-place-discrimination-poll_n_3480243.html.
75. Ibid., p. 2.
76. The cases were *U.S. v. Windsor* and *Hollingsworth v. Perry*.

Section II

Broken Institutions

5

Diminished Public Investment

In his *The Post-American World*, Fareed Zakaria worries about American complacency, short-sided policies, and a nation caught up with its past successes in a rapidly changing world. Yet, at the end of the day, Zakaria emerges as an optimist for America's future. Whatever this country's shortcomings, he writes, "America has succeeded not because of the ingenuity of its government programs but because of the vigor of its society. It has thrived because it has kept itself open to the world—to goods and services, to ideas and inventions, and, above all, to people and cultures."[1] Zakaria's words of hope and praise are predicated upon the assumption that American culture has a "can do" mentality, and that what has happened in the past will surely continue in the future. We confront imposing challenges and overcome them. That kind of thinking assumes an underlying foundation of agreed national purpose and citizen execution of those goals.

Historically, he has a point to a degree. The United States has had great moments—engaging and conquering the totalitarian enemy in World War II, landing a man on the moon, and vanquishing cruel diseases such as polio and small pox are seminal triumphs in American history where society took pride in its accomplishments and where its population thrived from working as one.

However, such notable successes did not stem from the strong determination of society alone. In virtually every instance, these historic achievements were the outgrowths of government commitments and policies that responded to the demands of the people who willingly supported sweeping programs and services designed for the public good. If the prescription to conquer disease meant more government-funded research, so be it. Higher taxes for national goals? Fair enough, as long as they are used for the public good. Commitment of Americans to fight just wars? Anything to preserve our republic and democratic values. Simply put, America has succeeded in the past because of the strong partnership between a willing people and proactive leaders housed in forward-looking political institutions. These two invaluable elements, leaders and institutions, have been just as important to our national achievements as our "get the job done" culture.

The lockstep moments heralded by Zakaria and others are from an era now mostly viewed through America's rearview mirror, and they become more distant over time. Rather than embrace the collective good, we have turned our backs on the fundamental building blocks of American society, leaving individuals to fend for themselves in an increasingly divided nation economically, politically, and culturally. With conflicting expectations from government based on narrow individual demands in place of basic societal benefits, consensus is the rare exception to the rule. Meanwhile, policy makers have replaced leadership with a dour complacency now commonplace throughout the land. It just seems too hard for most of them to cobble together essential services and programs for the general public even as the few benefit at the expense of the many. And so we drift every day with a little less collective purpose and a lot more individual agendas, the results of which fuel the incremental deterioration of American society from within.

As with other aspects of American life, the costs of our disrepair are hardly distributed equally. Many of those at or near the bottom of the economic ladder have no alternatives other than failing public schools, polluted water systems, or increasingly unaffordable energy costs. They are de facto second-class citizens struggling in a society that preaches equal opportunity—a disconnect to be sure. In fact, most people work harder today with a lower standard of living. Those at the other end of the economic spectrum send their kids to private schools, drink bottled or filtered water, and reap the benefits of solar energy, courtesy of generous government tax breaks. And all too many are all too happy to abandon their tax obligations to the country that enabled their success.

The fundamental problem is not necessarily the differences between the "haves" and "have-nots," although that growing chasm is certainly part of the mix. Rather, the concern lies with the inadequate basic services for all of us, but particularly those mired at the bottom and doomed to stay there. These are the people who suffer disproportionately from diminished public investment that those with resources are unwilling to support through higher taxes and other revenue streams that might intrude upon their standard of living.

America's decay has not been a complete downward spiral. Some basic needs have been addressed over the years. The creation of Social Security in 1935 established a minimum income floor for most Americans in their twilight years. The passage of Medicare in 1965 represented a major step toward helping the elderly with medical costs. And enactment of the Patient Protection and Affordable Care Act in 2010 expanded the opportunity for most Americans to acquire health insurance at reasonable prices, although the newness of this legislation suggests there will be tweaking and resistance in some quarters for years to come. Yes, these are success stories, but they exist as exceptions in an otherwise flagging society.

This chapter addresses the diminished investment by government and others in American society. Much like a rotted-out tree, the decomposition of the country is not easily noticed upon casual examination; nor has it occurred in a rapid fashion that might set off alarms. In fact, we still have a public education system and reap some benefits from government-sponsored research and development. We continue our everyday lives by attending and matriculating from education institutions, driving on highways and bridges, and anticipating that the lights will glow when we flip the switches. Sure, there's an occasional power blackout or collapsed bridge, but for the most part, everything seems to be pretty operational. *Seems* to be.

But similar to the rotted-out tree, what occurs inside the bowels of our infrastructure provides a much different picture than superficial appearances. Simply said, America's socioeconomic infrastructure is slowly falling apart, making existence incredibly dangerous for our citizens and increasingly costly to properly address. Moreover, we continue to ignore the deterioration almost in tacit recognition that our problems are too overwhelming to address. Our decay is also leaving us increasingly disadvantaged compared to other nations. Yet, putting off until tomorrow what we must do today only exacerbates the extent of our problems and increases the difficulty of solving them. That is the essence of our short-sightedness and the fundamental cause of losing our place in the world.

This is the essence of the frustration Americans feel, although we tend not to fully understand the context or consequences.

A POORLY EDUCATED NATION

Education is a key measuring stick for the overall well-being of a society, particularly in democracies.[2] But the benefits of education ripple in other directions too. Economist Jeffrey Sachs has observed that education and economic development are interdependent elements of growth. As societies move up the development ladder from subsistence economies to commercial economies, and then again to emerging market economies and technology-based economies, they demand and become increasingly dependent upon more education.[3] Much like a slingshot, advancement in education permits an economy to excel yet again and again, with more and better training demanded along the way to accelerate the economy even more. That's the theory, anyway.

Against that backdrop, we turn to the condition of public education in the United States. It's no secret that the American public education system is steeped in profound race-based inequality. And it is just as well documented that inequality has changed little in spite of potentially impactful legislation and once historic U.S. Supreme Court decisions (see Chapter 2). On the face of it, this seemingly permanent condition denies millions of Americans the same opportunities as others. An equally compelling concern, however, exists with the extent to which American education has slipped far from the top to mediocre status when compared to the education successes of other countries. This development has cast a pall on the entire nation.

The decline of American public education costs us dearly with respect to our competitive standing among nations around the world, as well as commitment to once treasured core values such as equality and upward mobility. Benjamin Barber connects the dots by explaining that "schools are the public nurseries of our future, and their wanton neglect entails a kind of silent social suicide. What happens today in a third grade classroom or a college seminar determines whether tomorrow the great American community flourishes or fails."[4] Indeed, the future for most of us begins a lot earlier than we imagine. Thus, with the lack of adequate investment in public education, the United States suffers externally and internally—a double whammy that harms us economically as well as from the standpoint of long-term citizen commitment to the political system.

K–12 Public Education

Compared with other nations, the U.S. government spends relatively little on public education. That's because the lion's share of the responsibility for public education lies with the states. This tradition heralds from the earliest days of the republic when the framers failed to include public education as a guarantee at the constitutional convention. Thus, the responsibility fell to the states. On this matter, the United States stands as one of a distinct minority of nations. One recent study of 188 countries finds that only 32, including the United States, do not guarantee education as a fundamental public right.[5]

With states serving as the primary funding sources of universal public education, outcomes vary wildly with the investment and student composition. Compulsory public education emerged in a patchwork quilt-like fashion over a period of more than 100 years. The last state to include the requirement, Mississippi, waited until 1918 to mandate education for its citizens. (Alaska and Hawaii, the 49th and 50th states, were admitted to the union with compulsory public education already in place.) Thus, when we consider the place of American public education in the world, we need to remember that any national numbers reflect the averages of the 50 states.

Public Education as an Investment

International comparisons of the public education product are tricky at best because of a litany of variables. Some nations promise only universal government funding for primary education, while others require parental investment as part of the mix. Other nations still mix religious instruction with secular instruction. Despite the differences in guarantees and support, the fact remains that 156 nations pledge *some* form of universal public education to their citizens.

Against this unusual backdrop, the quality of K–12 public education in the United States has plummeted from among the best in the world to mediocre status. Much of the problem lies with investment. A World Bank report in 2012 listed the United States as tied for 44th (with Mongolia!) in terms of the percentage of gross domestic product (GDP) dedicated to

K–12 public education, a position far from the top.[6] Another study of the 31 countries belonging to the Organization for Economic Cooperation and Development (OECD), a group of economically advanced nations, found that between 2005 and 2010, the United States was one of five countries that reduced its commitment to public education.[7] Clearly, the United States has been backsliding with respect to support of a key infrastructure component.

Public Education as a Commitment

Of course the issue is about more than money: it's about the quality of education, which begins with the time spent in the classroom and the quality of instruction. The average number of school days per year in the United States hovers around 180. Other countries require considerably more attendance. One recent study found that students in Singapore, for example, attend school 280 days per year in year-round fashion. Japanese students study 240 days per year. Yes, these examples are exceptional. However, when examined on a larger scale, European nations average 195 school days per year—3 weeks more than the United States. East Asian countries average even more, 208 days per year.[8]

Does more time necessarily guarantee better-educated students? Not necessarily, but time provides at least the opportunity for instruction and socialization, and countries that commit more time tend to produce students with achievement scores that exceed those in the United States. The relationship is hardly rocket science.

Quality of Instruction

Time in school is important, but time isn't worth much without quality instruction, which takes us to teacher preparation and performance. Simply put, American teachers are not as equipped to do the job as they need to be. In a seven-nation study of some of the world's most advanced nations, 35 percent of U.S. English teachers did not have English as an undergraduate major. The disparity was almost as severe in science, where 29 percent of all U.S. secondary teachers taught without a major in that field.[9] With respect to math, an international assessment of math teachers in 46 countries found that American math teachers rank 21st in qualifications. And why? One reason is because less than half of our math teachers major in math as undergraduates![10]

Indeed, teacher training in the United States seems something of an afterthought. The authors of the seven-nation study put it best when they wrote, "In the United States, teaching as an occupation has an unusually ambivalent character. Compared with other occupations and professions, teaching is relatively complex work, with low pre-employment entry requirements, but nevertheless with relatively high scrutiny and skepticism of the requirements that do exist."[11] Moreover, inadequate training in the United States has reached epic proportions. One account finds that at least 50,000 individuals begin teaching each year "without full training, most of them assigned to teach the nation's most vulnerable students in the highest-need schools."[12] Given that framework, how can we expect our teachers to succeed? If they do, it seems to be only the result of an uphill battle driven more by perseverance than institutional support.

Teacher Pay

In the United States and almost universally elsewhere, compensation serves as an indicator of the value of work performed. With respect to the teaching profession, American educators are not valued very highly by society. A 2010 study of 27 countries by the Organization for Economic Cooperation and Development of teachers with 15 years experience compared the compensation of full-time teachers to the value of a college degree. American teachers earned less than 60 percent of the average pay for full-time workers with a 4-year degree, placing the United States 22nd among the 27 participating countries. Moreover, in several other countries, teachers were paid between 80 and 100 percent of the typical college-educated worker.[13]

The irony is that Americans view teachers positively by huge margins, both for their work and as role models in society. Two-thirds actually see the teaching profession as a desirable vocation for their children. Nevertheless, whatever praise public opinion may bestow upon the teaching profession, such applause does not translate into financial compensation.[14]

The result is an increasingly high departure rate of teachers from the profession, which leads to profound instability for students as well as a sense of defeat for those who have chosen the field. At the end of the 2008–2009 school year, an estimated 269,800 teachers choose to leave the public education profession, amounting to 8.0 percent of the education community. Just 20 years earlier, 132,300 left the profession, equal to 5.6 percent of the educator population. Thus, over a 20-year period, teacher departures increased by nearly 50 percent.[15] The percentage doubles when the exits include those teachers who transfer from one school to another because of undesirable working conditions.[16] And while compensation is not the only reason for leaving the profession, it is among the reasons most cited, along with poor administration, stress, and deplorable working conditions.[17] Meanwhile, the number of first-year teachers swelled during the same period to more than 200,000 annually, from 65,000 new teachers two decades earlier.[18] The unstable teaching environment is hardly a setting that gives our students the best opportunity to succeed with skilled, seasoned talent.

Test Scores

The foregoing provides a rich foundation for discussing student academic performance. Given an overall environment consisting of less classroom instruction time, poor teacher preparation, and relatively low compensation, how can we expect that our students will be taught by the best and the brightest? We can't. Predictably, American student test scores generally reveal a nation whose students are not competing with the best, which adds to this nation's inability to compete with other nations around the world.

A plethora of data tell the story. A 2011 international study of students in member countries of the Organization for Economic Cooperation and Development found American fourth grade math students ranking 11th among students from 50 countries; eighth grade students performed slightly better, ranking ninth in a group of 47 countries.[19] With respect to science knowledge, American fourth grade students ranked seventh among students from 50 countries; the data dipped among eighth grade students, with Americans placing 10th among students in 42 countries.[20] A similar study of 45 nations in literacy showed U.S. students ranking sixth among fourth grade students.[21] Other data focus on more fundamental capabilities, such as general cognitive skills and the ability to reason. Here too, the information on American students is less than stellar. A 2012 report by the OECD shows American students ranking 17th among the 40 participating countries.[22] Translation: American students do not conceptualize issues and problems on abstract levels nearly as well as students elsewhere.

Combined, the takeaway from these studies shows that U.S. students are somewhat above the average but nowhere near the top. Simply put, Americans do not compete at the elite level when it comes to education performance.

Tinkering on the Margins

Ironically, the United States has been in a quasi-catch-up mode with the introduction of two major federal initiatives: No Child Left Behind (NCLB) under the George W. Bush presidency and Race to the Top (RTTT) under the Barack Obama presidency. Both attempts have been disappointments in terms of moving U.S. students to the next level of educational competence.

Passed as the signature education reform legislation in 2001, NCLB required all students to become proficient in reading and math by aggressively designed target dates. As a means of inducing success, the program offered extra federal funds for schools that met proficiency deadlines and sanctions for schools that did not. That all sounds good in theory. The problem is that each state was left to define proficiency, and many watered down the meaning of the term in order to qualify for federal assistance.[23] For this reason, NCLB has done little to move the bar on quality education.

Race to the Top represented an attempt by the Obama administration to put more teeth into education reform, with the main thrust connecting student test scores with teacher evaluations. The $4 billion program dangled extra funds before schools willing to fuse instruction with test scores and create innovative education settings such as charter schools. RTTT rewarded "transformation" strategies, with teachers often called upon to make sweeping changes in their pedagogies. Hoopla notwithstanding, the evidence finds relatively few long-term success stories.[24]

The results from these reforms? A double failure according to leading education experts. Test scores can be part of the teacher evaluation experience if they track the growth in overall student knowledge, including the environmental conditions that frame the student experience. However, reliance upon test scores as the most significant barometer for student success is misleading, particularly if those scores stem from "teaching to the test" or other disingenuous means of securing a surge in performance. And that's a major concern with the two recent federal programs. As education expert Diane Ravitch concludes, "NCLB created—and Race to the Top sustained—the unwarranted belief that standardized tests are an accurate, scientific gauge of education achievement. They are not.... The test scores provide a way to rank children, but the labeling in and of itself serves no educational purpose." As a result, teachers are moved in and out, schools are closed down, and students are subjected to countless interruptions in their lives that do little more other than slow down their educational growth.[25]

What about Post-Secondary Education?

Given the dreary state of K–12 education, it should be no surprise that the United States is losing ground in the post-secondary education setting. Ironically, more Americans than ever have college degrees; as of 2012, 33 percent of all American adults between 25 and 29 years of age earned 4-year degrees, up from 28 percent in 2001 and twice the percentage in 1971.[26] That's the good news.

The bad news is that the United States has been losing ground to other nations. Whereas the United States once produced a higher percentage of college graduates than any other nation, we have slipped to near the middle of the pack, ranking 12th of 36 developed nations. This includes 21st-century STEM fields—science, technology, engineering, and mathematics.[27] Thus, while the United States has gained in the percentage of college graduates, we are falling behind other countries that are producing college graduates at higher rates.

Public Education Investment in Perspective

As the world has moved through the 21st century, the United States continues to operate with a 20th-century education mentality focused on artificial benchmarks and inferior quality. American investment in public education is considerably below the rate of that of competing nations, and the product reflects the commitment. Increasingly, students-turned-workforce members can't compete with their counterparts elsewhere. A 2013 study of adults in 23 industrialized nations found Americans near the middle in literacy and almost at the bottom in math and technology.[28] It's not surprising, therefore, that as the United States falls behind the globalization curve, other nations benefit from the gains of their educated populations in the form of better jobs and more successful economies. Given the results of the 2013 study, U.S. Secretary of Education Arne Duncan lamented, "Our education system hasn't done enough to help Americans compete—or position our country to lead—in a global economy that demands increasingly higher skills."[29] When it comes to preparing our population for the best opportunities, Americans are on the outside looking in, and the cost of the unpreparedness grows each year.

DECAYING INFRASTRUCTURE

The disintegration of a nation can be physical as much as it can be political or sociological. The lack of attention to aging structures, facilities, and services tells us much about the extent to which our society is committed to a solid foundation. Maintaining an infrastructure operates no differently than maintaining one's automobile or home. As needs develop, one must decide whether to address problems immediately or defer repairs until later.

In the United States, "deferred maintenance" has become the mantra for those who would rather deal with infrastructure issues down the road. After all, why allocate precious resources to structures and facilities if they seem to be in good enough condition? A recent international study assessing the 2012–2013 period ranks the U.S. infrastructure 25th in the world, behind nations including Oman and Barbados, and just above Qatar.[30] That position doesn't bode well for a superpower, which ranked 23rd the previous year.

The problem is that aging structures and out-of-date systems do not necessarily reveal deterioration even when they are coming apart. Only when a bridge collapses, a dam bursts, or a train comes off the track do authorities tend to the matter, viewing such occurrences as freak accidents.

With declining standards for excellence, increasing elements of the nation's infrastructure have been found to be at risk, often causing problems for the economy as well as jeopardizing people's lives. The combination has produced a downward spiral. As the bills for repairs approach astounding numbers, the tendency to defer maintenance grows accordingly. Sadly, the results of this shortsightedness are all too predictable. Below we examine the conditions of key components of America's framework.

Highways and Bridges

Roads are the web-like backbone of the nation's transportation network; they move not only people, but also endless amounts of products and goods essential to a humming economy. Historically, the nation's roads and highways have been maintained mostly by the federal and state governments. Lately, neither level of public authority has had the political will or financial capability to keep our roads in good shape, and we're all paying the price for the lack of commitment.

The data are daunting. According to the Federal Highway Administration, 45 percent of the nation's major highways and roads are in poor shape. Those conditions cost American motorists $67 billion annually in vehicle repairs and otherwise unnecessary operating costs.[31] Regular maintenance of highways and roads would shave repair costs to a fraction of the annual incurred by automobile drivers and trucking companies.

With respect to bridges, the news isn't much better. According to federal statistics, one out of four bridges in the United States is structurally deficient.[32] The recent collapses of well-traveled bridges in population centers such as South Padre Island, Texas (2001), Minneapolis (2007), and Seattle (2013) underscore the point. These and other tragic events shouldn't be a surprise, given that the average age of the nation's 607,000 bridges is 42 years old. The federal government has been spending $12.8 billion annually just to repair these transportation conduits, yet the American Society of Civil Engineers estimates that governments need to dedicate $20.5 billion annually just to keep up on a $78 billion maintenance bill that only gets larger every year.[33]

A sizable portion of the funding for many of the nation's most traveled roads, highway building, and maintenance has been provided by the Federal Highway Trust Fund. By collecting a tax of 18.3 cents per gallon of gasoline (24.4 cents per gallon for diesel) from motorists, the fund has generated about $40 billion annually for road construction and upkeep. The tax percentage was last increased in 1993, which is significant given that the increased miles per gallon have produced cars that use much less fuel. At the same time, Americans take to the roads today in record numbers. The result has produced fewer dollars for more highway work.

A related concern centers on the deteriorating relationship between federal highway tax revenues and inflation. The Congressional Budget Office calculates that between 1993 and 2013, the tax structure failed to keep up with the Consumer Price Index, eroding the value of the tax by 36 percent. Had the tax kept up with inflation, motorists in 2013 would be paying 29 cents per gallon and 38 cents for diesel.[34]

The situation is so untenable that experts have predicted without additional financial sources, the Federal Highway Trust Fund may be out of money as early as 2015.[35] That's because the federal government has actually been spending more money each year than it collects. In 2011, for example, the trust fund spent $44.5 billion for roads and bridges while collecting $36.9 billion.[36] Recognizing the potential shortfall, Congress added funds to the program on a temporary basis as part of a 2-year highway act in 2012. Yet, the demands of sequestration, a congressional commitment to reduce discretionary federal spending each year for a decade, make additional allocations from Congress unlikely in the near term. Thus, pressure has fallen on the states.

States and local governments account for about three-quarters of the annual spending for highways, roads, and bridges. As a general rule, these governments raise only about one-third of the transportation spending funds through gasoline taxes, other motor fuel taxes, and toll road fees, leaving the rest to come from other sources.[37] But state and local governments are hindered even more than federal government in raising transportation revenues, thanks to resistance from conflicted legislators or uninformed voters to tax increases. So these governments hope in desperation for rescue from the federal government. Yet, aside from a one-time temporary federal infusion from the American Reinvestment and Recovery Act in 2009 to cope with the Great Recession, the federal road commitments of states and local government have been stuck at the same percentages for decades.

As with the federal government, states have been reluctant to raise gasoline taxes, lest they face the rancor of angry taxpayers. But states are hamstrung much more than the federal government. Because of debts associated with lengthy bond financing, these governments simply lack the capability to stretch their investments beyond maintaining what they already have—this as bridges crumble and roads deteriorate in the wake of increasing traffic and inadequate maintenance.[38]

Clearly, the United States is suffering from a deteriorated road and bridge network that shows no sign of significant improvement in the coming years. Yet, public opinion polls show that Americans want better roads and are willing to pay for them.[39] If nothing else, there is a serious disconnect between the governments that provide transportation funding and those who use the transportation network.

Airports, Seaports, and Rail Systems

Roads are only part of the multifaceted transportation network. Inasmuch as the United States is a hub for international commerce, the movement of products and people depends upon a web of modern airports, water ports, and rail systems. Over the past few decades, the United States has lost its once preeminent position in transport, making facilities more expensive and less desirable for use. On one level, the poor condition of the transportation network represents a psychological blow; on another, the cost of international commerce extracts a huge loss in the name of lost jobs.

Airports

Four of the world's 10 busiest airports are in the United States,[40] although, like so many other global transformations, such prominence may soon fade away. Among the 25 fastest-growing airports with annual traffic of 15 million passengers or more, 24 are in Latin America, the Middle East, or Asia.[41] With respect to cargo, only 2 of the world's 10 busiest airports are in the United States.[42] Hong Kong became the world's busiest in 2012, overtaking Memphis, Tennessee, the home of Federal Express. Combined, these data reveal a changing world, with the United States struggling to keep up. Perhaps the most disconcerting evidence about U.S. airports lies in their popularity, or lack thereof. A 2013 survey of airports throughout the world found the most admired American facility ranked 30th, and that was Cincinnati/Northern Kentucky, hardly a large international transportation center! Denver ranked 36th, San Francisco 40th, and Hartsfield-Atlanta 48th. Meanwhile, Washington-Dulles, Washington-Reagan, and New York–LaGuardia didn't even crack the top 100.[43]

U.S. airports face huge bills for construction and maintenance, yet if the past is any guide to the future, they have little hope of realizing such needs met in the near term. A 2013 report of the Airports Council International–North America shows capital development and maintenance needs for U.S. airports of $71.3 billion between 2013 and 2017, or $14.3 billion annually. Yet, available government funds amount to no more than $13.4 billion annually over the same period. That's a deficit of almost $1 billion annually just to keep up with basic needs.[44] The report concludes that "the existing federally-mandated funding system fails to meet U.S. airport capital needs for modernizing and expanding airport capacity which is critical for a safe, efficient and globally competitive aviation system."[45] Here again, the United States is falling behind the infrastructure curve.

Container Ports

Shipping by sea is the most common method for transporting large amounts of cargo. Movement by this method comprises 90 percent of the world's international trade. Of the 10 largest container ports, 5 are in Asia;

only 1, Los Angeles, resides in the United States. Singapore, the largest container port, ships 471 million tons annually. Number 10, Los Angeles, transports 60 million tons annually. Still, American seaports are critical components of the U.S. economy, processing more than $42 trillion in goods annually, or about 20 percent of all moving commerce around the globe.

As with other infrastructure facilities, American container ports have failed to keep up with global transport demands. Predictably, this neglect has taken a toll on the American economy. Experts calculate that immediate repairs alone would cost a minimum of $30 billion, yet only $14 billion have been earmarked by the federal government to satisfy these needs. The American Society of Civil Engineers has determined that the failure to address port repairs could cost the U.S. economy $270 billion by 2020 as well as 738,000 jobs.[46] And these numbers don't even take into consideration expansion to keep up with the competition.

With respect to growth, most U.S. ports are not prepared to deal with the super-size ships, known as post-Panamax vessels, scheduled to begin passing through the enlarged Panama Canal in 2015. These next-generation container ships are much larger and wider than previous vessels because of the expansion of the Panama Canal. Within a few years, they will approximate 62 percent of all Panama Canal traffic and, as such, require deeper channels, increased rail connections, and considerably larger port capabilities to manage their cargoes. One report by the U.S. Army Corps of Engineers estimated that as much as $5 billion would be required to prepare American ports for the new ships,[47] yet no such allocations have been committed by the federal government or elsewhere. Without these upgrades, American ports will be unable to accommodate most 21st-century container shipments, leaving the ships and the jobs that go with them loading and unloading in other locations.

Los Angeles and three other West Coast ports (Long Beach, Oakland, and Seattle) can accommodate post-Panamax ships, but East Coast and Gulf Coast ports are lagging. Aside from inadequate funds, these locations are plagued by a variety of factors, including low bridges, jurisdictional disputes, and environmental concerns. Additional worries center on too many East Coast and Gulf Coast ports fighting over too few expansion funds, leaving few—if any—winners.

Meanwhile, other countries have expanded their ports to capture more business. Mexico, Chile, and Colombia have moved full throttle to handle post-Panamax ships. They have joined Vancouver, Canada, in the race to move commerce via super-size container vessels. As other countries become more targeted in their post-Panamax port expansion efforts, efforts in the United States suffer from excessive competition and inadequate funds.

Rail

American railroads are unheralded workhorses of transportation, moving large numbers of both people and goods. Trains may not seem as flashy as the newest generation of jet aircraft or automobiles, but they move their contents with less energy and lower costs than their counterparts, particularly over intermediate distances of several hundred miles often traveled on the East Coast.[48]

With respect to intercity travelers and commuters, 32 million passengers travel the rails every year. About 20 million passengers journey on Amtrak, with another 12 million commuting up and down the very busy northeast corridor that extends from Boston to Washington, D.C., before continuing down the East Coast. Originally funded with $40 billion in start-up funds by the U.S. Congress as a for-profit government corporation in 1971, Amtrak's subsidies have been reduced over time. Today, Amtrak receives about $2.5 billion in government support for its steadily increasing ridership. Another half-dozen smaller independent railroads operate throughout the nation, many of which receive subsidies by the states they serve, but the lion's share of passenger traffic travels on the 22,000 miles of Amtrak rails that meander through 46 states.

Railroad travel has thrived in the United States over the past few years. Between 1997 and 2012, Amtrak boardings jumped by 55 percent, nearly triple the passenger increases of air traffic (20 percent), more than three times the economic growth of the nation (17 percent).[49] Yet, with all its commercial success, passenger rail in the United States is anything but a first-class experience. A 2010 study by the Federal Transit Administration found a deferred maintenance backlog for railroad tracks and related facilities of $59.8 billion, with the difference between needs and funding growing every year.[50] Meanwhile, high-speed rail, travel at 150 miles per hour or more, remains something of a pipe dream in the United States, despite its use in at least 14 countries, as well as another 10 rapidly ramping up service. A somewhat paltry effort to kick-start high-speed rail was made by the Obama administration in 2009, when the American Recovery Reinvestment Act set aside $8 billion to facilitate development of high-speed rail in congested corridors. More than 40 states submitted funding requests totaling $100 billion,[51] leaving any federal commitments to advanced passenger rail service clearly a drop in the mass transit bucket.

Transportation: Going Nowhere Fast

The state of America's transportation network is in disrepair. One recent study of international access, including transportation, trade, and telecommunications, finds that the United States ranked 12th among 75 industrialized nations. The same study showed that other countries had the 10 largest infrastructure projects in progress, consisting substantially of labor-intensive rail and airport developments.[52] These days, the United States does not show the commitment to improving this infrastructure component in any significant manner. Instead, our facilities function much like the operations of developing nations with far fewer resources than ours.

The Power Grid

Imagine 2.7 trillion miles of heavy-duty transmission lines connected at thousands of junctures throughout the nation, moving electricity where it's needed to provide power 24 hours each day for manufacturing plants, transportation systems, public facilities, and homes. It almost boggles the mind, yet 3,200 utilities with 5,800 major power plants support the power grid that moves $400 billion worth of electricity each year. Most of the electricity comes from fossil fuel (coal, natural gas, and oil); other sources include hydroelectric and nuclear sources, and small, yet increasing percentages are generated from "green" energy sources such as solar power plants and wind farms. Regardless, whatever the source, energy is useless without efficient, reliable distribution throughout the power transmission grid.

The enormous electricity transportation system in the United States is a source of good news and bad news. The good news is that the grid enables energy to be moved from areas with plentiful supplies to those places where it's needed the most; think of the way that massive amounts of hydroelectric power in the northwestern part of the nation are routinely shipped to the parched southwest. The bad news stems from the good news. Because of the interconnectivity, if a problem delivering electricity develops in one part of the nation, it can spill over to other parts, quickly leaving large, often densely populated areas without power until the original sources of the outages are found and repaired. That's why a healthy, reliable power grid is essential to a strong infrastructure, and that element does not exist in the American power transmission network.

The problem is that the U.S. power grid is anything but healthy or reliable. According to the U.S. Department of Energy, at least 679 power outages occurred between 2003 and 2012, mostly because of severe weather problems, with costs to the economy between $18 and $33 billion annually. On occasion, the costs have spiked because of extreme natural disasters; estimates from the power outage losses alone from Superstorm Sandy in 2012 were between $27 and $52 billion.[53] During that event, 8.5 million customers suffered power outages, while 50 people lost their lives specifically because of power stoppages. Sandy might have been out of the norm, but plenty of others have been occurring with increasing frequency.

While scientists and others debate the causes of growing numbers of weather-related disasters, there is little debate about the condition of our transmission and delivery system or the fact that the power grid is not adapting to climate changes. Simply put, the United States is not keeping up with electricity transmission maintenance and construction needs. A 2012 study by the American Society of Civil Engineers found 70 percent of transmission lines and transformers are at least 25 years old and in need of replacement. Moreover, the study found that at least $673 billion in maintenance and updates would be needed by 2020 to avoid severe breakdowns.[54] These figures are well beyond any allocations that have been provided or proposed by the U.S. government and energy companies. They show no sign of changing direction on these needs in the coming years, according to projections.[55] As a result, electrical engineers and other safety experts can do little more than wait for the next disaster, with few tools other than to patch up an antiquated power network yet again. This is not the way to run the power grid of the world's most powerful industrialized nation, yet this is, in fact, the case.

Selling Infrastructure: Short-Term Gains, Long-Term Losses

One of the most familiar sayings about an individual's shortsightedness is "fool me once, shame on you; fool me twice, shame on me." The idea behind the saying is that anyone can be victimized or tricked once, but when the same victim suffers a similar fate a second time, any original sympathy for the victim becomes an indictment of irresponsible behavior.

And so it is with the nation's attention to our infrastructure. Virtually every part of the U.S. transportation system suffers from inattention, placing the economy at risk and costing untold numbers of jobs. Not once, but many times, the nation has been ill-prepared for electricity-related disasters. Each time such events occur, people look around sheepishly for explanations that have been staring us in the face for decades. The United States has an antiquated infrastructure that can be repaired and modernized if we put our minds to it. Yet, the gravity of the problem notwithstanding, public policy makers have done little to improve the conditions.

RESEARCH AND DEVELOPMENT

Despite endless debates over the extent to which government should intersect with the private sector, few people connected with innovation would call for a diminishing role in sponsoring research and development. Focusing on new technologies, biomedical research, and engineering applications, to name a few areas, can spawn products for new markets, changing the course of history along the way. As the authors of one study conclude, "Research and develop drives innovation and innovation drives long-run economic growth, creating jobs and improving living standards in the process."[56] One recent study concludes that the $423 billion dedicated to research and development by the U.S. government and private sector in 2012 generated nearly 2.5 million full-time and part-time U.S. workers, and ultimate employment of another 8.7 million people in related sectors.[57]

Historically, government-supported research and development has helped the United States maintain its preeminent position in the world. These days, however, the commitment is questionable, raising concerns about the future prowess of the nation.

Dwindling Government Support

In recent years, the United States has lost standing in the community of nations that pursue research and development. A 2013 report found that between 1999 and 2009, the U.S. share of global spending on research and development declined to 31 percent from 39 percent.[58] During the same period, the number of U.S.-granted patents slipped with respect to the rest of the world. Until 2007, more patents were awarded in the United States than the rest of the world; from 2008 to the present day, the United States has not only lost the lead, but also continued to lose share relative to the rest of the world.[59] The publications of findings by U.S. authors have also declined. The number of U.S.-authored peer review research articles declined by 30 percent between 1995 and 2005 alone.[60] Patents and research papers are important indicators of commercial applications yet to come. Simply put, without robust attention to research, there are few findings to present.

The lack of government support is part of a slow, yet steady downward path. In 1967, the United States invested 17 percent of all discretionary spending for research and development. By 2007, only 9 percent of discretionary spending was designated for research and development.[61] Between 2012 and 2013, government spending fell by nearly 1 percent, when controlled for inflation.[62] This is significant because in the United States, the government contributes more than two-thirds of all funds for R&D. Meanwhile, other nations have increased their R&D commitments, paving the way for product developments and application, with accompanying economic successes downstream.

Higher Education

Universities are often the pulse of the research and development engine. Operating in relatively open and benign environments, these institutions avail the brightest minds and creative ideas for the pursuit of untested ideas and concepts, and account for about 80 percent of all government-supported research. But such efforts are difficult to undertake without funding. According to a recent study of 30 advanced nations, the United States now ranks 22nd in university-funded research, when viewing the government's commitment as a share of the gross domestic product.[63] In other words, 21 nations dedicate more of their resources in this area than the United States, yet another sign of a dim future for this country when it comes to transforming ideas into marketable products. Worse yet, the sequestration, automatic cuts in discretionary spending associated with the Budget Control Act of 2011, portends sharp reductions in future university research and development funding.[64]

The situation is just as unfortunate with respect to government support for private sector initiatives. Data from the 30-nation study cited above ranks the United States 23rd in supporting business-funded research efforts.[65] Whether for university scientists or potential commercial partners, the U.S. government has reduced its commitment to funding research and development.

Nurturing the Private Sector

Finally, there is the question of research and development support solely within the private sector. Here again, the United States is falling behind other nations. Between 1991 and 2008, corporate research and development declined by 3.2 percent.[66] Conditions remained much the same between 2008 and 2011, when business-supported research increased by a fragmentary 0.3 percent.[67] Viewed overall, business-supported research and development support has remained flat for more than two decades.

One reason for the drop-off of corporate support in the United States lies with growing support of American companies for research and development abroad. A study by Booz & Company found that for every dollar that foreign companies spend on R&D in the United States, American-based companies spend $2 abroad. In 2007, the year of the study, the differential was more than $40 billion—that's $40 billion in R&D and all the jobs with it going abroad, instead of remaining in the United States.[68] While companies complain about dwindling federal support, they don't hesitate to send their research and development dollars elsewhere.

Success Stories

When government and private resources are devoted to research and development, good results may follow. Two recent examples are the commitments to clean technology and space flights, both of which show promise for American hegemony, economic security, and employment opportunities for years to come.

Clean Energy

Unlike fossil-based fuels, clean technology focuses on natural sources of energy such as solar, wind, and hydroelectric means of production for goods and services. The chief benefits of clean energy are that it is renewable and tends to deposit few, if any, greenhouse gases into the atmosphere. Given the concerns of climate change (sometimes referred to as global warming),[69] clean energy offers the opportunity to minimize the deleterious impacts of a planet susceptible to excessive environmental shifts.

As of 2011, the annual commitment to clean energy research and development by the U.S. government amounted to $35 billion.[70] The effort has produced commendable results. Between 2000 and 2011, electricity generated by renewable sources jumped from 9.4 percent to 12.8 percent of all electricity in the percent, helping to reduce fossil fuel consumption and improve the environment. Equally important, experts forecasted that the number of clean energy jobs approached 700,000 by 2012, with clean energy employment growing at 2.5 times the national average.[71]

Space Travel

Government-funded research and development for space travel is another area that produced meaningful results. Until recently, the National Aeronautics and Space Administration (NASA) exercised virtually complete control over space travel by determining contractors to deliver space vehicles. Between 1981 and 2011, NASA conducted 135 missions with five manned space shuttle craft, many of which landed at the International Space Station, where astronauts conducted various experiments over various periods of time. The program ended in 2011 because of concerns that the shuttle had become too costly and old to fly safely. That left the United States in the uncomfortable position of being dependent upon Russia, a space station partner, for space station transport.

Beginning in 2009, NASA sponsored competitive research and development for next-generation space flight in the private sector, thus creating the opportunity for better products at less cost than government-controlled efforts. The first effort came with $3.5 billion in support for the development of a space shuttle to transport astronauts and cargo to the international space station. Several companies entered the competition, supplementing federal grants with their own resources, thus providing public-private partnerships. By 2013, Orbital Sciences Corporation and Space Exploration Technologies (SpaceX) successfully launched vehicles, with SpaceX landing at and returning from the space station with an unmanned vehicle. These companies and others offer the promise of next-generation space craft with at least 10,000 well-paying jobs supporting the effort during the first 5 years alone, offsetting some of the losses from NASA's program.[72]

The Bottom Line

Research and development efforts are indicators of a nation's commitment to innovation and the jobs that follow. They represent investments in the future. To the extent that such investments grow, societies are more secure with brighter tomorrows. To the extent that such investments lag, societies fall behind others and suffer accordingly in prestige, competitiveness, and economic well-being. Other than a few prominent exceptions, the United States is fast losing its place in the world of research and development, and that loss does not bode well for future generations.

LEAVING THE FUTURE BEHIND

If nothing else, government exists to provide citizens basic services and programs that they can't provide for themselves, or manage only at substantial cost or with great difficulty. Such basic provisions range from national defense to clean air. People with good intentions differ on which responsibilities should be carried out by governments and which should be left to individual management. Determining nature and conditions of those services and programs has been a source of rich debate throughout the course of our national history, and that debate will not be settled here.

Still, there are circumstances where government involvement in public matters provides collective benefits for society, as demonstrated through commitments to clean energy and space transport. But for the most part, the federal government is not investing in the nation today as it has in the past. The private sector has been as much or more disregarding of commitments to research and innovation in this country. Basic building blocks such as public education, national infrastructure, and research and development—once centerpieces of American excellence and global dominance—have declined in some cases and crumbled in others, leaving the United States less competitive with other nations around the world, less self-reliant, and vulnerable to second-class status in the world of nations.

As a result of our shortsightedness, millions of Americans today are denied the basic benefits and opportunities they would have enjoyed in the past. The threat from such unraveling not only affects America's prestige, but also harms the ability of the nation's population to thrive. On an individual level, limited skill sets, aged facilities, and a reluctance to invest in the future will leave millions of Americans at risk as other nations relentlessly invest in their workforces and infrastructure.

Americans know from their own experience that public investments pay off in spades. Consider the Apollo space program launched by President John Kennedy in 1961, which endeavored to land a man on the moon by the end of the decade. Over that period, the federal government spent $25 billion (the equivalent of more than $250 billion in today's dollars) to complete the project on time. The program's success brought tremendous prestige to the United States. Moreover, it provided endless technology spin-offs, including health devices, lubricants, textiles, and water filtration systems—all of which brought untold numbers of jobs along with societal benefits to Americans.[73] Similarly, within months after the 1957 launch of the first *Sputnik* satellite by the then Soviet Union, Congress passed the National Defense Education Act, which provided more than $1 billion for university loans, scholarships, and fellowships. The legislation was designed to kick-start higher education training in the sciences, mathematics, and foreign languages, and did so in remarkably fast fashion.[74]

All of which takes us back to the pervasive theme of this book—the predicament of a nation whose members have been left behind by an inattentive government, assisted by a self-consumed private sector. Without national investment, Americans are denied opportunities to excel at the highest levels. That loss translates to higher unemployment as well as a collective sense of discouragement and disdain for the government. No wonder that Frank Newport, director of the Gallup Poll, found in 2013 that "Americans are now more likely to name dysfunctional government as the most important problem facing the country than to name any other specific problem,"[75] including the economy. It's yet another indication of the extent to which Americans feel disconnected from their government.

ENDNOTES

1. Fareed Zakaria, *The Post-American World*, New York: W.W. Norton and Company, 2008, pp. 257–258.
2. See Anne Colby, Elizabeth Beaumont, Thomas Ehrlich, and Josh Corngold, *Educating for Democracy*, San Francisco, CA: Jossey-Bass, 2007.
3. Jeffrey D. Sachs, *Common Wealth*, New York: Penguin Press, 2008, pp. 209–210.

4. Benjamin R. Barber, *An Aristocracy of Everyone: The Politics of Education and the Future of America*, New York: Oxford University Press, 1992, p. 263.
5. www.right-to-education.org.
6. "Public Expenditures in Education," World Development Indicators 2012, World Bank, Washington, DC, http://hdrstats.undp.org/en/indicators/38006.html.
7. "Education at a Glance, 2013," Organization for Economic Cooperation and Development, Paris, 2013, p. 7, http://www.oecd.org/edu/eag.htm.
8. Richard G. Neal, "Extended School Day and Year Are under Review across the Country," *Heartlander*, February 1, 2008, http://news.heartland.org/print/22698.
9. Richard M. Ingersoll, Ding Ging, Sun Meilu, Kwok Chan Lai, Hidenori Fujita, Ee-gyeong Kim, Steven K.S. Tan, Angela F.L. Wong, Pruet Siribanpitak, and Siriporn Boonyananta, "A Comparative Study of Teacher Preparation and Qualifications in Six Nations," Consortium for Policy Research in Education, Philadelphia, PA, 2007, p. 12.
10. Motoko Akiba, Gerald K. LeTendre, and Jay P. Scribner, "Teacher Equality, Opportunity Gap, and National Achievement in 46 Countries," *Educational Researcher*, October 2007, pp. 375–376.
11. Ibid., p. 2.
12. Linda Darling-Hammond, "Teaching as a Profession: Institutional Lessons and Professional Development," *Phi Delta Kappan*, 87(3), 239, 2005.
13. See Jack Jennings, "Teacher Pay: U.S. Ranks 22nd out of 27 Countries," *Huffington Post*, August 30, 2011, http://www.huffingtonpost.com/jack-jennings/teacher-pay-us-ranks-22nd_b_940814.html.
14. "U.S. Parents Want Teachers Paid on Quality, Student Outcomes," Gallup Poll, August 25, 2000, http://www.gallup.com/poll/142664/Parents-Teachers-Paid-Quality-Student-Outcomes.aspx.
15. Ashley Keigher and Freddie Cross, "Teacher Attrition and Mobility: Results from the 2008–09 Follow-Up Survey," National Center for Education Statistics, U.S. Department of Education, Washington, DC, 2010, p. 9.
16. Ibid.
17. Molly H. Fisher, "Factors Influencing Stress, Burnout, and Retention of Secondary Teachers," *Current Issues in Education*, 14(1), 2011, http://cie.asu.edu/.
18. Diane Ravich, *Reign of Error: The Hoax of the Privatization Movement and the Danger to America's Public Schools*, New York: Alfred A. Knopf, 2013, p. 132.
19. "Highlights from TIMSS 2011: Mathematics and Science Achievement of U.S. Fourth-Grade and Eighth-Grade Students in an International Context," Institute of Education Sciences, U.S. Department of Education, Washington, DC, December 2012, pp. 11–12.
20. Ibid., pp. 42–43.
21. *Digest of Education Statistics*, National Center for Education Statistics, U.S. Department of Education, Washington, DC, 2012, http://nces.ed.gov/programs/digest/.
22. "The Learning Curve, 2012 Report," Pearson and *The Economist*, http://thelearningcurve.pearson.com/.
23. Chester E. Finn Jr., "Dumbing Education Down," *Wall Street Journal*, October 7, 2007, p. A6.
24. Debra Viadero, "'Race to the Top' Said to Lack Key Science," *Education Week*, October 2, 2009, http://www.edweek.org/ew/articles/2009/10/07/06research_ep.h29.html?tkn=U POF0gr3VyWzsRnnw33eZ7vcUVPTNDFp7Mqd&print=1.
25. Op. cit., pp. 315–316.

26. "One-Third of Young People Have a Bachelor's," *USA Today*, November 5, 2012, http://www.usatoday.com/story/news/nation/2012/11/05/college-graduates-pew/1683899/.

27. See "Once in First Place, Americans Now Lag in Attaining College Degrees," *New York Times*, July 23, 2010, and "Percentage of Bachelor's Degrees Conferred in Science, Technology, Engineering and Mathematics Fields," U.S. Education Dashboard, U.S. Department of Education, Washington, DC, 2010, http://dashboard.ed.gov/moreinfo.aspx?i=m&id=6&wt=0.

28. "U.S. Adults Fare Poorly in a Study of Skills," *New York Times*, October 8, 2013, pp.A12, A13.

29. Ibid.

30. "America's Infrastructure Ranks … 25th in the World," *Business Insider*, January 26, 2013, http://www.businessinsider.com/us-infrastructure-behind-developed-world-2013-1.

31. "Condition of State Roads and Bridges," Council of State Governments, August 2010, http://knowledgecenter.csg.org/drupal/system/files/FF_Roads_and_Bridges.pdf.

32. "GAO: 1 in 4 U.S. Bridges Deficient," *PaintSquare News*, June 19, 2013, http://www.paintsquare.com/news/?fuseaction=view&id=9789&nl_versionid=3156.

33. "2013 Report Card for America's Infrastructure," American Society of Civil Engineers, http://www.infrastructurereportcard.org/.

34. Kim P. Cawley, Chief, Natural and Physical Resources Costs Estimates Unit, Congressional Budget Office, "Status of the Highway Trust Fund," testimony before the Subcommittee on Highways and Transit, Committee on Transportation and Infrastructure, U.S. House of Representatives, July 23, 2013, p. 5.

35. "Federal Road Fund Could Go Broke By 2015," *Stateline*, April 24, 2013, http://www.pewstates.org/projects/stateline/headlines/federal-road-fund-could-go-broke-by-2015-85899471023.

36. "Highway Statistics Information, 2011," U.S. Department of Transportation, May 2013, Table FE-210, http://www.fhwa.dot.gov/policyinformation/statistics/2011/fe210.cfm.

37. Joseph Henchman, "Gasoline Taxes and Tolls Pay for Only a Third of State and Local Road Spending," Tax Foundation, January 17, 2013, http://taxfoundation.org/article/gasoline-taxes-and-tolls-pay-only-third-state-local-road-spending.

38. Alex Marshall, "States, Localities Are Failing to Seize Their Infrastructure Moment," *Governing*, June 2013, http://www.governing.com/columns/eco-engines/col-states-localities-failing-to-seize-infrastructure-moment.html.

39. See "New Poll: Americans Support Investment to Increase Transportation Choices, Favor Expanding Transit over Building New Roads," National Resources Defense Council, September 12, 2012, http://www.nrdc.org/media/2012/120912.asp, and Asha Weinstein Agrawal and Hilary Nixon, "What Do Americans Think of Federal Tax Options to Support Public Transit, Highways, Streets and Local Roads? Results from Year Four of a National Survey," Mineta Transportation Institute, San Jose, CA, June 2013.

40. They are Atlanta (1), Chicago (5), Los Angeles (6), and Dallas (8).

41. "Where Is the World's Busiest Airport," CNN, September 27, 2013, http://edition.cnn.com/2013/09/26/business/whats-the-worlds-busiest-airport/index.html.

42. They are Memphis (2) and Anchorage (5).

43. http://www.forbes.com/sites/eamonnfingleton/2013/04/16/the-worlds-best-airports-and-the-only-u-s-airport-to-make-the-top-30/.

44. "New Report Examines U.S. Infrastructure Needs," AIN Online, January 21, 2013, http://ainonline.com/aviation-news/ainalerts/2013-01-31/new-report-examines-us-airport-infrastructure-needs.
45. "Airport Capital Development Needs, 2013–2017," Airports Council International–North America, Washington, DC, January 2013, p. 30.
46. "Urgent Need to Upgrade U.S. Ports Infrastructure," Thomas.Net News, September 25, 2012, http://news.thomasnet.com/IMT/2012/09/25/urgent-need-to-upgrade-u-s-ports-infrastructure/.
47. "U.S. Army Corps of Engineers Releases the U.S. Port and Inland Waterways Modernization: Preparing for Post-Panamax Vessels Report," Washington, DC, June 21, 2012, http://www.iwr.usace.army.mil/DesktopModules/DigArticle/Print.aspx?PortalId=70&ModuleId=29453&Article=11016.
48. Paul Krugman, "Planes, Trains, and Automobiles," *New York Times*, March 2, 2011, http://krugman.blogs.nytimes.com/2011/03/02/trains-planes-and-automobiles/.
49. Robert Puentes, Adie Tomer, and Joseph Kane, "A New Alignment: Strengthening America's Commitment to Passenger Rail," Brookings Institution, Washington, DC, March 2013, p. 6.
50. "National State of Good Repair Assessment, 2010," Federal Transit Administration, Washington, DC, June 2010, p. 3.
51. "Final Applications Submitted for the Corridor-Level High-Speed Rail Grants," *The Transport Politic*, October 5, 2009, http://www.thetransportpolitic.com/2009/10/05/final-applications-submitted-for-corridor-level-high-speed-rail-grants/.
52. "The Transportation Challenge: Moving the U.S. Economy," Cambridge Systematics, prepared for the National Chamber Foundation of the U.S. Chamber of Commerce, 2008, p. 105.
53. "Economic Benefits of Increasing Electric Grid Resilience to Weather Outages," Executive Office of the President, Washington, DC, August 2013, p. 3.
54. "U.S. Electric Grid Gets Regulatory Jolt into the 21st Century," *Bloomberg View*, October 10, 2012, http://www.bloomberg.com/news/print/2012-10-10/u-s-electric-grid-gets-regulatory-jolt-into-21st-century.html.
55. "Economic Benefits of Increasing Electric Grid Resilience to Weather Outages," op. cit., p. 7.
56. Robert D. Atkinson and Luke A. Stewart, "University Research Funding: The United States Is Behind and Falling," Information Technology and Innovation Foundation, Washington, DC, May 2011, p. 1.
57. "2013 Global R&D Funding Forecast," *R&D Magazine*, December 2012, p. 10.
58. "Brainbox Nation," *The Economist*, March 16, 2013, p. 5.
59. "Patents By Country, State, and Year—All Patent Types," U.S. Patent and Trademark Office, Washington, DC, December 2012, http://www.uspto.gov/web/offices/ac/ido/oeip/taf/cst_all.htm.
60. "Research and Development: Essential Foundation for U.S. Competitiveness in a Global Economy," National Science Board, Washington, DC, January 2008, http://www.nsf.gov/statistics/nsb0803/start.htm.
61. "U.S. Scientific Research and Development 101," *Science Progress*, February 26, 2011, p. 2.
62. "2013 Global R&D Funding Forecast," op. cit., p. 6.
63. Op. cit., p. 10.
64. Op. cit., p. 12.
65. Op. cit., p. 3.

66. Op. cit., p. 3.

67. See "Business R&D Performance Increased in the United States, 2011," National Science Foundation, Washington, DC, September 2013, 13-335, and "Business R&D Performed in the United States Cost $291 Billion in 2009 and $288 Billion in 2008," National Science Foundation, Washington, DC, March 2012, 12-309.

68. "Booz & Company Study Finds Top Corporate Spenders on R&D Boosted Investments to Nearly Half a Trillion Dollars in 2007," Booz & Co., October 21, 2008, http://www.booz.com/global/home/press/article/42808596.

69. For more on the perils of global warming, see Michael Brune, *Coming Clean: Breaking America's Addiction to Oil and Coal*, San Francisco: Sierra Club Books, and Spencer R. Weart, *The Discovery of Global Warming*, Cambridge, MA: Harvard University Press, 2008.

70. *2011 Renewable Energy Data Book*, Washington, DC: U.S. Department of Energy, 2013, pp. 23, 107.

71. Kate Gordon, testimony before the Senate Subcommittee on Green Jobs and the New Economy, February 15, 2011, Center for American Progress Action Fund, Washington, DC, http://www.americanprogressaction.org/issues/green/report/2011/02/15/9099/green-jobs-and-trade/.

72. "Running in the Commercial Space Race," *Dawnbreaker*, Spring 2010, http://www.dawnbreaker.com/about/phase3_spr10/space.php.

73. "Apollo Spinoffs," NASA, Washington, DC, May 1, 2011, http://spinoff.nasa.gov/apollo.htm.

74. See Wayne J. Urban, *More Than Science and Sputnik: The National Defense Education Act of 1958*, Tuscaloosa, AL: University of Alabama Press, 2010.

75. "Dysfunctional Gov't Surpasses Economy as Top U.S. Problem," Gallup Poll, October 9, 2013, http://www.gallup.com/poll/165302/dysfunctional-gov-surpasses-economy-top-problem.aspx.

6

Policy-Making Institutions at a Crossroads

The more advanced a society becomes, the more complex its governmental arrangements. The logic is inescapable: as human interaction becomes ever more intertwined, some problems can't be managed without some form of organized political organization, which Samuel P. Huntington defines as "an arrangement for maintaining order, resolving disputes, selecting authoritative leaders, and thus promoting community."[1] The meaning of *community*, of course, runs the gamut from primitive social groupings with little collaboration to modern arrangements defined by extensive human interaction and interdependence. With the most developed economy in the world, the United States falls into the latter category and, as such, exhibits an equally complex system of governmental institutions.

Government is the authoritative component for maintaining relative harmony in a society. Leaders in power are tasked with managing society's problems to the extent that they rise to the level requiring some kind of response. In representative democracies such as ours, government must consider entreaties in ways that at least recognize the concerns and needs of those who petition for assistance. This is a difficult task, given that beyond the general commitment to the basic political apparatus, American society is anything but a monolithic body politic. Difficult or not, it's incumbent upon elected officials to remain connected with those who put them in power and depend upon their attention.

From the earliest days of our education, we are instructed that the national government is a tripartite arrangement consisting of the legislative, executive, and judicial branches. Those officials who serve in these institutions collectively create policies for American society. Each has its own separate part in a process that cannot succeed unless the others cooperate.

Of course, the framers provided for and even encouraged some of this at the Constitutional Convention through the "checks and balances" organization of government. By providing a means for one branch to prevent the actions of the other two, the framers hoped to prevent tyranny while encouraging compromise and a "balancing of interests."[2] That approach has worked well, maybe too well. In the present era checks are so powerful that policy makers are rarely able to produce any balance in terms of outcomes. Increasingly, there are few policies of substance inasmuch as disagreements among national leaders over values yield little more than stalemate on critical issues of the day. For the disengaged, those Americans hungering for guidance and relief, unresponsive government only exacerbates their sense of powerlessness, for they feel unheard.

As noted in earlier chapters, Americans disagree on an array of fundamental issues, yet leaders must somehow enact rules, procedures, and policies that at a minimum exhibit the mantle of fairness. That sounds good in theory but is difficult to do on a consistent basis. In a democracy, Donald F. Kettl writes, the challenge for government is "to translate public wants and needs into policy [and] to marshal expertise to answer the wants and provide for the needs."[3] All this must take place in the context of a diverse society with competing claims and insufficient resources to satisfy the totality of demands. As a result, government decision makers are often in the thankless position of satisfying some and disappointing others. These exchanges take place at all sectors of government, from the national level to local school districts.

Policy makers are not alone in their disappointing behavior. On this note, the public bears responsibility for general disinterest about the organization of government and the work performed by those we put into power. Almost cavalierly, we elect people with little knowledge of who they are or what they advocate. When the campaign ends, we quickly disengage from the brief political courtship, assuming that officials will follow through with vague preelection promises. Some do, and some don't, in varying degrees. But by refusing to remain part of the process and hold leaders accountable to their agendas, those voters who walk away from political engagement are just as responsible for any post-election disarray as those who act without regard for the voters who put them in positions of authority.

This chapter explores the relationship between the national policy makers and the governed in American society. For many citizens, the relationship tends to be fickle on the best days, and downright dysfunctional on other days. It is one where those elected to power often lose sight of that precious interaction, leaving the public confused and unaware of who really does what, how, and why, or just as important, why seemingly nothing gets done at all. But most of all, it is a relationship where policy making occurs in an almost sleight-of-hand political environment that would make a magician blush. The result is an unnecessarily confusing set of institutions that leave policy making almost impossible to understand.

CONGRESS: A BRANCH IN DISREPAIR

Members of Congress are at the heart of the policy-making experience. Simply put, their most fundamental responsibility is to make laws, although they have major roles in oversight and investigations and, in the case of the Senate, deciding the fates of presidential nominees to key positions. Lawmaking may seem straightforward enough, but carrying it out is another matter altogether. As critical conduits between citizens and government, members of Congress are in the crosshairs of the policy-making process. They need to listen to their constituents, who often speak in many voices, compare what they hear with the issues at stake, and then determine the best course of action with their votes.

The work of legislators is performed in a demanding political environment filled with nuances. To begin with, the members of the House of Representatives and Senate serve different constituencies, smaller districts for those elected to the House versus entire states for those elected to the Senate, and each chamber operates with a different set of rules. There is also the matter of competing political values and ideologies as expressed through political party affiliations. Democrats and Republicans, loosely organized as they are, tend to coalesce around different sets of solutions to the same problems. As the authors of one book on Congress state, "Everything about the organization and operation of Congress is shaped by political parties."[4] Even then, the two big tents under which Republicans and Democrats govern have members with sometimes widely divergent opinions on the same issues.

Other factors interface with Congress as well, including pressures from the executive branch, elements of the bureaucracy, interest groups, influential campaign contributors, and the leadership hierarchies in their respective chambers. Combined, these cross-currents make it difficult for almost any proposal to sail through Congress very easily. As Burdette Loomis and Wendy Schiller observe, "In a political environment that discourages cooperation across party lines and rewards the promotion of individualism, generating the succession of majorities necessary to pass important legislation has grown more and more difficult."[5] Yet, somehow it is the task of these 535 individuals to legislate.

It used to be that committee organization, a hallmark of both chambers, provided a framework for the majority and minority to work through competing ideas and reach resolution, before sending proposed legislation on to their respective full complements. Negotiations within committees during the "markup," or construction of legislation, provided the basis for compromise and deference. As of late, however, Congress has been the most polarized in memory. On key issues of the day, open bitterness and disrespectful behavior have replaced civility and comity, while stark ideological divisions have for the most part poisoned the ability to forge compromise. Deliberation, once a key ingredient of bipartisanship, has been replaced by fewer meeting days, less committee work, and the orchestration of policy making (to the extent that any exists) by a few party leaders at the top of the organizational hierarchy.[6] As a result, gridlock has become the order of the day, with an emotionally exhausted American public twisting in the wind.

Below we focus on three aspects of the dysfunctional Congress: lawmaking gridlock as exemplified by the brinkmanship associated with endless federal budget impasses, bitter internal organizational implosions that blur traditional roles, and modern election formats that harden already deep divisions. These characteristics have produced a 21st-century Congress with little ability to govern.

Budgeting and the National Debt

For government to provide its various services and functions, it must be able to secure the necessary revenues through taxation and then determine spending priorities and their attendant financial commitments. Congress is at the heart of this process, which represents the blueprint of national direction. As one scholar notes, "The federal budget is the monetary manifestation, or a sort of skeletal structure of our political system and public philosophy."[7] By definition, of course, skeletons are the frames for larger masses, such as bodies. With respect to Congress, our skeletal structure has been ripped apart by conflicting values over the annual budget and debates over raising the national debt. These twin financial issues have brought the legislative branch to a near standstill, leading to the inability of the government to carry out its most basic obligations.

Budgeting

The differences of opinion in Congress over U.S. federal spending practices have been fueled by a long-simmering debate over annual budget deficits and how to stop them from occurring. The chasm has been so great that the Congress failed to pass an annual budget for 4 years in a row (between 2009 and 2013), resorting instead to a series of continuing resolutions that maintained the status quo.

In recent years, some members of Congress, particularly Republicans, have stopped the funding process, which has led government to cease or reduce services and programs. This idea of shutting down government as a tactic for controlling the budget standoff and potential outcome is fairly new to American politics. Such efforts have exempted military defense, postal service, and Social Security, viewed as necessary expenditures. Virtually everything else, however, has been left on the table. Shutdowns occurred a half-dozen times during the Ford, Carter, and Reagan administrations, usually for only some government services and for a matter of hours before combatants reached a truce. Two particularly contentious shutdown events occurred during the Clinton administration, with the second lasting 17 days before both sides came to terms. In each case, the breakdown centered on different approaches to the budget deficit.

The shutdown possibility took on an ominous twist in 2013. After several threats, Republican opponents in Congress forced a cessation of most domestic spending. They acted because of the budget deficit particularly as it related to the costs associated with implementation of the Patient Protection Affordable Care Act, which was passed by a Democratic-led Congress and signed by President Barack Obama in 2010. On more than 40 occasions between 2011 and 2013, House Republicans passed budgets tied to slow down, change, or end Obamacare, as they called it; not once did the Democratic Senate go along. And so, with no federal budget in place on October 1, 2013, the federal government was forced to cease operations in most domestic policy areas. The shutdown led to layoffs of 400,000 government workers and tens of thousands of others in the private sector with government contracts, and lasted for 16 days before Republicans relented.

Beyond the disruption of curtailed federal programs and services, there were economic and political costs for the 2013 shutdown. Economically, the shutdown cost the economy as much as 120,000 jobs in economic growth and as much as $24 billion in lost productivity. Standard & Poor's, an independent economic forecast consulting company, pared its prediction of national economic growth in the fourth quarter of the year to 2 percent from 3 percent.[8] All this occurred in the midst of a shaky economy still attempting a full recovery from the Great Recession.

Meanwhile, the budget fiasco extracted a political cost as well. A public opinion poll conducted by the Associated Press in the middle of the shutdown found 62 percent blaming Republicans. Democrats didn't fare much better, with about half of those surveyed assigning responsibility to Democrats in Congress or President Obama for the event. Worst of all, only 5 percent of the respondents gave Congress a positive approval rating.[9] Toward the end of the shutdown, another poll was more one-sided, with 70 percent assigning blame to Republicans for the shutdown. Even more depressing was the public mood: 78 percent believed that the country was going in the wrong direction, compared with only 14 percent who believed the United States was heading in the right direction.[10] The public lost faith in Congress on a deeper level than any in recent memory, yet for those elected officials hailing from safe districts, the message went without acknowledgment.

Congress reached a truce of sorts in December 2013, when the two chambers agreed to a 2-year budget program that freed up some of the mandatory sequestration cuts while reducing the national debt by $22.5 billion. Still, the legislators failed to reach agreement on tax reform and entitlement reform, the drivers of the ongoing political stalemate. Resolution of these issues would have to wait until another day, and delaying such matters further will only increase both the political pain and the financial costs. Yet, such procrastination seems to have become a mantra in American politics.

The Debt Ceiling

The shutdown occurred precisely at the time when Congress was confronted with increasing the ceiling on the national debt, the money owed by the United States to all of its creditors at home and abroad. The national debt exists because of the inability of Congress to pass balanced budgets. Until recently, votes to increase the debt occurred with little fanfare other than the near-universal (and gratuitous) acknowledgment that the United States needs to be a better manager of taxing and spending. Such calls, almost always partisan, traditionally have been accompanied with exhortations from the Democrats to increase taxes and demands by Republicans to reduce spending, culminating with an increase in the ceiling. Regardless, any failure to lift the debt high enough to manage the nation's obligations would leave the United States forced to make draconian spending cuts to avoid defaulting on bills immediately due. Nevertheless, the stage was set for a deadly game of political chicken.

Early in 2013, the president asked Congress to increase the debt ceiling from $15.5 trillion to $16.7 trillion, as part of an agreement he negotiated with Congress in 2012. After much wrangling over excessive spending and Obamacare, House Republicans reluctantly agreed to lift the ceiling through another short-term fix to $16.7 trillion. A sluggish recovery from the Great Recession required another increase, which only raised the ire of Republicans, who were unhappy about the lack of spending cuts, which the president insisted would not take place without additional taxes. Meanwhile, Treasury Secretary Jack Lew warned that failure to act by October 17 would cause financial chaos in the United States and around the world; leaders across the globe concurred.[11] Economists warned of an economic crunch that could cost as many as 3 million American jobs and a new recession.[12]

Again, House Republicans attempted to connect any action on the debt to dismantling Obamacare, but they had little support. One national poll had Americans against tying together the budget and health care by a lopsided margin of 64 percent to 27 percent.[13] At the last moment, the Republican leadership in Congress relented and lifted the ceiling for four months, when the fight would ensue yet again. Yet the tone of persistent brinkmanship had been set. Lamented one financial expert, "We'll be back here in January [2014] debating the same issues. This, I fear is a permanent feature of our budgetary process."[14] Meanwhile, a weary public was forced to cope with every gut-wrenching twist and turn of the budget roller coaster, never certain about whether or when government programs would cease or move forward.

A Legislative Body without Discipline or Control

Congressional management of the budget and the national debt have been reduced to day-to-day political combat that leaves government agencies unable to plan and the public uneasy about what to expect. This isn't the way to run a country. After witnessing endless budget and debt ceiling fights, one assessment by Standard & Poor's concluded that American policy making had become "less stable, less effective, and less predictable than what we previously believed."[15] As Congress lunges from one skirmish to the next, its efforts become less and less predictable for a world that longs for political and economic certainty from the most powerful country on the planet.

Chamber Issues

Without question, Congress now operates in a poisoned political environment bereft of trust and cooperation. No doubt, much of the acrimony stems from the changing makeup of the institution. Democrat members tilt to the left, while Republican members swing even more so to the right. With few moderates to bridge the two sides, composition of the legislative branch stands as the most polarized since the end of the Reconstruction Era in the late 1870s.[16] Two recent examples of the great divide are seen with adoption of the nuclear option by Democrats in the U.S. Senate to overcome persistent Republican filibusters and rule by the Tea Party faction of the Republican Party in the House of Representatives. Each points to the loss of political moderation. More to the point, each reflects an effort to circumvent traditional relationships, leaving observers perplexed about the process and the efforts to bypass it.

Nuclear Option in the Senate

Forget about majority rule in the U.S. Senate as the basis for passing legislation and confirming presidential nominations. Because of the filibuster, in reality the majority must capture 60 votes of the 100-member body to overcome any organized resistance. This is done through cloture, a Senate tradition since the 1880s. The procedure was tweaked in 1975, when the Democratic-led Senate was able to reduce the cloture requirement to 60 votes of the membership in place of the two-thirds requirement that had previously guided that august body.

Under the filibuster, no other Senate business can take place as long as someone speaks in opposition to a pending nomination or legislation before the body. To that end, most of us think of the delaying tactic as a tool for a Senator or perhaps a group of Senators to speak in opposition for so long until the majority gives in or manages to gather the 60 votes necessary to invoke cloture.

Use of the filibuster increased dramatically during the 1970s, when Senators introduced the silent filibuster, defined as their *intention* to speak against a nomination or proposal. Knowing what was likely to come, the majority dropped legislative efforts. This new tool has become the way the minority forces an end to a procedure unless the majority can round up 60 votes. By one account, the silent filibuster was used 380 times almost exclusively by Senate Republicans between January 2008 and December 2012.[17] When combined with the more traditional filibuster resistance, the increase in the total number of filibusters has been nothing short of staggering, rendering the Senate to little more than a legislative graveyard. According to one account, between 2011 and 2012, more than 400 bills passed in the House died in the Senate.[18] Here's an even more dramatic statistic: filibuster records were first kept on a consistent basis starting in 1949. From that year until 2009, 69 presidential nominations were blocked by filibusters.[19] During the first 5 years of the Obama administration *alone*, Republicans blocked 79 nominations. Clearly, the use of this parliamentary tool has changed the very concept of lawmaking from a proactive to a reactive policy-resisting mechanism.

Filibustering bills ended the journey of countless proposed laws, but Senate Democrats were particularly angered about the extent to which executive branch appointees and federal judicial nominees were denied confirmation repeatedly through the filibuster. Time and time again, Senate Majority Leader Harry Reid attempted to work out compromise with Minority Leader Mitch McConnell on unplugging the Republican-led filibuster obstruction. Occasionally, Senate Republicans relented, but only momentarily. Increasingly, agitated Senate Democrats threatened to change the filibuster rules, a change that soon became known as the nuclear option because of the way it might permanently harm Senate relationships. The threat did little to change what Democrats considered Republican obstruction.

Finally, on November 21, 2013, the Democratic majority in the Senate voted for the nuclear option and lowered the cloture requirement on most presidential executive branch nominees and judicial nominees (except for the U.S. Supreme Court) to 51 votes. Democrats ended the confirmation barrier, but at what cost remained uncertain. In offering a "what's good for the goose is good for the gander" assessment, Minority Leader McConnell warned, "I say to my friends on the other side of the aisle, you'll regret this. And you may regret this a lot sooner than you think."[20]

McConnell's warning may come to pass when the Republicans regain the majority in the Senate. In fact, Republicans threatened to do the same thing to the Democrats just a few years earlier,[21] so perhaps it was inevitable that the rule change would take place. But McConnell's threat missed the larger point. In an attempt to circumvent endless and perpetually hostile Republican opposition by rewriting the filibuster rules, Democrats added another chapter to the already boiling polarized environment in the Senate.

The Tea Party Sets the House Table

Whereas the Senate has suffered from a partisan breakdown, the House of Representatives has hemorrhaged from an intraparty conflict. The heart of the intraparty fight is housed in what has become known as the Tea Party, which is a philosophical movement at the extreme right-wing end of the Republican Party. The crusade took its name in honor of the Boston Tea Party, which occurred in 1773 when American colonists threw a supply of tea into Massachusetts Bay as a nonviolent protest against new taxes imposed by the British government.

The modern American version of the Tea Party began in 2009 on similar terms in that its supporters opposed the actions of government, which they viewed as forced upon citizens without their consent. Originally, Tea Party supporters and their sympathizers rebelled against the burgeoning national debt and unbalanced budgets, which had been particularly out of whack largely because of issues related to the Great Recession stemming from lower federal tax revenues and higher government expenses to fight off the economic collapse. Soon after the 2010 election, the economic core of the Tea Party movement was broadened to include opposition to various social programs, ranging from food stamps to the Patient Protection Affordable Care Act, which ultimately was enacted with virtually no Republican support. Meanwhile, the Tea Party Caucus was created in Congress with the goal of promoting its ideals from within government rather than outside of it.

With the help of Freedom Works and similar libertarian organizations opposed to what is defined as excessive government, Tea Party groups endorsed Republican candidates across the nation in the 2010 congressional elections who were loyal to their ideals. Some candidates won, although not nearly as many as who lost. A post-2010 election assessment found 39 Tea Party-supported candidates won election to the House of Representatives, while 82 candidates were defeated—a piece of history that has been overlooked particularly by proponents.[22] In the Senate, five Tea Party candidates won their elections, while two lost. The Senate gains, while important, did little to change the complexion of the Republican minority other than conservatives elected in place of moderates.

In the House, however, the Tea Party victors became a powerful counterweight to new Republican Speaker John Boehner. Boehner, who had gained a reputation as a conservative capable of working with the other side, found himself on the hot seat. Prior to his election as Speaker, Boehner had said he would use his new leadership position to reduce partisan rhetoric.[23] But that didn't last long. The two Republican leaders next in line, Majority Leader Eric Cantor (Virginia) and Majority Whip Kevin McCarthy (California) had close alliances with the Tea Party block. They, along with soon-to-be House Budget Committee chair and future 2012 vice presidential candidate Paul Ryan, authored a book, *Young Guns: A New Generation of Conservative Leaders*,[24] which described the importance of tax cuts and small government, and the imperative to stop compromising with the other side.

Even though their numbers in the House were only a healthy slice of the party membership, Tea Party supporters have threatened to run candidates against moderately conservative Republican incumbents in future elections. That possibility put Boehner in a tough spot. As the leader of his party, Boehner has espoused many Tea Party tenets to the satisfaction of some conservative activists. Nevertheless, as the leader of the House, Boehner has found himself in trouble with the Tea Party Caucus when he has attempted to negotiate budget and deficit ceiling agreements with Democrats in the Congress and the Obama White House. In seeking to please two "masters," he has satisfied none. That conundrum drove Boehner to refuse fully funding a budget in 2012, which resulted in the shutdown that seriously hurt the Republican brand. Moreover, the agreement to resume government was negotiated by Senate Republicans and the president, leaving Boehner appearing powerless. Still, Tea Party advocates were incensed that Boehner blinked with a vote on the budget and lifting the deficit ceiling.

While Boehner attempted to contain the rancor among House Republicans, plenty of criticism mounted from fellow Republicans outside the chamber. Senate Republicans viewed the House position on the shutdown as costly and unnecessarily combative. Republican Senator John McCain termed the Tea Party wing as "wacko birds."[25] Fellow Republican Senator Lindsay Graham described the shutdown as a useless "time of lost opportunity."[26] Even some House Republican loyalists couldn't resist expressing exasperation over Tea Party Republicans changing the rules in midstream.[27]

Tea Party reformers were beside themselves with anger over the mainstream Republican retreat when Speaker Boehner elected to end the shutdown. "Goose egg, nothing, we got nothing," groused one. Another said defiantly: "I'll vote against the Senate plan [to end the shutdown]."[28] In fact, only about one-third of the House Republicans joined the Democrats in the vote to end the shutdown stalemate, indicating the state of hemorrhage within the party. Nonetheless, if nothing else, the Tea Party rebellion showed intraparty factionalism as the root of the dysfunctional condition of the House of Representatives, leaving Americans perplexed over a government paralyzed by a foolish power play.

Gerrymandering

Contrary to the way they organized the U.S. Senate to have its members representing entire states, the framers of the Constitution designed the House of Representatives as the most direct link between the people and their government. Each state would be guaranteed at least one representative, with additional members awarded to states with larger populations. Unlike the selection of senators by state legislatures (later changed to direct election through adoption of the 17th Amendment), representatives would be elected in their districts by citizens, thereby ensuring a direct connection between the people and this portion of government. Referring to the organization of the House, constitutional architect James Madison explained, "As it is essential to liberty that the government in general should have a common interest with the people, so it is particularly essential that the branch of it under consideration (the House) should have an immediate dependence on, and intimate sympathy with, the people."[29] Brief 2-year terms would cement the imperative for representatives to remain in close contact with constituents.

Under federal law, states must organize their congressional districts after each national census, which is conducted every 10 years. With the nation's population growing and moving, almost every state routinely redesigns its newly allocated portion of the 435 congressional districts to reflect equal population. Most of the time, the responsibility is managed by state legislatures and governors, although in recent years some states have opted for more clinical and less overtly political independent commissions.[30] All this organizational information is straightforward enough—House members are intimately connected with their districts on short political strings "to ensure that they do not stray too far from public opinion."[31] But what if the members do not reflect the values of their districts in spite of the carefully designed electoral mechanism? If carried out on a widespread basis, such a disconnect could certainly threaten the body's intended overall composition. This quandary takes us to the questionable relationship between election systems and officeholders and the specific issue of gerrymandering.

Gerrymandering refers to the ability of policy makers to carve out legislative districts in ways that distort the proportions of some populations more than others, while keeping to the numeric requirements of equal size. By altering the compositions of districts, those who employ this tool can alter election outcomes. The name comes from a Massachusetts governor, Albert Gerry, who drew oddly shaped congressional boundaries after the census in the early 19th century, with one of the districts almost appearing like a salamander, to help ensure a safe Democratic district in an otherwise Republican environment. Ever since, governors and state legislatures have skewed the designs of district lines in ways to benefit one political party over another, and more recently, one race or ethnic group over others.

Gerrymandering comes in two forms. Some gerrymandered construction has utilized packing, a technique that squeezes disproportionately large numbers of like-minded voters into few districts, thereby minimizing their influence elsewhere in the state. Another construction has utilized racking, a technique that disperses like-minded voters over several districts to dilute their influence in any single district.[32] As a result, Ross Baker notes, House districts often are "astonishingly atypical of the nation at large."[33] Equally important, safe districts, districts where one party has a commanding control over the other, dominate the political landscape, giving little reason for incumbents at one end of the political spectrum to find common ground with incumbents at the other end of the political spectrum.

Since its creation, gerrymandering has been used successfully by Democrats and Republicans alike, depending upon which political party has dominated the various statehouses. Republicans have benefited the most in recent years. For example, after the 2010 elections, Republican House members enjoyed a 242–193 margin over the Democrats, even though nationwide Democrats won 1.1 million more votes than the GOP. After the 2012 elections, Republicans held a slightly smaller margin of seats, 234 to 201, yet Democrats won 550,000 more votes. Much of the difference stemmed from Republicans controlling the redistricting process in states with 40 percent of the congressional seats, compared with Democrats controlling the process in states with 10 percent of the seats.[34] The remaining 50 percent of congressional districts were designed by non-partisan committees and, as such, generally yielded representatives that reflected district compositions.

More than ever, congressional districts are yielding exaggerated election results because of the ways they are organized. With respect to the 113th Congress (2013–2014), 51 percent of the Democratic winners captured two-thirds of the vote or more in their districts; among Republican winners, 67 percent collected two-thirds of the vote or more. Nearly 40 percent of the House membership contained winners from districts with virtually no competition.[35] An analysis of the 2014 House races by the Cook Report found 199 of the 234 Republican-held seats as safe. For Democratic-held seats, 162 of the 199 seats were considered safe. At the other extreme, the Cook Report considered only 29 seats (14 Democratic and 15 Republican) in the "toss up" category.[36] Such assessments scream political impasse. Not only do the partisans from each side have little in common, but also they have even less reason to seek common ground. Moreover, the numbers of safe incumbents from one-sided districts have escalated dramatically over the past 40 years.[37] Finally, while there have always been socioeconomic differences between the elected and those who elect them, gerrymandering has ensured that the political makeup of Congress, particularly the House of Representatives, is far removed from that of the nation as a whole.

CHANGING BOUNDARIES OF THE EXECUTIVE BRANCH

Whatever their disputes about the design of the legislative branch, the framers were more than comfortable that the country should be guided collectively by individuals sent to the nation's capital from their respective states. Their experience with colonial and early state legislatures had provided that necessity. Life under the Articles of Confederation, the nation's first governmental arrangement, revealed a somewhat rudderless nation, and convinced most of the constitutional framers of the necessity of an executive branch, which they ultimately decided would be led by a president.[38]

Over time the presidency has grown in stature and power in tandem with dramatic changes in technology, communications, and international relations. Given the fast-paced nature of the 21st century, it's hard to imagine the nation without a strong, powerful president. That said, some evolutionary traits of the office have created a sense of confusion about the extent to which the presidency may have assumed authority historically left in other hands. Here we speak of war making and signing statements. The expanded use of power in these areas has left the public confused about the appropriate roles of public policy makers and their institutional responsibilities.

War Making

Built into Articles I and II of the U.S. Constitution are specific responsibilities for the nation to entertain the idea of going to war. In Article II, the president must ask Congress for authority to declare war if he believes the nation needs to use military force against or in response to another nation; if such authority is granted, the president prosecutes the effort in his capacity as commander in chief. In Article I, Congress is tasked with declaring a state of war between the United States and its adversaries, and if the legislative branch is so disposed to such a declaration, it has responsibility for raising the funds necessary to carry out the military undertaking.

All of this sounds rather drawn out and almost clumsy within the framework of a fast-paced 21st century. That very division of responsibilities was intentionally created by the framers to ensure agreement and cooperation between the branches of government to "avoid concentrating too much power into a single branch."[39] It's one of many examples of the separation of powers concept designed to promote unity of purpose while preventing excessive, independent power in any single branch of government.

So much for intent. Modernity has reshaped the distribution of war-related responsibilities between the branches of American government even if the Constitution has not. Rather than reconstruct the balance in any abrupt fashion, incremental movements by the executive branch and generally tacit acceptance of those movements by the legislative branch have positioned the president as the indisputable authority in war making.

For the most part, American presidents refrained from sustained independent activities until the 20th century. In both world wars, presidents sought congressional permission. During World War I, President Woodrow Wilson asked for and received a declaration of war. The U.S. role was almost gratuitous, assisting European allies in the waning days of conflict. With respect to World War II, President Franklin Roosevelt asked for and received a declaration of war first against the Japanese, who attacked Pearl Harbor, and shortly thereafter against Germany and Italy.

There have been no declared wars since World War II. Nevertheless, presidents have dispatched American troops and, more recently, instruments of war with increasing frequency, often in the vague, yet forceful flag of protecting national security.[40] One account has presidents using military force abroad unilaterally on at least 300 occasions, none of which included a formal declaration of war.[41] A report by the Congressional Research in May 2013 listed 45 instances of American military activity just since 2001. It included American forays into Bosnia, East Timor, and Liberia, as well as many other examples.[42]

Recent presidents have authorized the use of military with little regard for congressional input. President Richard Nixon particularly offended Congress when he assigned several thousand American troops in Vietnam to invade Cambodia in 1970. In a rare political slap at what appeared to be an almost casual abuse of war-making authority, Congress passed the War Powers Resolution, which required presidents to consult with Congress before sending troops to war and the return of those troops to U.S. soil if Congress refused to endorse the action within 60 days. The policy may sound tough, but subsequent presidents have skirted it with regularity ever since.[43]

Since the War Powers Act, presidents have routinely dispatched American armed forces or instruments of war abroad with little or no formal congressional consultation, behaving almost as if the act never existed. Most of the engagements have been "preemptive initiatives"[44] to defend the United States abroad in order to avoid engaging the enemy at home. Others have been conducted in the name of promoting democracy or protecting human rights, although the selection of intervention targets has followed anything but a consistent pattern other than American self-interest. Ronald Reagan defended the U.S. invasion of Grenada as a response for help by the Lebanese government, Bill Clinton explained the U.S. invasion of Haiti as carrying out the will of the United Nations, and George H.W. Bush championed the placement of U.S. troops in Somalia as a humanitarian operation rather than a military exercise. In each case, the presidents saw no need to secure congressional approval.[45]

Yet, the United States has never invaded Middle East ally Saudi Arabia, a monarchy with a terrible human rights record and incubating source of the Al Qaeda terrorist network.[46] Nor has the United States taken action against authoritarian regimes with appalling human records in Central Asia, which just happen to house vital oil pipelines[47] and provide support for strategic U.S. military bases engaged in the Afghanistan military initiative.[48] None of this is to suggest that presidents need to be even more aggressive than they already are. Rather, these examples point to the inconsistent use of presidential authority in promoting U.S. interests abroad without anything but the most superficial congressional oversight or involvement.

In recent years, presidents have relied more upon unmanned aerial vehicles (UAVs), unofficially known as drones, to complement—and in some cases replace—on-site troop presence in the pursuit of antiterrorism efforts abroad. Although long used as high-flying vehicles of surveillance, drones have been armed as military weapons since the early days of the 21st century. The benefit from the application of drone attacks lies with the reduced risks of military personnel on the ground and less loss of innocent lives that come with large-scale combat. Yet, because of the minimized risk of life—particularly American lives—drone activity is often overlooked as part of the U.S. military machine.[49]

The president has constitutional authority to use drones as interpreted through his role as commander in chief and previous legislative acts of Congress,[50] stemming all the way back to the National Security Act of 1947. More recently, the National Defense Authorization Act of 2001, a response to the Al Qaeda terrorist attacks of September 11, 2001, added further authorization for presidential discretion in the use of drones. Technically, drone attacks are conducted by the Central Intelligence Agency (CIA), but only after final approval by the president. Also, technically, Congress has oversight. But the simple fact remains, as expert Gregory McNeal notes, "The executive branch simply knows more about how they conduct targeted killings than the legislature that oversees them."[51] In effect, the president can and does pursue the use of drones with precious little accountability to anyone else.

The issue here is not the use of military forces or drones per se. Rather, the issue is that the president now conducts military campaigns with little involvement from Congress or anyone else. That ability has altered the balance of responsibilities between the two branches of the national government, reducing the significance of the checks and balances doctrine that helps to frame Constitution.

Signing Statements

Expanded use of presidential authority goes well beyond American foreign relations. For example, modern presidents have used the federal bureaucracy with regularity to shape various domestic and foreign policy initiatives through the regulatory process. Rule making provides all the details either omitted or overlooked in the creation of laws, and is commonly left to the executive branch.[52] Citing "we can't wait" as his driving force for activism, Barack Obama used the executive branch to roll out a series of regulatory changes during his administration on environment, immigration, and public education, among others.[53] In this sense, Obama was no different than his predecessor, George W. Bush, who also issued a series of "guidance documents" for his version of regulatory reform.[54] Only the political goals differed, not the tactics. Furthermore, the regulatory reforms in either case traveled through a reasonably transparent process. Presidential directives, often executive orders, give the president great flexibility to get things done. Depending upon their level of controversy, these action steps can draw a good deal of public attention.

Signing statements have followed a different path. Their origin dates back to Article II, Section 3, of the Constitution, which requires that the chief executive "take care that the laws be faithfully executed." Most scholars on the subject believe that President James Monroe (1817–1825) wrote the first signing statement in 1822, when he informed Congress that part of the congressional bill he was signing into law seemed confusing. For decades afterward, presidents used the signing statement as a technical explanation to clarify how or when the law signed would be carried out.[55] With occasional exceptions, they were sparingly used and administrative rather than political in design and intent. Until the 1980s, presidents collectively had written fewer than 75 signing statements.

From the 1980s to the present day, signing statements have emerged as rather powerful arrows in the chief executive's policy-making quiver. Beginning with the Ronald Reagan administration, signing statements were employed for different reasons, primarily to reject some provisions or actually challenge the constitutionality of some aspects of the bill the president was signing into law.[56] Reagan alone wrote 16 signing statements containing 22 constitutional challenges to the laws. Then the floodgates opened. George H.W. Bush, Reagan's successor, wrote 71 signing statements with 150 constitutional challenges. Bill Clinton, the next president, wrote 16 signing statements with 39 constitutional challenges.

George W. Bush became the signing statement champion with 63 signing statements and 386 constitutional challenges.[57] One of the most controversial signing statements by Bush centered on a bill, the Detainee Treatment Act, sponsored by Senator John McCain in 2005, and passed by the Congress shortly thereafter. The heart of the act declared that no U.S. interrogating agency should subject any person to "cruel, inhuman, or degrading treatment or punishment" while in custody. The topic was dear to McCain, who suffered 6 years of torture during the Vietnam War. During congressional deliberations, Bush publicly opposed the law as an intrusion on presidential responsibilities. Nevertheless, fellow Republican McCain warned the president that bipartisan support was sufficiently great that even a presidential veto would be overturned, should Bush be so disposed. Bush checked the political climate and publicly agreed to support the bill when it reached his desk. On December 30, 2005, Bush signed the Detainee Treatment Act with a smiling John McCain among those present looking over the president's shoulder. Shortly thereafter, Bush wrote a signing statement that declared he would interpret the ban "in a manner consistent with the constitutional authority of the president."[58] With his action, Bush completely undermined the protection provided in the McCain bill. As a leading expert on the Constitution noted, "The whole point of the McCain Amendment was to close every loophole.... The president has re-opened the loophole by asserting the constitutional authority to act in violation of the statute where it would *assist* in the war on terrorism."[59] Added another authority, "The signing statement is saying, 'I will only comply with this law when I want to, and if something arises in the war on terrorism where I think it's important to torture or engage in cruel, inhuman, and degrading conduct, I have the authority to do so and nothing in this law is going to stop me.'"[60] Simply put, Bush's actions undermined the guarantees provided by the legislation.

When Barack Obama campaigned for president, he promised to avoid the use of signing statements whenever possible. In late 2007 he declared,

"While it is legitimate for a president to issue a signing statement to clarify his understanding of ambiguous provisions of statutes and to explain his view of how he intends to faithfully execute the law, it is a clear abuse of power to use such statements as a license to evade laws that the president does not like or as an end-run around provisions designed to foster accountability."[61] Nevertheless, during the first 3 years of his presidency Obama wrote 10 signing statements and 78 constitutional challenges.[62] For example, within 3 months of taking office, after Congress authorized $108 billion for the International Monetary Fund with conditions, Obama signed the bill and attached a statement that he would not be bound by the conditions.[63] Other signing statements have followed since then.

Although they occur in a somewhat public environment, the uses of signing statements to modify congressionally passed bills are commonly found in the distant shadows of the public ceremonies surrounding the hoopla and presidential signature of congressional action. Often, by the time the press gets wind of the additional language, the original law and its issues are long forgotten by all except those closest to the issue. Thus, by virtue of his position as the last person to speak on a law, the president has unequaled power, a luxury rarely understood by citizens, who at best will only remember the original intent of the new law.

The expanded use of presidential power has ruffled more than a few feathers among those familiar with the Constitution and the lawmaking process. In 2006, the American Bar Association, the nation's most prestigious organization of attorneys, warned that the signing statement had become a tool "contrary to the rule of law."[64] It had good reason for concern.

SUBTLETIES IN THE JUDICIARY

For many Americans, the judiciary is the undiscovered branch of American government. They have much more familiarity with the executive and legislative branches of the U.S. government than their judicial counterpart. When it comes to the role of the judiciary, particularly the U.S. Supreme Court, the institution and its justices lead fairly anonymous existences.[65] A 2007 national survey by the Annenberg Public Policy Institute found that 31 percent of the respondents knew that the

U.S. Supreme Court was the nation's court of last resort. In the same survey, only 15 percent were able to name John Roberts as the Chief Justice; yet 28 percent, nearly twice as many, named entertainer Paula Abdul as a talent judge on the popular television show American Idol.[66] Another survey found that 77 percent of Americans could name two of Snow White's dwarfs, compared with only 24 percent who could name two justices of the U.S. Supreme Court.[67] Such data points speak volumes of public awareness, or the lack thereof.

Oddly, even though people know little about the U.S. Supreme Court or how it works, the public trusts the justices more than either the president or Congress.[68] Much of the court's popularity stems from the ways the justices package their work and comport themselves. They meet and discuss cases mysteriously prior to their decision making and within the confines of the ornate building where they hear arguments. After careful thought, research, and deliberation, they solemnly deliver their decisions.[69] In these respects, the Supreme Court functions as a truly unique element of American political theater. Nevertheless, the pageantry only scratches the surface of the important work carried out by the most elevated members of the American judicial system.

Judicial Review

The American judiciary began as the weak sibling of the policy-making triplets otherwise known as the three branches of national government. The framers at the Constitutional Convention recognized that the Articles of Confederation had failed in part because of the lack of an independent judiciary to resolve disputes. And so, the new Constitution included Article III, which begins, "The judicial Power of the United States shall be vested in one supreme Court, and in such inferior Courts as Congress may from time to time ordain and establish." Over the next 15 years, Congress added "inferior" courts, although the complete structure of district, circuit courts of appeal, and the U.S. Supreme Court was not completed until 1911.[70] Still, in the early years particularly, the framers had difficulty agreeing on the extent to which the Supreme Court should interpret the legality of laws and possibly offset the intentions of policy makers in the other branches.

Much of the confusion was clarified with *Marbury v. Madison*, an 1803 case that questioned the legality of some low-level judicial appointees by President John Adams immediately prior to his departure from office in 1801. In this case, the Supreme Court majority nullified the appointments on the grounds that a portion of the Judiciary Act of 1789, a law enabling them, was unconstitutional. The court's self-appointed ability to overturn the congressional statute became known as judicial review.

Anti-Federalists, those who feared an excessively strong national government formed by the new Constitution, were furious over the *Marbury* decision inasmuch as the Constitution awarded no such specific authority to the judicial branch. Still, the argument for a powerful court was hardly new, and had been articulated by Federalist Alexander Hamilton, who wrote in *Federalist Papers* No. 78 that "the complete independence of the courts of justice is peculiarly essential in a limited constitution."[71] In fact, Hamilton's argument reflected Section 2 of Article III, which reads: "The judicial Power shall extend to all Cases, in Law and Equity, arising under this Constitution." Given such authority, the Supreme Court justices believed they had the room to act, and they did.

With *Marbury*, precedent was set for the court's new power. Still, that power has been used sparingly over the past two centuries largely because of the significance of the actions of one branch reversing those of another. In fact, after *Marbury*, the Supreme Court did not exercise judicial review again until the *Dred Scott* decision that struck down the Missouri Compromise 54 years later. Since then, the Supreme Court has declared more than 140 federal laws and about 1,100 state laws unconstitutional.

In recent years, the Supreme Court has shied away from judicial review, almost as if to minimize its role. During the tenure of Chief Justice John Roberts, the U.S. Supreme Court has overturned federal, state, or local laws in 3.8 percent of the cases between 2005 and 2013. These percentages are much lower than during the William Rehnquist court (1986–2005), which overturned laws 6.4 percent of the time; the Warren Burger court (1969–1986), which overturned laws 8.9 percent of the time; or the Earl Warren court (1953–1969), which overturned laws 7.1 percent of the time.[72] As Henry J. Abraham notes, there is good reason for such caution: "Conscious of the nature and purpose of federalism and, especially, the need to permit legislative bodies to act in accordance with their judgment, no matter how unwise that may be at times, courts are understandably loath to invoke the judicial veto."[73] On the surface, it would appear that the Supreme Court has become more cautious in its decision making in recent years. But there is more to the story.

From Judicial Review to Judicial Circumvention

When Supreme Court justices use their authority under judicial review to declare an act unconstitutional, they provide a clear explanation of how and why their actions change the meaning of law. This is critical, given that the court by its actions takes on another branch of government. But in recent years, the U.S. Supreme Court has been less forthcoming by handing down decisions that overturn key components of laws without overturning the law altogether. Some might view such efforts as skillful fine-tuning of the existing law to maintain established precedent, but they actually give the misleading impression of protecting the status quo when, in fact, the status quo has been all but uprooted with an almost sleight-of-hand maneuver.

The Roberts court has been particularly adept at crafting decisions that undermine the essence of a law without overturning it. By acting in this way, the court has avoided appearing unduly activist and controversial at a time when the nation is so divided, particularly on major social and political issues. Consider three recent examples: desegregation, voting rights, and campaign spending limits.

Desegregation

Brown v. Board of Education (see Chapter 2), in 1954, describes the historical role of the Supreme Court in declaring racial segregation unconstitutional under the Equal Protection Clause of the 14th Amendment. Despite the clarity of the 9–0 decision, management of future cases by the Supreme Court has emasculated the *Brown* decision and made race, the centerpiece of the ruling, all but irrelevant. In 1991, the Supreme Court ruled that desegregation efforts could end after a "reasonable time" even if such efforts had not been entirely successful.[74] Four years later the court determined that desegregation efforts could end when states had done everything "practicable" to solve the problem.[75] The final blow came in 2007 when the court held that race could not be used as a tiebreaking factor in determining the racial balance in segregated schools.[76] Writing for the majority, Chief Justice John Roberts Jr. made it clear that the U.S. Supreme Court would no longer promote desegregation as a constitutional necessity, stating, "The way to stop discrimination on the basis of race is to stop discrimination on the basis of race."[77] Thus, while racial segregation remained unconstitutional courtesy of *Brown*, the court no longer believed in any institutional means to guarantee it. Without enforcement by laws and government agencies, desegregation will not work.

Voting Rights

No right is more fundamental to a democracy than the right to vote. Through the vote, individuals declare their opinions of how they want their government to work and who should be its stewards. That sounds simple enough, yet given the history of discrimination in the United States, the right for all Americans to vote has been difficult to gain and even more difficult to preserve despite various constitutional provisions providing the guarantee.

During the post-Civil War 19th century and most of the 20th century, voter suppression of racial minorities existed throughout the United States, and particularly in the South.[78] For the bulk of that period, several Supreme Court decisions and national laws focused on the right to vote, yet discrimination persisted. Clarity finally emerged with the Voting Rights Act of 1965, which not only restated the right to vote for all, but also provided enforcement, including the requirement of southern states (and portions of a few others) to obtain approval from the U.S. Department of Justice before changing any local laws or procedures. The results from the "preclearance" requirement were stunning, with a surge in African American voter registration, candidates, and ultimately elected officials.[79]

For nearly a half century after the 1965 Voting Rights Act, changes came and went through the federal courts to no avail. But matters changed considerably in 2013 when the U.S. Supreme Court struck down Title V of the act. Chief Justice Roberts wrote that preclearance had served its purpose and was therefore no longer necessary.[80] Once again, the justices did not overturn the law per se. Nevertheless, by striking down Title V, they destroyed the heart of the legislation. Now southern states were free to fashion their own laws with new requirements and restrictions, and they did. Yes, the law remains on the books, but in a radically different form from its design.

Campaign Spending Limits

Large amounts of untracked money have long been a concern for those who worry about its undesirable impact on elections. As the authors of one book on the subject write, "The means by which money is raised and how it is spent in political campaigns have been issues since the beginning of the republic."[81] Congress attempted to install oversight on funding with the Federal Election Campaign Act in 1971, which led to the Federal Election Commission (FEC). The FEC set limits on campaign spending and contributions, most of which were rejected by the U.S. Supreme Court a few years later. In 2002, Republican Senator John McCain and Democratic Senator Russell Feingold successfully co-sponsored the Bipartisan Campaign Reform Act (BCRA), which allowed the FEC to control "soft money," unregulated money donated to political parties, and excessive independent expenditures.

In 2003, the U.S. Supreme Court upheld most of the provisions, thereby preventing "a flood of money into national politics that had all but swamped a previous generation's effort of regulation."[82] Less than a decade later, however, the court reversed course. In *Citizens United v. Federal Election Commission*, a 5–4 majority of the justices declared that placing limits on campaign contributions amounted to censorship and a violation of free speech spelled out in the First Amendment. With this reversal, the court removed all limits of campaign spending by corporations and unions, gutting the most important authority of the Federal Election Commission. Nevertheless, as with other decisions, the court did not overturn creation of the Federal Election Commission; rather, it removed its most important responsibility.

A Sagging Reputation

The recent actions of the U.S. Supreme Court have come at a cost. Although still viewed more favorably by the public than the other two branches of national government, the Supreme Court's once lofty standing as an institution above politics has dropped considerably over time. A national survey conducted by the *New York Times* in 2012 found that 44 percent of the public approved of the court, down from 66 percent in the late 1980s. The same survey found that 55 percent of the public believed that the justices decided cases "mainly based on personal or political views," compared with 32 percent who believed the court decided cases "based on legal analysis."[83]

The court has lost prestige abroad as well. Whereas the judiciaries of other nations relied on U.S. Supreme Court decisions as guideposts for their own thinking, increasingly they look elsewhere. Instead, they model their decisions after the European Court of Human Rights and other international court systems that have more liberal views on issues like equality, liberty, and cruelty. Some scholars believe that the recent aversion to the U.S. judiciary stems from an aggressive U.S. foreign policy that has been unpopular in many parts of the world. Others think it has to do with the conservative leadership and decisions of the past two decades. Whatever the reasons, American courts no longer carry the badge of leadership in international circles.[84]

Given the American public's lack of knowledge about the work of the judiciary, the meaning of the drop in prestige is hard to assess. At a minimum, however, these data suggest yet another aspect of the political system that has lost support from the American public, as well as international audiences, over a fairly brief period of time. That alone should be reason for concern.

INSTITUTIONS ON SHAKY GROUND

Making modern governments work is difficult under any conditions. Add to that task the context of an operational democracy and the task becomes even more onerous. But it's the core responsibility for policy makers who we choose to somehow get the job done within our constitutional framework. Their challenge is even greater given the polarized condition of American society where the "haves" and "have-nots" live in two different worlds with two radically different sets of hopes and expectations. Yet, somehow, those we put into power must find a way to fulfill their obligations in a civil fashion. But the problem these days lies with the manner that policy makers exercise their authority.

American government has become a confusing enterprise in the 21st century. Congress is plagued by extremism, yielding a near-perpetual stalemate that has cost the legislative branch public respect. The presidency has taken up much of the authoritative slack, which, while carrying on some of the nation's business, has done so in a manner that has blurred the traditional separation of powers. And the judiciary has virtually exercised the once rare tool of judicial review to overturn basic constitutional principles without clearly stating the implications of its actions.

Combined, we now have a government much more complex than in the past, deadlocked, and almost duplicitous compared to the simple three-part diagram that neatly separates the policy-making authorities and their responsibilities. It often consists of officials who appear to do one thing while doing another, and who operate in a fluid environment of loose rules—or sometimes changed rules—just to "get the job done." That pressing demand comes at the cost of institutional credibility and a bewildered, if not discouraged, public. It's yet another reason why so many Americans are disengaged from the political system.

ENDNOTES

1. Samuel P. Huntington, *Political Order in Changing Societies*, New Haven, CT: Yale University Press, 1968, p. 8.
2. J.W. Peltason, *Corwin & Peltason's Understanding the Constitution*, 8th ed., New York: Holt, Rinehart and Winston, 1979, p. 24.
3. Donald F. Kettle, *The Transformation of Governance*, Baltimore, MD: Johns Hopkins Press, 2002, p. 151.
4. Roger H. Davidson, Walter J. Oleszek, Frances E. Lee, and Eric Schickler, *Congress and Its Members*, 14th ed., Thousand Oaks, CA: CQ Press, 2014, p. 32.
5. Burdett A. Loomis and Wendy J. Schiller, *The Contemporary Congress*, 5th ed., Belmont, CA: Thomson Wadsworth, 2006, p. 146.
6. Thomas E. Mann and Norman J. Ornstein, *The Broken Branch*, New York: Oxford University Press, 2008, p. 170.
7. Daniel P. Franklin, *Making Ends Meet: Congressional Budgeting in the Age of Deficits*, Washington, DC: Congressional Quarterly Press, 1993, p. 9.
8. "Obama Adviser Furman Says U.S. Shutdown Cost 120,000 Jobs," Bloomberg.com, October 22, 2013, http://www.bloomberg.com/news/2013-10-22/obama-economic-adviser-furman-says-shutdown-cost-120-000-jobs.html.
9. "Government Shutdown 2013: Republicans Mostly Blamed for Shutdown, AP Poll Shows," WJLA.com, October 9, 2013, http://www.wjla.com/articles/2013/10/government-shutdown-2013-republicans-mostly-to-blame-for-shutdown-ap-poll-shows-95085.html.
10. "Poll Finds GOP Blamed More for Shutdown," *Wall Street Journal*, October 11, 2013, p. A13.
11. "How the World Sees the U.S. Shutdown," CNN.com, October 8, 2013, http://globalpublicsquare.blogs.cnn.com/2013/10/08/how-the-world-sees-the-u-s-shutdown/.
12. "Analysis: U.S. Debt Ceiling Crisis Would Start Quiet, Go Down Hill Fast," Reuters, October 15, 2013, http://www.reuters.com/article/2013/10/15/us-usa-fiscal-debtceiling- analysis-idUSBRE99D0R320131015.
13. "CNN Poll: Majority Says Raise Debt Ceiling," CNN.com, October 2, 2013, http://www.cnn.com/2013/10/02/politics/cnn-poll-debt-ceiling/index.html.
14. "Obama Signs Bill to End Partial Shutdown, Stave Off Debt Ceiling Crisis," CNN.com, October 17, 2013, http://www.cnn.com/2013/10/16/politics/shutdown-showdown/index.html.
15. Quoted in Thomas E. Mann and Norman J. Ornstein, *It's Even Worse Than It Looks*, New York: Basic Books, 2012, p. 4.

16. See Dylan Matthews, "How Tuesday's Elections Made Congress More Polarized, in One Chart," *Washington Post*, November 8, 2012, http://www.washingtonpost.com/blogs/wonkblog/wp/2012/11/08/how-tuesdays-elections-made-congress-more-polarized-in-one-chart/?print=1 and Ezra Klein, "14 Reasons Why This Is the Worst Congress Ever," *Washington Post*, July 13, 2012, http://www.washingtonpost.com/blogs/wonkblog/wp/2012/07/13/13-reasons-why-this-is-the-worst-congress-ever/?print=1.

17. Joyce Appleby, "Disarm the Filibuster," *Los Angeles Times*, January 2, 2013, p. A15.

18. Garrett Epps, "How the Senate Filibuster Went Out-of-Control—And Who Can Rein It In," *The Atlantic*, December 27, 2012, http://www.theatlantic.com/national/archive/2012/12/how-the-senate-filibuster-went-out-of-control-and-who-can-rein-it-in/266645/.

19. "Harry Reid Says 82 Presidential Nominees Have Been Blocked under President Barack Obama, 86 Blocked under All Other Presidents," *Tampa Bay Times*, November 21, 2013, http://www.politifact.com/truth-o-meter/statements/2013/nov/22/harry-reid/harry-reid-says-82-presidential-nominees-have-been/.

20. "Senate Vote Curbs Filibuster Power to Stall Nominees," *New York Times*, November 22, 2013, pp. A1, A16.

21. "Showdown in Senate on Judicial Filibusters," *San Francisco Chronicle*, May 18, 2005, pp. A1, A8.

22. "How Tea Party Candidates Fared," *New York Times*, November 4, 2010, p. 8.

23. Michael Grunwald and Jay Newton-Small, "Mr. Speaker," *Time*, November 15, 2010, p. 35.

24. Paul Ryan, *Young Guns: A New Generation of Conservative Leaders*, New York: Simon & Schuster, 2010.

25. Margaret Carlson, "Boehner to Tea Party: Shut Yourself Down," Bloomberg.com, October 15, 2013, http://www.bloomberg.com/news/2013-10-15/boehner-to-tea-party-shut-yourself-down.html.

26. "Republicans Back Down in Fiscal Stalemate," *New York Times*, October 17, 2013, pp. A1, A20.

27. "Team Player Chides His Own," *Wall Street Journal*, August 3–4, 2013, p. A4.

28. "Republicans Back Down in Fiscal Standoff," op. cit., p. 19.

29. James Madison, "The Federalist No. 52," in Alexander Hamilton, James Madison, and John Jay, *The Federalist*, edited by Edward Mead Earle, New York: The Modern Library, 1937, p. 343.

30. For the 2011–2012 cycle, 43 states relied upon state legislatures; 7 used independent commissions.

31. Davidson et al., op. cit., p. 7.

32. For a discussion of these terms and their consequences, see Royce Crocker, "Congressional Redistricting: An Overview," Congressional Research Service, November 21, 2012, Report R42831, pp. 5–6.

33. Ross K. Baker, *House and Senate*, 4th ed., New York: W.W. Norton, 2008, p. 87.

34. "How Maps Helped Republicans Keep an Edge in the House," *New York Times*, December 14, 2012, http://www.nytimes.com/2012/12/15/us/politics/redistricting-helped-republicans-hold-onto-congress.html?pagewanted=all.

35. Doug Mataconis, "38% of Congressmen Represent 'Safe' Districts," *Outside the Beltway*, October 7, 2013, http://www.outsidethebeltway.com/38-of-congressmen-represent-safe-districts/.

36. "The 2014 Political Environment," *The Cook Political Report*, December 20, 2013, p. 17.

37. See Charles Gibson, "Restoring Comity to Congress," Joan Shorenstein Center on the Press, Politics and Public Policy, Discussion Paper Series, Harvard University, Cambridge, MA, January 2011, p. 6.
38. For a review of the issues related to creation of the presidency, see Richard J. Ellis, *The Development of the American Presidency*, New York: Taylor & Francis, 2012, pp. 1–19.
39. Louis Fischer, *The Politics of Shared Power: Congress and the Executive*, 3rd ed., Washington, DC: CQ Press, 1993, p. 145.
40. James M. McCormick, *American Foreign Policy and Process*, 4th ed., Belmont, CA: Thomsom Wadsworth, 2005, p. 189.
41. Ryan Henrikson, *The Clinton Wars: The Constitution, Congress and War Powers*, Nashville, TN: Vanderbilt University Press, 2002, p. 1.
42. Barbara Salazar Torreon, "Instances of Use of United States Armed Forces Abroad, 1798–2013," Report 42738, Congressional Research Service, May 3, 2013.
43. Loch K. Johnson, *Seven Sins of American Foreign Policy*, New York: Pearson Longman, 2007, p. 139.
44. Thomas E. Cronin and Michael A. Genovese point to preemptive initiatives emerging as a major foreign policy power of the president in the 21st century. See their *The Paradoxes of the American Presidency*, 4th ed., New York: Oxford University Press, 2013, p. 134.
45. See Glenn P. Hastedt, *American Foreign Policy*, 8th ed., Boston: Longman Pearson, 2011, pp. 181–183.
46. *The 9/11 Commission Report*, New York: W.W. Norton, 2003, p. 35.
47. Gerald Sussman makes this point in his "The Myths of 'Democracy Assistance': U.S. Political Intervention in Post-Soviet Eastern Europe," *Monthly Review*, 58(7), 2006.
48. One such base is in Uzbekistan, which is described by Human Rights Watch as a country where "torture remains endemic in the criminal justice system." See "World Report 2012: Uzbekistan," http://www.hrw.org/print/world-report-2012/world-report-2012-uzbekistan.
49. John Sifton, "A Brief History of Drones," *The Nation*, February 27, 2012, http://www.thenation.com/article/166124/brief-history-drones#.
50. James Joyner, "Oversight or Not, Drones Are Here to Stay," *World Politics Review*, July 27, 2012, http://www.worldpoliticsreview.com/articles/12207/oversight-or-not-drones-are-here-to-stay.
51. Gregory McNeal, "The Politics of Accountability for Targeted Killings," *Lawfare*, http://www.lawfareblog.com/2013/03/the-politics-of-accountability-for-targeted-killings/.
52. For a discussion of rule making in the executive branch, see Cornelius M. Kerwin, *Rulemaking: How Government Agencies Write Laws and Make Policy*, 3rd ed., Washington, DC: CQ Press, 2003.
53. "Shift on Executive Power Lets Obama Bypass Rivals," *New York Times*, April 23, 2012, pp. A1, A12.
54. Andrew Rudalevige, "The Decider," in Colin Campbell, Bert A. Rockman, and Andrew Rudalevige, eds., *The George W. Bush Legacy*, Washington, DC: CQ Press, 2008, p. 142.
55. Irwin L. Morris, *The American Presidency: An Analytical Approach*, New York: Cambridge University Press, 2010, p. 74.
56. James P. Pfiffner, *The Modern Presidency*, 6th ed., Belmont, CA: Wadsworth Cengage Learning, 2011, pp. 158–160.
57. "Obama Shifts View of Executive Power," *Wall Street Journal*, March 30, 2012, pp. A1, A12.
58. "Torture Ban? What Torture Ban?" *Salon*, January 4, 2006, http://www.salon.com/2006/01/04/torture_54/.

59. "Bush Could Bypass New Torture Ban," *Boston Globe*, January 4, 2006, http://www.boston.com/news/nation/articles/2006/01/04/bush_could_bypass_new_torture_ban/.

60. "Torture Ban? What Torture Ban?" op. cit.

61. Quoted in Barack Obama's Q&A, *Boston Globe*, December 20, 2007, http://www.boston.com/news/politics/2008/specials/CandidateQA/ObamaQA/.

62. "Obama Shifts View of Executive Power," op. cit.

63. "President's Signing Statements Anger Lawmakers," *Wall Street Journal*, July 15, 2009, p. A6.

64. "ABA Targets 'Misuse' of Presidential Signing Statements," *U.S. News & World Report*, August 9, 2006, http://www.usnews.com/usnews/news/articles/060809/9signing.htm.

65. Lawrence Baum, *The Supreme Court*, 9th ed., Washington, DC: CQ Press, 2007, pp. 18–19.

66. "Fewer than a Third of Americans Know That Supreme Court Rulings Are Final," The Annenberg Public Policy Center of the University of Pennsylvania, Philadelphia, September 13, 2007, http://www.annenbergpublicpolicycenter.org/fewer-than-a-third-of-americans-know-supreme-court-rulings-are-final/.

67. "Seven Dwarfs versus Supreme Court Justices," UPI, August 14, 2006, http://www.upi.com/Odd_News/2006/08/14/Seven-Dwarfs-vs-Supreme-Court-justices/UPI-14791155596541/.

68. In a 2005 Fox News poll, respondents were asked, "Of the three branches of the United States government, which branch do trust the most, the U.S. Congress, the legislative branch, the President, the executive branch, or the Supreme Court, the judicial branch?" Answers: the legislative branch, 20 percent; the executive branch, 22 percent; the judicial branch, 33 percent. See Karlyn Bowman, "AEI Public Opinion Study," American Enterprise Institute, Washington, DC, July 8, 2009, p. 47, http://www.aei.org/files/2009/07/08/20050729_SupemeCourt0729.pdf.

69. Barbara A. Perry draws out this distinction in her *The Priestly Tribe: The Supreme Court's Image in the American Mind*, Westport, CT: Praeger Publishers, 1999, pp. 7–23.

70. For a discussion of the evolution of the federal court system, see G. Alan Tarr, *Judicial Process and Judicial Policymaking*, 4th ed., Belmont, CA: Thomson Wadsworth, 2006, pp. 28–31.

71. Alexander Hamilton, "Federalist #78," in Michael Kammen, ed., *The Origins of the American Constitution: A Documentary History*, New York: Penguin Books, 1986, p. 229.

72. "How Activist Is the Supreme Court?" *New York Times*, October 13, 2013, p. 4.

73. Henry J. Abraham, *The Judicial Process*, 6th ed., New York: Oxford University Press, 1993, p. 272.

74. *Board of Education of Oklahoma City Public Schools v. Dowell*, 111 S.Ct. 630.

75. *Missouri v. Jenkins*, 515 U.S. 70.

76. The two cases were parents involved in *Community Schools v. Seattle School District No. 1*, 05-908, and *Meredith v. Jefferson County Board of Education*, 05-915.

77. Quoted in "Justices, 5–4, Limit Use of Race for School Integration Plans," *Los Angeles Times*, June 29, 2007, pp. A1, A20.

78. For a history of the right to vote in America, see Tova Andrea Wang, *The Politics of Voter Suppression: Defending and Expanding Americans' Right to Vote*, Ithaca, NY: Cornell University Press, 2012.

79. Ibid., pp. 111–114.

80. See "Justices Rein in Voting Rights Act," *Los Angeles Times*, June 26, 2013, pp. A1, A9.

81. Matthew J. Burbank, Ronald J. Hrebrenar, and Robert C. Benedict, *Parties, Interest Groups, and Political Campaigns*, 2nd ed., Boulder, CO: Paradigm Publishers, 2012, p. 97.
82. Quoted in "Justices, in a 5-to-4 Decision, Back Campaign Finance Law That Curbs Contributions," *New York Times*, December 11, 2003, pp. A1, A24.
83. "Approval Rating for Justices Hits 44% in Poll," *New York Times*, June 8, 2012, pp. A1, A16.
84. "U.S. Court, a Longtime Beacon, Is Now Guiding Fewer Nations," *New York Times*, September 8, 2008, pp. A1, A26.

Section III

A Tale of Two Economies

7

An Economic System That Divides Its Members

Most Americans operate with the assumption that the United States is a land of great uniqueness, a place where just about anyone can make his or her mark and secure a rewarding sense of contentment as a result. For Americans with this perspective, only hard work and dedication separate those who will succeed from those who will not succeed, due in no small part to the endless opportunities afforded in this special nation. As historian Daniel Boorstin wrote shortly after World War II when the United States emerged as the world's most powerful nation, "No nation has been readier to identify its values with the peculiar conditions of its landscape: we believe in *American* equality, *American* liberty, *American* democracy, or, in sum, the *American* way of life."[1] And so it is—America, the great exception, where the level playing field allows everyone to excel. The idea of the American way is enshrined everywhere—in the school lessons we learn, the economic ladders we aspire to climb, and the flags we proudly place outside our homes each holiday, reminding us of the special place we call the United States.

Boorstin is not alone in his analysis. Plenty of contemporary thinkers embrace such sentiments in the present day, believing that the individual is limited only by self-imposed constraints. Thomas Sowell contends that those at the bottom of the economic ladder live there by choice: "The image of 'the working poor' who are 'falling behind' as a result of society's 'inequities' bears little resemblance to the situation of the people earning the lowest 20 percent of income in the United States, however much such rhetoric may be fashionable in the media and elsewhere."[2] Many of those at the bottom, he adds, are retired, have chosen to work part-time, or are illegal immigrants whose lack of skills explains their absence from the workplace. Together these groups distort the data.[3] Moreover, their economic conditions are created by their choices, not others holding them down.

To the extent that such conditions exist, we might be tempted to walk away from any remedies for poorly compensated workers, for there would be little reason to assist those who choose not to help themselves. But powerful data suggest that the description offered by Sowell and his contemporaries misses the mark. Economic research by Lawrence Mishel and his colleagues finds that poverty stems in large part from imposed conditions *within* the workplace environment, not outside of it. Examining data from the last quarter of the 20th century through the first years of the 21st century, they find the working poor benefited from economic gains at less than half the rate of those at the top.

Some might counter that those near the bottom fail to improve their incomes because their skill sets limit productivity. Yet, Mishel and his colleagues find that during the first decade of the 21st century, "the workforce was highly productive, yet poverty increased."[4] In fact, poverty does not exist out of choice or out of economic dominos that benignly fall because of cyclical issues or individual life choices, but rather as a result of corporate management decisions and government policies that produce it. Thus, employment is not simply an innocent function of supply and demand, but rather determined by circumstances often well out of the control of those seeking work.

Under these circumstances, we now can see why government policies can mitigate the conditions of the working poor, whether they come in the form of health insurance subsidies, food stamps, education assistance, job training, or any other programs designed to help elevate the less advantaged members of society from their precarious conditions. Thus, 4 years after recovery from the Great Recession, President Barack Obama stated in his 2013 State of the Union speech, "There are millions of Americans whose hard work and dedication have not been rewarded.... Too many people still can't find full-time employment. Corporate profits have rocketed to all-time highs—but for more than a decade, wages and incomes have barely budged."[5] It seems that recovery from the Great Recession has meant much more to some than others.

No one expects everyone to earn the same amount of money or enjoy the same status. Obviously, people bring different skills and talents to the employment table. Still, the differences between those most advantaged and least advantaged in the workplace have grown over time, and continue to accelerate to this day, creating a huge underclass in the American economy not seen since the Great Depression. The low-wage workforce has grown for several reasons. Educated workers and older members of the workforce, groups once unaffected or little affected by the ability to generate incomes, now find themselves among the long-term unemployed, often with substantial intervals before securing employment—if at all. Corporations have restructured full-time jobs with generous benefits to temporary or part-time jobs with few, if any, benefits. Unions, once powerful engines for raising wages, particularly in the private sector, have lost much of their clout in a world where companies now squeeze wages to remain competitive in the global economy. In addition, many of today's American workers lack critical job skills that match jobs available by hungry employers.

Which takes us to the focus of this chapter. In the following pages, we explore the immense differences in compensation between workers at the bottom of the American economic stratum and those at the top. Even as the American economy has recovered from the Great Recession, discrepancies between those at either end have accelerated, giving question to the once cherished belief that those clinging to the bottom rungs of the economic ladder can ever climb out of their collective despair. Meanwhile, efforts to create and manage government programs to assist those most in need increasingly are met with stiff resistance and scorn, often by those who benefit from low wages as a way of maintaining corporate profitability and giddy stockholders. With these disparities reinforced generation after generation, it's little wonder that so many Americans feel discouraged and left behind in a country that they have worked hard to build.

THE UNEVEN 21ST CENTURY WORKPLACE

The nature of the American workforce is changing, in some ways more noticeably than others. We know, for example, that the United States has become much more of a services nation than a manufacturing nation due to increasing global competition.[6] We also know that U.S. companies have extended their operations beyond American shores as a way of meeting competition with a less costly workforce.[7] But what we sometimes overlook is that for those working at home, major changes have taken place for most with respect to their education and training, employment opportunities, and compensation.

C-Level versus Those at the Bottom

It's not very often when the workers make more money than their bosses. We see it in unusual circumstances like sports, where athletes earn salaries many more times than their managers; we sometimes find it in the public sector, where the heads of state universities or medical programs make higher incomes than governors or other prominent elected government officials. These, of course, are the exceptions to the rule. In fact, we expect business owners, CEOs, and high-level corporate managers who sometimes oversee the efforts of thousands of employees to earn much more than those who work in less responsible positions. After all, they're the ones who have invested the capital, taken the financial risks, obtained special training, gained valuable experience, and endured countless problems that revolve around running an enterprise. But how much more do they make? Perhaps the more important question might be: How much more *should* they make? To that we ask: Is there a point where amounts earned by those at the top are so extreme that they discourage those at the bottom? And finally, we add the question: Where does fairness fit into this discussion?

Let's put the fairness question aside for a moment and examine the facts. According to data gathered by the Economic Policy Institute, in 2011, the average CEO earned 231 times the amount of a typical private sector worker.[8] Twenty years earlier, the average CEO/typical worker disparity was about 100 to 1. And 50 years ago, the compensation difference was only 18 to 1. As the data indicate, the current gap is not the result of a temporary fluke in the economy or measuring methodology. The growing differential has been accumulating for decades. And here's why: between 1978 and 2011, the compensation for American CEOs soared by 725 percent; meanwhile, compensation for the typical private sector worker grew by a relatively paltry 5.7 percent.[9] These numbers reflect only average CEO packages. In fact, several corporate managers earn well beyond the average. In 2012, the CEO of Dollar General received 1,007 times the average worker wage in his company, and the CEO of Starbucks made 1,096 times the average worker in his company. But the most lopsided disparity was found with the CEO of McDonald's, who earned a whopping 1,196 times the amount earned by the average employee in his company.[10]

Those who have suffered the most in the workplace are 1.6 million employees who are paid the federal minimum wage of $7.25 per hour and the 2.1 million employees who earn less than the minimum wage because of their status as full-time students employed by retail, service establishments such as restaurants, agriculture, or higher education institutions, and those who are impaired by physical or mental disabilities. With respect to restaurant servers, states can pay as little as $2.19 per hour as long as tips bring up the overall hourly wage to $7.25 or more. This formula has remained in place since 1991.[11]

But even the $7.25 per hour minimum wage is suspect in terms of purchasing power when controlled for inflation. A study by the Congressional Research Service in 2013 found that the current minimum wage lost 36 percent of its purchasing power since 1968[12]; in other words, in today's dollars, the real minimum wage is $4.64. Put these two groups together, and 3.7 million Americans earn the paltry minimum wage or less. Assuming a 40-hour workweek for 52 weeks, the annual salary of these people would be $15,080 in inflated dollars. For perspective, according to the U.S. Department of Health and Human Services, as of 2012 the poverty line for a family of four was $23,050.[13]

The poverty issue goes beyond the growing sector of the workforce earning the minimum wage. A 2012 study by the National Employment Law Project found that the Great Recession generated long-term changes in the composition of the workforce. According to the study, during the recession, lower-wage occupations represented 21 percent of all job losses, but during the recovery, lower-wage jobs accounted for 58 percent of new jobs. Meanwhile, mid-range occupations represented 60 percent of the jobs lost during the recession, but only 22 percent of the jobs generated during the recovery.[14] These structural changes portend long-term trends in the economy of the future—an economy that hurts increasing numbers of people. These tendencies are not new; indeed, they extend back before the Great Recession. Data gathered by the U.S. Department of Labor show that between the pre-Great Recession years of 2003 and 2007, when the U.S. economy was humming, incomes for high-wage earners increased by 12.9 percent, compared to 8.4 percent for the bottom 10 percent of the workforce.[15]

Post-Great Recession statistics have only exacerbated a wage divide that has a long, painful history for those at the bottom. Moreover, recovery from the Great Recession notwithstanding, there is little hope for low-wage earners to expect any real improvement. A 2012 study by the Economic Policy Institute (EPI) found that 28 percent of all U.S. workers were in low-paying jobs—employment paying $11.06 per hour, or $23,005 per year. That's just about the amount that full-time workers must earn to reach the official poverty line for a family of four. Worse yet, EPI predicted that 28 percent of all workers would continue in low-paying jobs through 2020.[16] For more than a quarter of the labor force, there appears to be no remedy for their condition any time soon.

Consider these data in light of the proposal by President Barack Obama in his 2014 State of the Union address to raise the federal minimum wage to $10.10. Even that amount wouldn't help the 28 percent escape the poverty line; rather, they would only get closer to it. Yet, within days of the proposal the National Retail Federation launched a $1 million campaign against the proposal as harmful to the American economy.[17] For a polarized Congress, that was reason enough to dither.

Demographic Differences

Today's workforce is built on a platform with many more obstacles for some than others. Opportunities to climb the economic ladder are hindered by a variety of factors. Some, such as gender and race, have been obvious for as long as experts have been gathering data. Other impediments, such as levels of education and age, are relatively new additions as barriers to attaining success. These groups and their persistently discouraging obstacles are discussed in the following paragraphs.

Gender

A long history exists of women being unable to reach the highest levels of corporate management.[18] As of 2013, only 23 women were CEOs of the Fortune 500 companies, a number that translates to 4.6 percent.[19] But even the few who succeed do so at a substantial "discount," inasmuch as they are rewarded with salaries equal to about 80 percent of what males earn.[20] With respect to general management, women hold 40 percent of these high-paid positions, even though they comprise a majority of the workforce. Clearly, the "good old boys" network is alive and well in the American workplace.[21]

Matters are just as disappointing at the other end of the workforce. With respect to the minimum wage, census data show that 6 percent of women are paid minimum wage, compared with 3 percent for men.[22] A study of 15 employment categories spanning the educational spectrum by the Bureau of Labor Statistics found that women earned less than men in 12 fields, exceeding male counterparts only in the low-paid jobs as food servers, bill collectors, and stock clerks. In the other areas, such as nursing, lawyers, pharmacists, computer managers, and retail, women earned less than men.[23] The differentials are less today than in the past, but they still remain significant.

Recovery from the Great Recession in the workplace has been harsher for women than for men. Between 2009 and 2012, male employment went up by 4.1 percent in the private sector, compared to 3.4 percent for women. With respect to the public sector, new male employment in the federal government grew by 5.3 percent, while female employment dropped by 3.7 percent.[24]

Some have argued that women earn less than men because of differences in education or other variables. That sounds convenient enough, but it's only partially the case. A study conducted by economists Francine Blau and Lawrence Khan examined differences in pay, adjusting for education, experience, race, industry, and occupation. With all those factors accounted for, women still earn 91 percent of what men earn.[25] All told, the picture is not pretty: women don't get the opportunities for the best jobs, and when they do, they are paid less. Moreover, compared to men, women have been left behind in the post-Great Recession workforce.

Race and Ethnicity

Any serious discussion of African American and Latino employment opportunities must connect present circumstances with past treatment; in fact, it's almost impossible to separate the two dimensions. More than 30 years ago, a report by the U.S. Commission on Civil Rights stated, "Past discrimination [of racial and ethnic minorities] continues to have present effects."[26] With few exceptions, that vicious cycle continues to this day.

According to the U.S. Bureau of Labor Statistics, the unemployment rate in December 2013 was 6.7 percent, the lowest since 2007, yet the rate was unevenly distributed throughout the population. Among non-Hispanic whites, unemployment stood at 5.9 percent; however, among Latinos, 8.3 percent were unemployed, and among African Americans, the unemployment rate was 11.9 percent.[27] These trends have been more exaggerated in stressful times. Thus, in the depths of the Great Recession, unemployment for whites climbed to 8.7 percent, but it soared for Latinos and African Americans to 12.5 and 16.0 percent, respectively.[28] Regardless of the economic conditions, unemployment for non-whites is always higher than for whites.

There is little question that much of the differences in employment stem from education patterns (see Chapter 4). Yet even when controlling for education, large disparities exist in incomes. For example, in 2008 African Americans with less than a high school education earned 61 percent of their white counterparts. Among those with bachelor's degrees, African Americans earned 74 percent of their white counterparts. The gap shrunk somewhat with advanced degrees; even here, however, African Americans earned 83 percent of their white counterparts.[29]

Latinos suffer similar opportunity losses irrespective of education. A study by Georgetown University finds Latinos with educations comparable to non-Hispanic whites trail in earning power at all educational levels, from high school dropouts to doctoral degrees. Latino professionals are likely to earn one-third less than whites over the course of their careers.[30] Latinos are also the least likely of the ethnic groups to have access to paid sick days or parental leave.[31]

Collectively, these data show that racial and ethnic minorities lack the same life chances as whites. Such disparities contradict the claim of "equal opportunity for all" in American society. Simply put, it's difficult to dismiss racial discrimination as a factor that at least in part accounts for different compensation patterns.

The Young

Young adults are quickly losing their place in the nation's workforce, and perhaps society. The unemployment rate for young adults has been running at twice the national average for years. Worse yet, the difference between employment opportunities for this age group and the rest of the workforce actually has widened since the 1980s, approaching epidemic proportions. As of 2013, the 5.6 million unemployed young adults (ages 18–24) accounted for a staggering 45 percent of the nation's unemployed workforce. Among 18- to 29-year-olds, only 43.6 percent were employed, a rate lower than at any time during the Great Recession. Less than 40 percent of young adults without a college degree held a full-time job. Among those with a college degree, only 65 percent were employed in full-time positions.[32] Thus, even high percentages of the educated young have not been able to put their skills to work. Added to their woes is the unenviable fact that as of 2012, the average college graduate left higher education with $29,400 in student loans.[33] It's hard to pay off loans without a job.

The lack of employment opportunities for young adults has stopped, if not hampered, careers before they have even started. The Center for American Progress estimates that the number of young people ages 20–24 unemployed for 6 months or more can expect to earn $22,000 less on average over the coming decade. Given the large numbers in this group, the aggregate loss of earnings and purchasing power would be $21.4 billion over the course of the period.[34]

Because of their inability to find jobs, record numbers of young people are living with their parents. A Pew Research study found that more than 21 million young adults ages 18–31 (36 percent of the age group) lived with their parents in 2012, up from 18.5 million in 2007 (32 percent of the age group). The study noted that somewhere between one-third and one-half of the young adults were attending college.[35] Still, even controlling for college attendance, the increase of young adults living at home is substantial.

It's an ugly combination, to be sure: living at home, with few employment opportunities, and watching potential incomes drifting by. And for many there is little hope. Even among those young workers who are employed in full-time jobs, only 11 percent see their current occupation as a career, and less than half believe they will be able to find another job if they lose or leave their current job.[36] Countless millions of America's future workforce can't even get started.

Older Workers

People who are near the end of their working careers share a status not found with other groups: their productive days in the workplace are numbered. With the approach of retirement, older workers don't have the time to make up for years of unemployment, underemployment, poor investments, or other adverse circumstances that have interrupted their income earning capabilities. They also have little incentive to retrain for jobs that they are not likely to hold for very long. In addition, large percentages are unprepared for life after work. Nearly 40 percent of those in the 55–64 age bracket, the period approaching retirement, have no retirement savings.[37] Thus, the members of this sector are particularly vulnerable to the conditions of their economic environment.

Older workers have responded to the increasingly uncertain American economy by sensing the need to work longer than they might have otherwise. According to the Social Security Administration, the median age for retirement from full-time jobs increased from 57 in the 1950s to 61 in 2000. A national workforce survey in 2013 found that 36 percent of those interviewed said they wouldn't retire until at least age 65, up from 11 percent in 1991. In the same survey, 7 percent responded that they would never retire. Another, more pessimistic study found that nearly three-quarters of all Americans intend to work past age 65, with 39 percent stating that working later was necessary to "make ends meet."[38] Moreover, of those displaced from their jobs in their sixties, 30 percent stated that they were forced to accept jobs that paid less than their previous employment.[39] The "work longer" trend seems to have taken hold. As to why they delayed their retirement, more than half of the respondents cited a poor economy, a change in employment status, or the lack of enough money to retire comfortably.[40] It's important to remember that these data were collected long after recovery from the Great Recession.

The fact that older workers now remain in the workforce longer has created something of a domino effect. With fewer positions available, younger workers have found it harder to break into the labor force. Because the young are unable to gain on-the-job experience, companies have tended to defer new hires, according to a 2013 Gallup workforce survey.[41] Thus, what benefits one generation has thwarted another.

The necessity of the would-be retired worker to continue in the workforce has produced circumstances far different from their expectations. For a large portion of these people, the "golden years" are a dream with little chance of ever becoming reality.

Labor Force Blues

The contemporary American labor market presents rich opportunities for some and terrible obstacles for countless others. Many who suffered temporary setbacks during the Great Recession have recovered and resumed successful careers. Others have been left behind with unanticipated impediments preventing them from pursuing their careers. Others still never had the same chances to begin with and, absent fundamental changes, are not likely to succeed in the future.

CHANGES IN THE WORKPLACE

There is little doubt that some people in the workplace have been denied the opportunities given to others because of their gender, race, or age. Beyond these discriminatory practices, other systemic factors have combined to change the composition of the American labor force. They include the corporate shifts from full-time employment to part-time employment, the use of overtime in place of additional hires, and mismatches between education skills and job openings. Outsourcing, a fourth component, stands as yet another impediment to the contemporary American workforce. This is discussed in Chapter 8.

Involuntary Part-Time Work

Those who work less than 35 hours per week are typically categorized as members of the part-time workforce, in which there are two subgroups. For some individuals, part-time work comes out of desire to keep busy lives, earn some extra discretionary income, or fill in their day with worthwhile activity; thus, their limited time at work is largely self-directed, rather than the result of imposed economic misfortune. But in the cases of involuntary part-time workers, their conditions result from circumstances beyond their control. These individuals want full-time employment and are unable to find it, or they are individuals who have been forced to accept fewer hours of work.

Involuntary part-time workers represent the lowest and most desperate link of the employment chain. In terms of the workforce, they approach second-class citizenship. Because these people do not work full-time, they are often not eligible for company retirement programs, lack union representation, have no job seniority or security, and are usually not eligible to compete for advancement opportunities with their employer.[42] They also commonly earn less per hour than full-time workers doing the same jobs.[43] Historically, part-timers were often excluded from company health plans as well, but with implementation of the Patient Protection and Affordable Care Act, beginning in 2015 companies with 50 or more employees who average 30 hours or more per week must provide their employees with health insurance. While those involuntary part-time workers who meet or exceed the 30-hour weekly threshold no longer have the health insurance concern, they account for a small portion of the involuntary part-time group.

The numbers of those who want to work full-time and can't find that kind of employment have grown considerably in recent years to unprecedented levels. Between 2007 and 2012, the involuntary part-time portion of the workforce more than doubled, rising from 3.6 to 7.8 percent—that's 3 million more people involuntarily stuck in part-time jobs than before the Great Recession. Recovery from the economic disaster may have been substantially complete for most Americans, but involuntary part-time workers have been left behind.[44]

Of concern is whether inflated numbers of involuntary part-time workers have become a permanent fixture of the workforce. Almost predictably, demographic studies show that they are disproportionately African American, Latino, recent immigrants, and high school dropouts. Collectively, they experience increasingly long intervals between jobs. In 2012, 24 percent of men and 31 percent of women who were involuntary part-time workers suffered at least 13 weeks of unemployment during the year.[45] Their growing numbers and lengthening periods of unemployment give these people little reason for hope.

Overtime

Not all members of the workforce have endured the problems encountered by part-time workers. Among those gainfully employed, many have had the good fortune of working overtime, thus increasing the sizes of their paychecks. This phenomenon has increased with the economic recovery, but at a cost to those hungering for work. Companies, especially in the manufacturing sector, choose the overtime route as a means of keeping a tight leash on expenses, lest the economic recovery turn out to be temporary or less robust than expected.[46] With a lean workforce, employers don't have to worry about the training and benefits costs connected with additional employees. Furthermore, they don't have to go through the painful layoff exercises of downsizing if the economy takes a turn for the worse. In short, the use of overtime helps 21st-century employers remain nimble.[47]

While these strategies may be good for employers, they are anything but helpful to those seeking employment. The consequences are staggering. One 2012 examination of the 12 million manufacturing employees in the United States calculated that if the overtime hours provided for just half that number were applied to the creation of new jobs, 500,000 employees would be added to the nation's labor force.[48] Such a strategy could go a long way toward spreading the wealth in a society where so many are left out of the opportunity to be meaningful participants.

Another related issue centers on the question of required overtime. The Federal Fair Labor Standards Act allows employers to mandate overtime for their staff as necessary; however, such efforts are typically limited to relatively low paid hourly workers. With the increases of overtime during the Great Recession as a means of stretching employee productivity, workers struck back at what they considered unfair demands with inadequate pay. In 2011, more than 7,000 wage-and-hour overtime suits were filed over the issue, many of which were class action suits affecting thousands of workers in a single case. That number nearly quadrupled the number of overtime suits filed in 2000,[49] indicating yet again the contentious divide between employers and their employees during a particularly rocky economy.

The practice of overtime has increased significantly in the 21st century. Even when used with worker cooperation, overtime has the effect of minimizing the addition of new employees. As a result, the workforce does not expand with a growing economy to the extent that it might if more workers replaced overtime hours. It's just another way that the number of unemployed workers remains unnecessarily high.

Job Mismatches

Mismatches between available jobs and those seeking employment represent a third phenomenon that now plagues the 21st-century American economy. Some of the disparity stems from the increasingly sophisticated and precise requirements for jobs, particularly those positions in the high-tech sector that focus on product design, engineering, or research. However, that's not the entire story. Compelling data suggest that the American education system is failing to inculcate basic thinking and reasoning skills in students almost across the board, leaving even the brightest untrained applicants unable to satisfy the requirements of millions of entry-level jobs.

Training Gaps

Specialization has become a watchword of 21st-century employment, as employers are having great difficulty in filling job vacancies.

The manufacturing jobs of the past require a different set of skills today. Factories have given way to advanced production centers, with employees requiring the ability to guide robotic components, design high-tech tools, and develop computer programs, along with problem solving and continuous development of new skill sets.[50] These attributes are sorely missing from large swaths of the workforce. A 2012 survey by Manpower found that 49 percent of U.S. employers had unfilled job positions, with more than half the respondents citing a dearth of applicants as the most important problem, and almost as many pointing to a lack of candidate experience.[51] As to how these impediments might be overcome, the most common response from American corporate leaders was the need for "additional training and development for existing Staff."[52] Thus, employers blame a poorly prepared workforce for the inability to hire more people, yet they have shown little commitment to dealing with the problem.

The Manpower survey results touch on an issue that is often overlooked—the lack of training from within. According to the findings, it turns out that despite the hue and cry from U.S. companies for better-trained employees, they are less willing than ever to deal with it. A study by Wharton School professor Peter Cappelli found that in 1979, American companies provided an average of 2.5 weeks' training per year for workers; by 1995, the typical company provided less than 11 hours per year. And in 2011, a similar study learned that companies provided training for only 21 percent of their employees over the past 5 years.[53] Of course, there are reasons for the drop-off in training. In a Business Roundtable survey of those who do not train employees, 76 percent cited cost as the primary reason. On the surface, that makes sense, except that labor accounts for an average of 15 percent of total corporate operating costs![54] Companies may complain about not finding suitable talent, but most are doing little to improve the talent they already have. In effect, they have placed virtually the entire burden on the public sector—a sector already overburdened with more obligations than resources.

Poor Education

None of this is to dismiss the lagging quality of American public education. For years, American students have been inadequately exposed to subjects that become the foundation of the fastest-growing and high-paying areas of the economy—science, technology, engineering, and mathematics, commonly referred to as STEM. One recent MIT study of young adults ages 16–25 found that 34 percent knew little about STEM fields, 33 percent found them too challenging, and 28 percent responded that they were not prepared enough in their education to pursue these fields.[55] The study's findings go along with a multinational assessment of U.S. students. According to a 2012 report of 15- and 16-year-old students in 34 industrialized countries by the Organization for Economic Cooperation and Development (OECD), the United States ranked 26th in mathematics, 21st in science, and 17th in reading.[56] The result: Fewer students are prepared in areas with significant job shortfalls. These deficiencies bubble up to university educations. Thus, in 1980, math, engineering, computer science, and technology students represented 11.1 percent of university graduates; as of 2011, the figure dropped to 8.9 percent.[57] The world may be embracing technology in the 21st century, but U.S. students are moving in the other direction.

Where does the lack of preparedness for the workforce begin? That answer is difficult to determine. But we do know that during the 4 years of high school, the last educational period before students go on to higher learning, a sizable proportion of these future members of the workforce are ill-prepared. According to the results from the 2013 College Readiness exam performed by ACT, 64 percent were college-ready in English, followed by 44 percent in reading, 44 percent in mathematics, and 36 percent in science. Moreover, only 26 percent were prepared in all four subjects. Worse yet, performance declined between 2009 and 2013.[58] Poorly prepared high school graduates are unlikely to find firm footing in the even more demanding college experience.

A Deteriorated Jobs Environment

Poor training and poor education produce a workplace that is unproductive, uncompetitive, and lacking for enough workers in skilled vocations. Industry leaders and educators may point fingers at one another, but in fact there is enough blame to go around. We also see more clearly than ever that difficulties in the workplace relate largely to a changed employment environment that has been neglected by business and government alike. Unfortunately, businesses often address shortages by importing workers from abroad. It may be the easy way out for them, but it doesn't address the basic problem of a society with inadequate numbers of skilled workers.

SAFETY NET PROGRAMS IN THE 21ST CENTURY: ON THE MONEY OR OUT OF TOUCH?

Thus far, we have examined the workplace and found challenges for several elements of American society. Some of the causes for employment have demographic components, others focus on inadequate or no corporate training, while still others center on the changing work environment in the 21st century. The point is that large segments of the population are disconnected from the workplace not by desire, but by a series of circumstances almost always beyond their control.

The employment opportunity field is anything but even. As modern economies evolve, so must their workforces. Therein lies some of the tension between the unemployed and underemployed members of society and the rest of working America. But what about the capabilities of the federal government? What about the idea of a safety net of last resort for those who have exhausted all other avenues to gainful employment? In the following pages, we will focus on government programs intended to rebuild the workforce in terms of their potential opportunities and outcomes.

Workforce Development

Conceding that many in today's workforce don't meet the requirements of the modern workplace, what can be done to fix the unbalanced economic equation? We begin with a discussion of government training programs and new education directions.

Training

The U.S. government has had a historical role in facilitating improvement of the nation's workforce. Beginning with the Great Depression, the U.S. government developed training programs for those seeking employment. Some programs such as the Civil Works Administration and the Works Progress Administration provided employment for infrastructure development such as national parks, dams, and roads. Others, such as the National Youth Administration, awarded stipends to the young so they could complete high school in preparation for employment. This was the model for getting people back to work and restoring the economy. Government attention to those seeking employment continued throughout the rest of the 20th century, depending upon the circumstances.

In recent years, the Workforce Investment Act has been the most important cornerstone of the government training-employment relationship. First passed in Congress by large margins and signed by President Bill Clinton in 1998, the most important component of the legislation was "its focus on meeting the needs of business for skilled workers and the training, education, and employment needs of individuals."[59] Those who were dislocated from their previous jobs, individuals new to the workforce, and the young were among the targets of the legislation that was based on federal funding and state implementation. The purpose of the act was to "provide quality employment and training services to assist eligible individuals in finding and qualifying for meaningful employment, and to help employers find the skilled workers they need to compete and succeed in business,"[60] thereby creating a win-win relationship for businesses and trained employees. The act was renewed periodically until 2013, although with less funding over time.

The lack of government investment has taken its toll. In 2012, federal funds for the Workforce Investment Act were 43 percent less than in 2000,[61] reduced from $2.1 billion to $1.2 billion, even though unemployment rose from 4.0 percent to 8.2 percent during the same period. Ironically, the employment assistance law was a success to the extent that funds allowed. A study in 2011 found that 77 percent of those who received training through the program found employment.[62] In 2009, the Obama administration was able to funnel an extra $4.0 billion into job training through the American Recovery and Reinvestment Act, but those funds dried up with the act's expiration in 2011. The temporary infusion notwithstanding, over time the U.S. government has provided fewer job-related programs and opportunities than at any time since the 1990s.[63]

Funding for the Workforce Investment Act dried up altogether in 2012, when the employment and training concept became caught with other potential government programs in the budgetary struggles of Congress. The Obama administration proposed extension of the act, with a focus on filling 3.6 million vacant jobs in high-tech manufacturing, alternate energy, healthcare, and other critically impacted sectors of the economy. The Democrat-run U.S. Senate passed a version comparable to the Obama request in 2013, but the Republican-run House of Representatives favored an alternative known as the Supporting Knowledge and Investing in Lifelong Skills Act (SKILLS) of 2013, which would have reduced workforce development funding by $1 billion.[64] A stalemate over social policies in general claimed both approaches as victims. Regardless of which version might ever pass, even the most generous would represent reduced funding at a time of record long-term unemployment.

Post-Secondary Education

Upgraded education is considered by many as the best way to meet the needs of the 21st-century economy because the required skill sets today are so different from those used in the past. A half century ago, a high school diploma opened doors to a range of upwardly mobile employment opportunities. Today, high school graduates have relatively few job prospects other than menial positions that offer little compensation and limited chances for advancement.

That takes us to the issue of university graduates. The U.S. education system has not produced enough college graduates to keep up with modern requirements. A 2012 report produced by the Organization for Economic Cooperation and Development (OECD) listed the United States as 14th among 34 industrialized countries in the percentage of college graduates, ages 25–34, slightly above average but well behind countries including Korea, Japan, and the Russian Federation.[65] Perhaps even more disconcerting in the OECD data was the finding that only 29 percent of young people whose parents lack university educations are likely to graduate from higher education institutions, a percentage that placed the United States 32nd among the 34 nations.[66] Thus, not only is the United States providing inadequate numbers of graduating students from universities, but also the opportunities to graduate are stacked against those from non-university families more than almost anywhere else. This lack of mobility runs smack into the concept of equal opportunity.

Along with the relative dearth of college graduates, those who do complete their educations do not match well with 21st-century needs, resulting in jobs that go wanting and applicants that go without. An examination of the 100 largest metropolitan areas in 2012 by the Brookings Institution found that 39 percent of the advertised job openings required a bachelor's degree or higher, yet only 29 percent of the population possessed such credentials.[67] This disparity not only contributes to long-term unemployment, but also results in employers looking outside the United States for trained labor.

In fact, both sides—would-be employees and employers in search of employees—feel the disconnection. A 2012 study by McKinsey learned that 44 percent of American students believed that their post-secondary educations improved their employment opportunities, yet the same study found that 45 percent of American employers cited skills shortages as a leading reason for entry-level job vacancies.[68] It almost seems that graduates and employers travel in two different worlds! One fact is clear: something is amiss. A study of unemployment during the Great Recession by the Federal Bank of New York estimated that one-third of the unemployment between 2008 and 2010 was due to the mismatch of skill sets between job seekers and employers.[69] Given these data, it's more than reasonable to conclude that the current secondary post-education system is not aligning enough students with 21st-century workforce needs.

Unemployment Insurance

Along with attention to employment training and education, the federal policy makers have had a long-standing commitment to providing unemployment insurance for dislocated workers. The interest emerged in the midst of the Great Depression as part of the Social Security Act of 1935, a massive piece of legislation that became the bulwark of the federal social safety net. Along with the Social Security program, the legislation included assistance for the aged, dependent children of single mothers, and the unemployed, the latter of which was set up under the Federal-State Unemployment Compensation Program. When people found themselves involuntarily out of work, unemployment insurance would provide a small weekly stipend to help them while they searched for, and eventually found, work. The money for payments comes from a trust fund that includes contributions from employers, the states, and the federal government.

Insurance, Not Welfare

It's important to remember that this program in no way constitutes welfare, where people are given something just because they need it. Rather, it's a system to tide people over through payments based on their length of employment. Moreover, unemployment insurance funds tend to average about one-third of what the unemployed would earn if they were working.[70] Clearly, such dependence is an undesirable situation and is designed to be a financial Band-Aid between jobs. During their unemployment, individuals are required to show evidence of employment searches to their state agencies as a condition of maintaining eligibility. According to the U.S. Department of Labor, approximately 97 percent of all wage and salaried workers are eligible.

Unemployment insurance was designed as a temporary fix for members of the workforce, with individuals typically permitted to collect money for up to 26 weeks, although in times of recession Congress has temporarily extended the period of eligibility. The most recent example of extending the eligibility period came during the Great Recession. In 2009, Congress extended unemployment benefits for 99 weeks. In 2012, Congress reduced eligibility to a maximum of 73 weeks, cutting off close to 500,000 people who had been unemployed for longer than that period.[71] In December 2013, the extended benefits expired for 1.3 million long-termed unemployed people, with another 1.7 million long-term unemployed expected within 6 months. President Obama asked Congress to extend the long-term unemployment benefits another 13 weeks, but Congress refused because of the lack of Republican support. As a result, the Center on Budget and Policy Priorities estimated that as many as 5 million newly and long-term unemployed would be denied benefits within 12 months.[72] Those out of the work the longest now find themselves without the benefits of an unemployment safety net. Meanwhile, a 2014 study of long-term unemployed workers found that of those out of work for 8 months or more, only 4 percent of job applicants were offered job interviews.[73] For many, the once touted safety net is no longer available.

Leaving the Workers Behind

How do we explain the drastic reduction in unemployment benefits for those who needed them the most? Some opponents such as Republican Speaker of the House John Boehner expressed a willingness to extend benefits if Congress would cut federal spending elsewhere—virtually impossible, given the dramatic reductions in spending because of sequestration. Others, such as Republican Senator Rand Paul, were direct in their equating long-term unemployment insurance with the inability of people to find work: "The longer you have it [unemployment insurance], that it does provide some disincentive to work," he said.[74] Absent from his assessment was the fact that there were 2.9 unemployed workers for every one job opening.

Unemployment insurance is a valuable component for propping up those who lose their jobs. But insurance alone is not enough. The only way to deal with long-term unemployment is for government to provide retraining programs. Yet, as noted above, Congress has been unwilling to make the investment. So, the takeaway is as follows: long-term unemployment persists in an environment with mismatched education and no government training. Meanwhile, the long-term unemployed pay the price for the inability or unwillingness of national policy makers to address the issue.

A GAP THAT MUST BE BRIDGED

When it comes to employment, American society is traveling in two radically different directions. Those at or near the top of the economic ladder are doing just fine, thank you. They were excelling before the Great Recession, and have been soaring even more since recovery from the Great Recession. Over time, this elite group has pulled far away from the rest of us in their ability to gain wealth and success. But they are the few among the many.

Many others, however, have struggled in the workplace, some more, some less. Large proportions of women, minorities, the young, and the old have not succeeded in the world of employment as have others. Some lack equal pay to others in spite of their competitive credentials. Others are overqualified for jobs they clutch until they can find something that fits closer to their skill sets. Others still have not been able to obtain the training they need in the 21st-century economy. The stories are different, but the unemployed and underemployed share space on the crowded bottom rungs of the economic ladder. Most at risk are those who have been separated from work for long periods; not only have they lost the contentment, dignity, and self-respect associated with work, but also they have suffered financially, accented with losing paltry unemployment benefits.

There are remedies for these tragedies, but they come at a price in the short term, although they pay off handsomely in the long term with respect to better jobs, more taxes, less unemployment, and a more content society. Nevertheless, we seem to be moving in the opposite direction from providing the resources necessary to help society thrive. Today our K–12 education system is losing millions of students before they even graduate high school, an obvious precursor to unemployment. Our production of college graduates is behind the rates of other nations, leaving those nations in the enviable situation of producing better-trained workforces.

Increasingly in the United States, we see a mismatch between unemployed workers and available jobs. Such a situation could readily be addressed through retraining programs, but federal government spending cutbacks have all but eliminated those funds as part of the effort to balance annual budgets. This new approach, the idea of letting those searching for employment fend for themselves, represents a dramatic departure from previous eras. Past government responses in the forms of workforce investment programs are now distant memories, despite their successes. Thus, we find ourselves with a 20th-century mentality in a 21st-century global economy—a condition that leaves larges numbers outside looking in as the country falls behind to other nations.

Many of those who are fortunate to have escaped unemployment or underemployment see no reason to spend precious resources such as education and employment training. There is no such need in *their* world; they already have what they need. But their world is a world of illusion and self-deception. The data point to increasingly large numbers of society who want to be meaningful participants, yet are ill-equipped to contribute. Their resentment of the other world will only grow over time, not necessarily because of jealousy, but because of their lack of life chances to succeed. That condition will be harmful to us all in the long run unless it is addressed.

ENDNOTES

1. Daniel P. Boorstin, *The Genius of American Politics*, Chicago: University of Chicago Press, 1953, p. 25.
2. Thomas Sowell, *Economic Facts and Fallacies*, New York: Basic Books, 2008, p. 129.
3. Ibid., pp. 129–131.
4. Lawrence Mishel, Josh Bivens, Elise Gould, and Heidi Shierholz, *The State of Working America*, 12th ed., Ithaca, NY: Cornell University Press, 2012, p. 444.
5. President Barack Obama, State of the Union Address, January 23, 2013.
6. Fareed Zakaria discusses this point and its consequences in his *The Post-American World*, New York: W.W. Norton, 2008, p. 185.
7. See Suzanne Berger, *How We Compete*, New York: Doubleday, 2005, pp. 113–120.
8. "CEO Pay 231 Times Greater than the Average Worker," Economic Policy Institute, May 3, 2012, http://www.epi.org/publication/ceo-pay-231-times-greater-average-worker/.
9. Ibid.
10. "CEO vs. Worker Pay: Walmart, McDonald's, and Eight Other Firms with the Biggest Gaps," *Christian Science Monitor*, December 12, 2013, http://www.csmonitor.com/layout/set/print/Business/2013/1212/CEO-vs.-worker-pay-Walmart-McDonald-s-and-eight-other-firms-with-biggest-gaps/AT-T.
11. "Proposal to Raise Tip Wages Resisted," *New York Times*, January 27, 2014, pp. B1, B2.
12. Craig K. Elwell, "Inflation and the Real Minimum Wage: A Fact Sheet," Report R42973, Congressional Research Service, Washington, DC, September 12, 2013, p. 1.
13. "One Version of the [U.S.] Federal Poverty Measure," Department of Health and Human Services, January 26, 2012, http://aspe.hhs.gov/poverty/12poverty.shtml.

14. "The Low-Wage Recovery and Growing Inequality," Data Brief, National Employment Law Project, August 2012, http://www.nelp.org/page/-/Job_Creation/LowWageRecovery2012.pdf?nocdn=1.
15. "Wage Divide Grows Wider," *Wall Street Journal*, April 18, 2012, p. A2.
16. "Low-Paying Jobs Are Here to Stay," CNN Money, August 2, 2012, http://money.cnn.com/2012/08/02/news/economy/low-pay-jobs/index.htm.
17. "Companies Ramp Up Fight against $10.10 Minimum Wage," CNN Money, May 6, 2014, http://money.cnn.com/2014/05/06/news/economy/companies-against-minimum-wage/.
18. For an in-depth study of the issue, see Raymond F. Gregory, *Women and Workplace Discrimination: Overcoming Barriers to Gender Equality*, New Brunswick, NJ: Rutgers University Press, 2003.
19. "The 23 Female CEOs Running Fortune 500 Companies," *San Jose Mercury News*, December 10, 2013, http://www.mercurynews.com/business/ci_24696574/23-female-ceos-running-fortune-500-companies.
20. "Still Few Women in Management, Report Says," *New York Times*, September 27, 2010, http://www.nytimes.com/2010/09/28/business/28gender.html?_r=0&pagewanted=print.
21. "Women in Management: An Analysis of Female Managers' Representation, Characteristics, and Pay," GAO-10-892R, Government Accounting Office, September 20, 2010.
22. "Characteristics of Minimum Wage Workers: 2012," U.S. Department of Labor, http://www.bls.gov/cps/minwage2012.htm.
23. "Women at Work," Bureau of Labor Statistics, March 2011, http://www.bls.gov/spotlight/2011/women/.
24. "Government Job Losses Hit the Young, the Less Educated, and Women the Hardest," The Urban Institute, February 23, 2013, http://www.urban.org/publications/ 412756.html.
25. See Francine Blau and Lawrence Khan, "The Gender Pay Gap: Have Women Gone as Far as They Can?" *Academy of Management*, 21(1), 7–23, 2007.
26. "U.S. Commission on Civil Rights," in Paula S. Rothenberg, ed., *Race, Class and Gender in the United States*, 8th ed., New York: Worth Publishers, 2010, p. 249.
27. Bureau of Labor Statistics, "Employment Status of the Civilian Population by Race, Sex, and Age," January 10, 2014, Tables A-2 and A-3, http://www.bls.gov/news.release/empsit.t03.htm.
28. Bureau of Labor Statistics, "Unemployment Rates by Race and Ethnicity, 2010," October 5, 2011, http://www.bls.gov/opub/ted/2011/ted_20111005.htm.
29. "Whiter Jobs, Higher Wages," Briefing Paper 288, Economic Policy Institute, Washington, DC, February 28, 2011, p. 2.
30. Anthony P. Carnevale, Stephen J. Rose, and Ben Cheah, "The College Payoff," Center on Education and the Workforce, Georgetown University, Washington, DC, August 5, 2011, p. 14.
31. Sarah Jane Glynn and Jane Farrell, "Latinos Least Likely to Have Paid Leave or Workplace Flexibility," Center for American Progress, Washington, DC, November 20, 2012, p. 2.
32. "In U.S., Fewer Young Adults Holding Full-Time Jobs in 2013," Gallup, July 26, 2013, http://www.gallup.com/poll/163727/fewer-young-adults-holding-full-time-jobs-2013.aspx?version=print.
33. "Average Student Loan Debt: $29,400," CNN Money, December 4, 2013, http://money.cnn.com/2013/12/04/pf/college/student-loan-debt/.

34. Sarah Ayers, "The High Cost of Unemployment," Center for American Progress, Washington, DC, April 5, 2013, p. 2.
35. Richard Fry, "A Rising Share of Young Adults Live in Their Parents' Home," Pew Research Center, Washington, DC, August 1, 2013, p. 3.
36. "Young, Underemployed and Optimistic," Pew Research Center, Washington, DC, February 9, 2012, p. 12.
37. Edward P. Glaeser, "Goodbye Golden Years," *New York Times*, November 20, 2011, pp. SR1, SR6.
38. See "Older Workers in U.S. Drive Competition in Labor Market," Bloomberg.com, June 26, 2012, http://www.bloomberg.com/news/2012-06-27/older-workers-in-u-s-drive-competition-in-labor-market.html.
39. Ibid.
40. "Changing Expectations about Retirement," 2013 RCS Fact Sheet 2, Economics Benefits Research Institute, Washington, DC, 2013.
41. "In U.S., Fewer Young Adults Holding Full-Time Jobs in 2013," op. cit.
42. Polly Callaghan and Heidi Hartmann, "Contingent Work," Economic Policy Institute, Washington, DC, 1991, p. 9.
43. "For Millions, Part-Time Work Is Full-Time Wait for a Better Job," *New York Times*, April 20, 2113, pp. A1, B6.
44. This point comes from Rob Valletta and Leila Bengali, "What's Behind the Increase in Part-Time Work," FRBSF Economic Letter, Federal Reserve Bank of San Francisco, August 8, 2013, pp. 4–5.
45. Rebecca Glauber, *Wanting More but Working Less: Involuntary Part-Time Employment and Economic Vulnerability*, Issue Brief 64, Carsey Institute, University of New Hampshire, Durham, Summer 2013, p. 3.
46. "Factory Overtime Cranks Up," *Wall Street Journal*, April 19, 2013, p. A2.
47. "How to Use Overtime," *Industry Week*, April 12, 2011, http://www.industryweek.com/articles/how_to_use_overtime_24356.aspx.
48. John R. Brandt, "Too Much Overtime," August 12, 2012, MPI Group, Shaker Heights, OH, http://www.nextgenerationmanufacturing.com/2012/08/15/too-much-overtime-3/.
49. "More American Workers Sue Employers for Overtime Pay," *USA Today*, April 19, 2012, http://usatoday30.usatoday.com/money/jobcenter/workplace/story/ 2012-04-15/ workers-sue-unpaid-overtime/54301774/1.
50. Richard Florida, "A Blueprint for a 21st Century Workforce," *The Atlantic Cities*, February 17, 2012, http://www.theatlanticcities.com/jobs-and-economy/2012/02/blueprint-good-21st-century-job/1214/.
51. "2012 Talent Shortage Survey Research Results," Manpower Group, Milwaukee, WI, 2012, p. 13.
52. Ibid., p. 14.
53. Peter Cappelli, *Why Good People Can't Get Good Jobs*, Philadelphia, PA: Wharton Digital Press, 2012, pp. 69–71.
54. Ibid., and "Business Roundtable 2011 CEO Economic Outlook Survey," Fourth Quarter, December 2011, http://businessroundtable.org/resources/ceo-survey/2011-Q4.
55. "Survey Reveals Potential Innovation Gap in the U.S.," MIT University, Cambridge, MA, January 11, 2011, http://web.mit.edu/newsoffice/2011/lemelson-invention-index.html.
56. "Country Note, Programme for International Student Assessment (PISA), Results from PISA 2012," Organizational for Economic Cooperation and Development, Paris, http://www.oecd.org/pisa/.

57. "So many U.S. Manufacturing Jobs, So Few Skilled Workers," Reuters, October 13, 2011, http://www.reuters.com/article/2011/10/13/usa-economy-jobs-idUSN1E79B 23O20111013.
58. "The Condition of College & Career Readiness, 2013," American College of Thessaloniki (ACT), Boston, http://www.act.org/research/policymakers/cccr13/pdf/ CCCR13-NationalReadinessRpt.pdf.
59. "The 'Plain English' Version of the Workforce Investment Act of 1998," U.S. Department of Labor, Washington, DC, September 1998, p. 1, http://www.doleta. gov/usworkforce/wia/Runningtext.cfm.
60. "Workforce Investment Act—Adults and Dislocated Workers Program," U.S. Department of Labor, Washington, DC, November 4, 2010, p. 1, http://www.doleta. gov/programs/general_info.cfm.
61. "Funds to Train Joblessness in U.S. Are Drying Up," *New York Times*, April 9, 2012, pp. A1, A13.
62. "U.S. Faces Uphill Battle in Retraining the Jobless," *Wall Street Journal*, August 1, 2012, pp. A1, A6.
63. Ibid.
64. "Side-by-Side Comparison of Current Law, House and Senate Legislation to Reauthorize the Workforce Investment Act," National Skills Coalition, September 2013, http://www.nationalskillscoalition.org/federal-policies/workforce-investment-act/wia-documents/2013-09-16_wia-house-senate.pdf.
65. "Education at a Glance: OECD Indicators 2012," Organization for Economic Cooperation and Development, September 12, 2012, p. 2, www.oecd.org/eag2012.
66. Ibid., p. 3.
67. Jonathan Rothwell, "Education, Job Openings and Unemployment in Metropolitan America," Brookings Institution, Washington, DC, August 2012, p. 9.
68. Mona Mourshed, Diana Farrell, and Dominic Barton, "Education to Employment: Designing a System That Works," McKinsey Center for Government, 2012, p. 15, http://mckinseyonsociety.com/downloads/reports/Education/Education-to-Employment_FINAL.pdf.
69. Atsegul Sahnin, Joseph Song, Giorgio Tapa, and Giovanni L. Violante, "Mismatch Unemployment," Federal Reserve Bank of New York, August 2012, no. 566, p. 36.
70. "Can You Live on $330 a Week?" MSN.Money, February 18, 2011, http://money.msn. com/how-to-budget/can-you-live-on-330-a-week-mainstreet.aspx.
71. "U.S. Winds Down Longer Benefits for the Unemployed," *New York Times*, May 28, 2012, http://www.nytimes.com/2012/05/29/business/economy/extended-federal-unemployment-benefits-begin-to-wind-down.html?pagewanted=all&_r=0&pagewanted=print.
72. Chad Stone, "Failure to Extend Emergency Unemployment Benefits Will Hurt Jobless Workers in Every State; Nearly 5 million Expect to Lose Out on Benefits in Next 12 Months," Center on Budget and Policy Priorities, Washington, DC, December 11, 2013, http://www.cbpp.org/cms/?fa=view&id=4060.
73. "Big Business Joins Obama Effort to Aid Long-Term Unemployed," *New York Times*, February 1, 2014, p. A10.
74. "Rand Paul Pooh-Poohs Unemployment Benefits," *Huffington Post*, January 5, 2014, http://www.huffingtonpost.com/2014/01/05/rand-paul-unemployment-benefits_n_4545033. html.

8

The Struggle for Corporate Inclusion

American corporations are complex enterprises. Operating in a hierarchical, yet coordinated managerial fashion, corporations hire people to perform a wide range of tasks to meet their varied needs. In turn, the employees of corporations use their salaries from their work for life's necessities. Because of their large sizes and access to capital, corporations "can undertake tasks beyond the reach of any single person."[1] Whether searching out raw materials, manufacturing products, or selling services, corporations collectively constitute America's economic engine.

Historically, American corporations and employees have relied upon each other to fulfill the corporation's objectives, which provided numerous private and public benefits. Unlike other nations, most have operated in the true spirit of capitalism, mining basically cooperative arrangements with few government constraints, ownership, or control.[2] This is not to say there haven't been moments of tension. The rise of the union movement added a new ingredient to the corporation-worker relationship, bringing about more than a little friction at times,[3] but the two sides have come to terms with this evolution over time. For the most part, the key to success has come with the value of the partnership. As early industrialist Henry Ford once said, "Coming together is a beginning; keeping together is progress; working together is success."

Some American corporation-employee relationships have been model pacts where each side has helped the other in good times and bad; layoffs have been at a minimum, and employee departures for other employment have been rare. In these arrangements, healthy corporate revenues have often resulted in profit-sharing programs, pension contributions, or other generous employee benefit programs. These arrangements have lived up to Ford's admonition of a win-win bond.

Other corporation-employee relationships have operated under contentious conditions because of mutual distrust and conflicting objectives. Unrealistic employer expectations, the threats of unions serving as feisty bargaining agents, disputes over salaries, and other areas of difference have contributed to a poisoned workplace environment underscored by scorched contempt.

In recent years, increasing numbers of corporations have moved much further away from Ford's dream. With the onset of globalization, they have become much more nimble enterprises, extending their workforce supply chain to locations far from the United States in the name of greater efficiency, reduced costs, and higher profits.[4] On the other side, employees have lost their affinity for the corporate "family" because of either management demands for salary and benefits concessions, unrealistic productivity requirements, or worse yet, jobs lost to outsourced workers willing to work for less.

The once tightly sown corporate management-employee fabric has frayed greatly in recent years. The ripple effects from this new dysfunctional arrangement have pierced the fabric of American society, signaling an end to a once sacred bond. In addition, corporate participation in the U.S. tax structure has declined greatly in the name of greater profits, giving further evidence of an ugly separation of business from American society. All of this has cast a pall on the great American corporation, which was once viewed as the bulwark of American capitalism for forging basically pleasant relationships between corporations and employees.

These changes have not gone without notice. Over time, a few layers of federal bureaucracy have touched the edges of modern corporations and the capitalist framework. The Securities and Exchange Commission regulates markets and portions of the financial industry; the Food and Drug Administration oversees elements of agriculture, the food supply, and pharmaceutical operations; and the National Labor Relations Board watches over delicate conditions between businesses and workers. There are other government agencies too, although any rarely make anything but the most superficial adjustments to the status quo. In fact, the only real potential menace has been the threat from organized labor, which has led the struggle for altering the corporation-worker dynamic. But in recent years, unions have lost much of their punch in the private sector, while managing some gains in the public sector. Today, only about 11 percent of the American workforce belongs to labor unions.[5]

Simply put, American corporations have been left largely alone by government to function as they see best and on their terms. But doing their best more than ever means primarily providing corporate benefits for the shareholders, often at the expense of the employee or government revenues. This change has not gone without notice. In a national survey conducted for the McClatchy newspapers in 2014, 75 percent of the respondents agreed that "U.S. corporations make their stockholders their top priority, over their employees," compared with 22 percent who believed otherwise.[6]

This evolution has been in the works for decades. For example, corporations have been left to define their share of taxes, thanks to their ability to keep billions of dollars offshore courtesy of federal tax loopholes. They have been free to reduce employee benefits through less rewarding pension plans. And in recent years, the most egregious corporate behavior has emerged with the dismissal of American workers in favor of workforces abroad, even as they expect American citizens to buy their foreign-made products and the American government to subsidize their research. Corporate America has become a one-way street with everyone else left behind in the name of profits for shareholders and just about nothing for anyone else.

This chapter focuses on the evolution of the modern American corporation and the increasing burdens endured by American society. Corporations have succeeded by minimizing the salaries and benefits of their employees, rather than working in partnership with them. They are American only when it comes to receiving tax breaks and subsidies; otherwise, they are allegiant only to the countries that provide the cheapest labor or best tax breaks. Their calls for better-trained American workers fail to mesh with their giddiness from relying upon foreign workers at a fraction of those costs, irrespective of working conditions or the repressive governments where they do business.

Ironically, at a time when millions of Americans are denied in their searches for work and better-paying jobs, American corporate profits are riding at record highs, often on the backs of underpaid foreign workers. Henry Ford's somewhat utopian 20th-century dream has deteriorated into a 21st-century nightmare, and with that decay, so have gone the dreams of millions of American workers.

LOYALTY TO SHAREHOLDERS FIRST, NATION LAST

Few Americans would begrudge any business making a profit, for profits are the gateway to shareholder satisfaction, employee paychecks, and most of all, a robust economy from which almost everyone benefits. Profits also pave the way for the payment of taxes that support government activities, programs, and services. For most of us, taxes are a given. So when Benjamin Franklin once wrote that "nothing is certain except death and taxes," he was referring to the inevitable relationship between the inflow of private sector taxes and the outflow of government arrangements for the public good.

Franklin's commonsense observation notwithstanding, corporate America has found ways to negate the financial obligation component of his truism. While the corporate adeptness to avoid taxes may bring smiles to managers and shareholders, such avoidance does a great disservice to the government's ability to the meet the nation's needs, while adding to unbalanced federal budgets. Furthermore, corporate abandonment of tax responsibility increases the burdens of those already paying into the revenue pot. This circumvention underscores a one-sided equation: corporate ability to benefit from government policies while giving back precious little in return to society.

Nor have corporations shared with their employees the money they might have paid in taxes. In 2012, roaring corporate profits comprised 14.2 percent of the entire national income, which represented the highest percentage since 1960. At the same time, 61.7 percent of total corporate income was set aside for employees, the lowest since 1966.[7] Defenders would view this combination as the ultimate formula for success: fewer, poorly compensated employees and minimal taxes equal higher profits. This helps to explain why corporate America is doing so well; it also explains why so many other Americans are not.

American in Name Only

These days it's hard to know just how much of America is in an American corporation. That's because increasingly, American corporations are turning abroad for various combinations of research and development, production, manufacturing, and services. As such, they are becoming multinational to the extent that large percentages of their products for sale in the United States are actually produced on foreign shores. There are two prominent elements of this phenomenon: the outsourcing of labor as a means of reducing costs and the loss of quality control. Both have profound consequences for American society, although neither seems to draw the concern of many corporations.

Outsourcing Labor

American corporations have become quite adept at investing abroad, more so than any other country. Moreover, the money American corporations spend abroad more than offsets foreign investments here. During the decade between 2004 and 2013, U.S. corporations spent more than all foreign investments in the United States in 9 of the 10 years. And the gap is substantial more times than not. During 2013 alone, U.S. corporate spending abroad topped $358 billion, more than twice the amount that flowed from foreign corporations to America.[8] About half of all U.S investments go to Europe, with most of the rest landing in Asia and Latin America. Regardless, it leaves here and goes elsewhere, building factories and hiring workers in the process.

Much of the investments by American companies have come in the form of offshore employment. As of 2011, they employed 22.8 million people abroad.[9] That amount is equal to a sizable percentage of the U.S. labor force, which stood at 155,460,000, with 10,236,000 unemployed in January 2014.[10] Now the offshore picture begins to become a bit more interesting. At the same time that more than 10 million Americans are unemployed, U.S. companies have twice that number on their payrolls abroad. Does that mean that U.S. unemployment could be wiped out if American companies made all of their hires at home? Of course not. Some jobs must be overseas for all kinds of logistical reasons, such as the presence of a sales force; in addition, not all specialized labor can be easily replicated. Still, even allowing some on-site foreign employment and specialization, the numbers of offshore jobs seem rather large. One only wonders how many of those jobs could be put to use on American soil.

It's difficult to capture the entire picture of offshore American corporate investments. American companies are rather quiet about their ventures abroad. After all, such information is not welcome as domestic news, especially when times are tough and when the same companies often ask for government assistance for "hardships" associated with doing business at home. Nevertheless, there are data, even if incomplete. For example, the U.S. Bureau of Economic Analysis found that in 2010, U.S.-owned multinationals grew their payrolls abroad by 1.5 percent, while adding just 0.1 percent of their new jobs at home. The same study showed that the percentage of Americans working for American corporations slipped from 79 percent of the overall workforce in 1989 to 67.7 percent in 2010.[11] Another examination of the 35 largest American corporations in 2012 by the *Wall Street Journal* found that they added 113,000 jobs domestically between 2009 and 2011, while increasing 333,000 jobs abroad during the same period.[12] In one case, Minnesota-based 3M Corporation grew to 87,677 employees in 2012 from 76,239 just 5 years earlier; of the 11,438 new positions, 10,830 were added overseas.[13] Offshore employment has taken its toll on the American workforce.

American multinationals are not shy about setting up shop where they get the best deals. For most involved with manufacturing, the biggest cost is labor. For the longest time, China was the country of choice because of an abundant labor force at a fraction of U.S. costs. But as the cost of Chinese labor has increased, companies have shifted to facilities in Thailand, Sri Lanka, and Indonesia—any place where the labor is cheap and the quality meets company standards.[14] Recently, several American companies have moved production to Mexico, which also has abundant labor at prices equal to or even below those of Asian companies. With a location close to the United States, Mexico has become the new factory of choice for American companies. More than 100,000 auto-related jobs have been located there since 2010, and American companies Ford and General Motors promise tens of thousands more in the near future.[15]

Sometimes, American corporations will hire third-party companies to manufacture their products. From a public relations perspective, this can be beneficial inasmuch as the American company is at an arm's length from pay, working conditions, housing arrangements, environmental degradation, and other negatives potentially harmful to the corporate citizen image. Walmart, Gap, Disney, and Nike are among the huge American corporations that have set up shop in Asia through foreign companies. They have attempted to inoculate themselves from criticism by hiring inspectors to check quality, working conditions, and building safety. Yet, studies show that the auditors are frequently poorly trained, misled by factory owners who subcontract, and given inadequate time to carry out their tasks. In other words, much of their work is superficial.[16] In 2013, after a fire swept through a Bangladesh factory that left more than 400 workers dead, Tommy Hilfiger and Calvin Klein, 2 of the 30 tenants, promised to support more rigorous worker and building safety as a condition of their occupancy, but Walmart and Gap resisted any formal agreement, lest they face legal consequences (and rising costs).[17] Arm's length or not, the arrangements of American companies abroad are fairly transparent in their lack of concern for anything but quality products at the lowest possible cost.

Apple stands out as the poster child for hiring third-party manufacturers. As of 2012, the company employed 63,000 workers on its payroll, 20,000 of whom worked overseas. But most of Apple's production has been provided by Foxconn, an independent Taiwanese corporation with factories throughout Asia. At the Foxconn facilities in China, as of 2012, nearly a quarter million employees lived in company villages, worked 12-hour days 6 days a week, and earned an average of less than $17 per day. Together, this massive workforce manufactures millions of iPhones and other "i" products, generating huge profits for Apple. The irony is that it wouldn't cost Apple that much more for those jobs to be in the United States. Studies by several academics and manufacturing experts in 2012 calculated that American labor would add no more than $65 per iPhone—a relatively small amount of money per unit in exchange for tens of thousands of Americans employed in manufacturing jobs.[18] That kind of job placement would barely make a dent in Apple's corporate profit structure, given that during fiscal 2013 alone, the corporation earned $37 billion in profits on revenues of $171 billion.[19] But bearing in mind the importance of the bottom line, Apple has kept almost all its production in China.

With all of the outsourcing, you might think that the international corporate shuffling stemmed from a troubled economy with weak corporate profits. Hardly. American corporations emerged from the Great Recession in great shape, contrary to the condition of the American workforce. In 2010, while U.S. unemployment remained at a stubbornly high 9.8 percent, all but 4 percent of the largest 500 corporations reported profits.[20] Given that salaries amount to 70 percent of the typical corporation's operating costs, we can see how companies have managed to be so profitable in good times and bad.

Uneven Quality Control

When U.S. corporations rely upon foreign companies to manufacture their products, they save money and earn higher profits for their offshore procurements, both of which are well received by investors and consumers. The financial trade-off, of course, comes in the form of reduced American manufacturing jobs because of low-wage costs abroad. Lost American jobs notwithstanding, a danger emerges because of the loss of the corporation's ability to control the quality of the products. In turn, that problem can cost the corporation money and jeopardize the lives of consumers. Below we focus on pharmaceuticals, automobile parts, and airplane maintenance as examples of poor quality control.

Pharmaceuticals

We begin with the beleaguered pharmaceutical industry. The supply chain for pharmaceuticals is long and convoluted, with products traveling through the hands of several producers along the way. The problem is that the geography with respect to production has been changing dramatically in recent years. Particularly since the beginning of the 21st century, American pharmaceutical companies have relied increasingly on foreign imports. Today, close to half of all finished drugs for U.S. consumption are produced abroad, with two-thirds of the manufacturing coming from India and China. In all, 80 percent of the ingredients in U.S.-manufactured drugs are actually created in other countries, although they are inside the packages of an American company.[21]

The unreliable supply chain has become a cause of great concern to the U.S. government. The U.S. Food and Drug Administration (FDA) has responsibility for overseeing pharmaceutical quality, but its annual inspection abilities are limited abroad to only a few dozen of the thousands of manufacturing plants because of limited resources.[22] Whereas U.S.-based facilities are inspected on an average of once every 2.5 years, foreign inspections occur on an average of once every 11 years, with Indian and Chinese suppliers receiving U.S. inspectors every 14 years![23] Moreover, a Government Accounting Office report found that when FDA inspectors gain access to foreign facilities, the inspections are often incomplete because of government interference, the lack of attention to original materials before they are processed, and the ability of foreign firms to cover up any issues because of advance inspection notice.[24] This inattention leads foreign sites to refrain from observing quality measures and replace called-for ingredients with cheaper or dangerous substitutes.[25]

The upswing in drug imports correlates with an increase in drug recalls by the FDA. Between 2006 and 2009, the number of recalls swelled from 384 to 1,742, an increase of 309 percent.[26] One independent source determined at least 165 of the recalls for a single year were from foreign sources, up 158 percent from the previous year.[27] The list goes on. In 2012, an Indian firm had a cholesterol drug recalled because of glass particles in the medication, and paid a $500 million fine for its sloppy manufacturing processes. Previously, the company had been banned from manufacturing U.S. drugs for its refusal to adhere to U.S. standards.[28] In 2013, a German company incurred a drug medication recall because of glass particles in its intravenous vials.[29] Under pressure to better manage the dissemination of pharmaceuticals, in 2013 Congress passed the Drug Quality and Security Act. The legislation addressed compounding practices, product reporting, the drug supply chain, and labeling, and the new law directed unannounced future visits to U.S.-produced drugs.

Note the emphasis on *U.S.-produced* drugs. The new law has done virtually nothing to change the haphazard and unsupervised conditions of foreign pharmaceutical manufacturing practices. In 2014, FDA Commissioner Margaret Hamburg became so concerned over the quality of Indian drugs exported to the United States that she traveled to India to express her displeasure about "recent lapses in the quality" of Indian drugs. She had good reason for her apprehension. The World Health Organization estimated in 2013 that 20 percent of the drugs coming out of India were counterfeit—reason for more than a little worry given that India provides 40 percent of the prescription drugs consumed in the United States. Meanwhile, India's drug regulating authority, the equivalent of the FDA, has 323 enforcement agents, 2 percent of the size of the number at the FDA in a country with more than three times the size of the population. Moreover, rather than cooperate, India's top drug regulator cautioned visiting FDA officials of "overregulation."[30] Nevertheless, U.S. companies continue to import bad drugs. After all, the price is right.

Counterfeit Automobile Parts

Check out the goods at almost any flea market on a given day and you will likely find what appear to be high-end, name brand hand bags, clothing items, automobile tools, and even machinery for a fraction of what you would expect to pay at a retail outlet. That's because in all likelihood, the flea market products are imitation or counterfeit "knockoffs." Some shoppers are fooled by the switch. Many others are aware of the distinction by the enormous price break alone, yet they are willing to go along with the charade for their own reasons. In the end, little harm occurs other than to the name brand store that has lost a sale or the reputation of the company, both of which are unfortunate in their own right. But counterfeit parts for moving machinery such as automobiles pose problems beyond style and appearances; indeed, counterfeit auto parts can be the cause of terrible tragedies, including deaths. These days, virtually no one is immune to the chicanery. Even the Department of Defense has been victimized repeatedly by counterfeit parts for automobiles as well as countless military components.[31]

The counterfeit auto parts business is thriving. A report in 2011 calculated that counterfeit auto parts generated $45 billion in business worldwide, nearly quadruple the amount in 2008.[32] More than $3 billion worth of counterfeit parts is sold in the United States alone each year. A 2007 report by the Ford Motor Company estimated that counterfeit parts cost the company $1 billion annually.[33] In 2013, federal law enforcement agencies and customs officials seized 50,000 ACDelco parts, including oil filters, gaskets, sparkplug wire sets, and windshields, in Saudi Arabia—all falsely packaged as original equipment—just before they were about to be distributed throughout Europe and the United States.[34] During the same year, the FBI arrested three people in New York for selling counterfeit auto parts, including brakes, brake pads, and antilock braking sensors, that were packaged as original Ford Motor Company and General Motors equipment.[35]

Most of the counterfeit parts come from China, but other culprits include Taiwan, Malaysia, and Thailand. One recent investigation found 15,000 nonregistered automotive component manufacturers interspersed with 10,000 legal manufacturers, a government regulator's nightmare. The fractured industry makes it difficult to know which parts makers are complying with American standards. Nevertheless, despite the problems of separating legitimate parts makers from illegitimate parts makers, American car companies have increased their commitments to foreign products because of their low prices. By 2010, GM and Ford alone were purchasers of $10 billion and $7 billion worth of auto parts and accessories annually from Chinese companies.[36]

In addition to costing American jobs, counterfeit auto parts can cost American lives. In 2012, the U.S. Immigration and Customs Enforcement seized more than 2,500 counterfeit air bags, the devices that blow up upon collision to protect passengers' lives. After the seizure, 10 were tested and all failed. Some failed to inflate, others inflated partially, and one exploded with metal shrapnel. The Immigration and Customs Enforcement director concluded, "These airbags don't work. They are not going to save you in an accident,"[37] yet no one knows how many have been inserted in cars by repair shops.

Clearly, there are great gaps in the quality of auto parts that come to the United States from abroad. Questionable quality control and a flood of counterfeit products blend with legitimate imports, with few purchasers the wiser. Yet, given the bargains perceived by American auto companies and repair centers, they see little reason to refrain from doing business.

Overseas Airplane Maintenance

One day in 2009, a U.S. Airways flight suddenly suffered a rupture in the pressure seal of the aircraft's main cabin door. The gash forced the pilot to make an emergency landing. Weeks before, the plane had been overhauled at a maintenance company in El Salvador by mechanics who had incorrectly installed a key part of the door.[38] There was nothing unusual about the maintenance facility. Like so many others, it operated with little expertise. These days, more than 45 percent of all U.S. commercial aircraft are shipped abroad to maintenance, repair, and overhaul (MRO) facilities in El Salvador, Mexico, Dubai, China, Korea, and Singapore. The price tag for such work was $21 billion in 2013, but it would have been much higher had the work been done in the United States. Then again, it would have been much safer, too.

The reason for overseas maintenance is simple enough: money. For example, when the U.S. Airways plane was serviced in El Salvador, mechanics earned between $4,500 and $15,000 per year; meanwhile, the average pay for an American aircraft mechanic at the time was $52,000 per year.[39] That's quite a difference in an industry known for high costs and low profit margins. Nevertheless, since the troubled travel days after the 9/11 attacks, five of the six largest U.S. airline companies have increased outsourcing dramatically to reduce their costs. In the process, they have laid off 25,000 U.S.-based aircraft maintenance technicians and mechanics.[40]

Of course, there is nothing wrong with saving money from offshore outsourcing of virtually any repair, assuming that the work performed is equal to that of the mechanics in domestic shops. Two factors leave that assumption in grave doubt. To begin with, offshore sites employ huge numbers of unlicensed aircraft mechanics. A study in 2011 of foreign repair centers found a facility in China with 2,500 unlicensed mechanics who serviced United Airlines jumbo jets under the supervision of five licensed mechanics; that's a ratio of 500 to 1! At an MRO facility in Mexico, 550 unlicensed mechanics serviced Delta MD80s under the supervision of 50 licensed mechanics; this time the ratio was only 11 to 1. In each case, almost all the unlicensed mechanics don't speak or read English, the language of the maintenance manuals. As such, they must rely upon overburdened licensed mechanics to do so, an impossible assignment given the numeric disparities. Those examples are contrasted with the in-house domestic facilities of

American Airlines in Tulsa, Oklahoma, and Fort Worth, Texas, where 1,500 unlicensed mechanics work alongside 5,000 licensed mechanics, a ratio of 1 to 3, and where, of course, English is the spoken and written language.[41]

The second factor centers on inspections. The Federal Aviation Administration (FAA) has responsibility for overseeing the work performed at all maintenance facilities, whether at home or abroad. The problem is the lack of balance in inspection assignments. The FAA uses 4,000 examiners to examine the work at approximately 4,200 MRO repair stations within the United States, but assigns only about 100 to inspect the work at more than 700 MRO facilities overseas. Numerically speaking, that's a ratio of about 1-to-1 inspection assignments at home, but 7 assignments for every inspector abroad in places often far from U.S. shores. Clearly, foreign repair centers are not getting the same attention as domestic facilities.

The irony is that these conditions have been going on for years. In 2003, the Office of the Inspector General of the U.S. Department of Transportation criticized the FAA for lax inspections, especially in overseas repair facilities. The FAA agreed with the bulk of the report and agreed to undertake remedial work to reduce poor maintenance.[42] Yet, a decade later, the Office of the Inspector General found more than half of the work orders contained errors "such as inadequate maintenance procedure training, use of tools with expired calibration tool dates, and inaccurate work order documentation." These problems were particularly the case in overseas maintenance facilities.[43]

The result goes something like this: over the past 15 years, the nation's leading airlines have traded 25,000 in-house competent mechanics for outsourced help. In nearly half of the cases, most of the mechanics work without credentials or supervision. These are the people who service the planes we fly, thanks to the policies of U.S. airline companies. Plainly put, airline companies are unnecessarily putting their passengers in harm's way in the name of the almighty overseas buck.

The High Price for Cheap Work

Everyone likes to keep costs down, because lower costs mean more profitable bottom lines. Still, there's a serious problem when the quality of the material produced abroad does not meet the standard set for it at home, whatever the product may be. Add to that concern the inability of American government to supervise abroad and we have a recipe for potential disaster, with the public—and sometimes the American repair shop or company marketing the product—unaware of the problem.

Cheap work comes at a high price with those Americans who are its victims, as well as those who may become victims. We count on the makers of goods to sell us products that work as intended, not products that fail at our peril. When the link is broken, the legitimacy of the company comes into question. When government institutions ignore their watchdog responsibilities, their legitimacy comes into question. Systemic examples such as those cited above leave Americans disconnected from membership in society, and it's increasingly hard to regain their trust.

The Symbolic Return of Corporate Jobs from Abroad

If nothing else, outsourcing means shifting American jobs abroad. That may be good for companies, but it's bad public relations at home. The substitution is especially awkward in times with a weak economy and high unemployment, as has been demonstrated in the United States until recently. As a result of bad press, some companies have brought back some manufacturing to American shores. Although the effort may look promising at first glance, the jobs are few, the requirements do not always match the available workforce, and the pay is far from what it was before the companies left.

Fewer Workers

According to the U.S. Bureau of Labor Statistics, the U.S. workforce surrendered 6.3 million manufacturing jobs to other nations between 1990 and 2010. But these data tell only part of the story. In fact, manufacturing in the United States has been on the decline for decades. In 1979, 21.6 percent of all U.S. workers held manufacturing jobs; by 2011, only 8.9 percent of American workers were employed in the manufacturing sector.[44] Here's an even longer horizon: in 1953, manufacturing accounted for 28 percent of the U.S. economy.[45] Simply put, the loss of American manufacturing has a history much longer than the economic freefall associated with the Great Recession. Nevertheless, the high unemployment rate during that period was a stark reminder of the new American economy. Recovery of the economy from the Great Recession began in 2009. Since 2010, about 500,000 manufacturing jobs have returned, but thanks to automation and productivity, fewer people are required to do what they used to do.

Of the half million or so recent manufacturing jobs, some have emerged as a result of "reshoring," the return of jobs that had been outsourced by American companies. According to the Reshoring Initiative, between

2009 and 2013, only about 50,000 manufacturing positions were brought back to the United States by companies through this process. Companies that have participated in this employee renewal process include Caterpillar, GE, Ford, Whirlpool, Google, and even Apple.[46] Could this be the beginning of a rebound in American manufacturing with high-paying jobs similar to the past? Not likely.

The reshoring movement is more illusory than reality. True, some companies have brought new manufacturing jobs to the United States, but their numbers are few and reflect little change in their commitments abroad. GE, for example, recently added 5,700 jobs in Louisville, Kentucky, to make refrigerators, washing machines, and other appliances, after removing 15,000 jobs between the 1970s and 2005. But while GE was adding those jobs, it was building plants in China, India, and several other foreign locations. Combined, its plants overseas still produce more than half of GE's revenues.[47] In 2012, Caterpillar opened a new factory in Texas, but had 9 factories under construction in China in addition to the 16 already there.[48] Foreign companies doing business with the United States are operating under the same principle. The list of companies with similar plans is long. In fact, a study of 330 business leaders' future employment plans concluded that reshoring by major manufacturers is symbolic, with few jobs in the offing.[49] The return of manufacturing can only be viewed as a trickle, not a torrent. Still, companies that engage in reshoring give the appearance that they are returning jobs to America.

Enter Automation

Why are there so few new manufacturing jobs in the United States? One reason centers on the move to modern manufacturing processes. With automation and robotics, it takes fewer people to do what many more once did, and they do so at a much lower operating cost. Step-by-step, automation is replacing humans at a bargain basement price. Once installed, robotic technology can pay for itself quickly, while yielding huge savings in labor and productivity.

Consider modern textile plants like Parkdale Mills in South Carolina. With robotic machinery, the plant uses 140 workers to produce 2.5 million pounds of yarn weekly; in 1980, the same production would have required the work of more than 2,000 employees.[50] A few years back, C&S Wholesale Grocers, the nation's largest grocery distributor, invested in a robotic system designed to automatically store and retrieve food items from its huge warehouse. As a result, 106 jobs were eliminated, amounting to 20 percent of the company's workforce.[51]

The nature of the manufacturing workforce has changed too. In 1960, assembly lines operated with manual processes, with employees using their physical abilities to assemble products. Today, fewer numbers of employees are required to manage automated assembly lines. Those who are hired come with more sophisticated skill sets than their predecessors of a generation ago. These days, more than half of U.S. factory workers have some college education, and 1 out of 10 possesses a graduate or professional degree.[52] The point is that jobs are coming back, but fewer than ever because of changes in the production process and changes in the requirements of those operating those processes. The American education and training network is not prepared for these requirements.

Losing Our Role in a Globalized Economy

Given the state of the world's labor force and nimble corporations, manufacturing will only decrease in the coming years. Sure, we'll always find token examples of companies bucking the inexorable trend—companies who have "brought back" jobs few in number and at low pay. These are pale imitations of the jobs we once had. The simple fact is that the world has changed and the American workforce has not changed with it. We're all affected in one way or another, but clearly, those struggling to hang on to blue-collar jobs and finding few of them are those who are losing the most.

LOW SALARIES, DIMINISHED BENEFITS

At the heart of employment lies the issue of employee compensation. As noted above, today's manufacturing employee tends to have a higher skill set because of the requirements of sophisticated equipment. Nevertheless, employee compensation on the whole is *less* today than when large amounts of manufacturing left the United States. It's another example where the corporation and the workforce now travel two distinctly different paths with two different sets of expectations. Still, it's fairly obvious that in the end, the employer has more leverage than the employee.

Lower Salaries

Today's salaries are more stratified than ever. In some cases, the newly hired workers join the "survivors" still on the lines at greatly reduced salaries. With both groups doing the same things, the two-tiered system represents a threat to employee morale. One study by the *New York Times* found that newly hired workers at expanded or new Ford and GE plants are paid $12 to $19 per hour, compared to longtime "legacy" workers who earn $21 to $32 per hour while performing identical tasks. That's a sizable difference over the course of a workweek. GE calls the new salary a competitive wage that allows the United States to compete with production costs in other nations,[53] yet it's questionable whether the company needs to pay such low salaries given its financial successes.

The competitive wage argument is based on the contention that U.S. salary and benefit packages are too high, and therefore uncompetitive in other work settings. As such, the argument goes, they need to be lower so that U.S. companies can compete with the wages paid abroad. In fact, they are not. Production costs are often lower—much lower in the United States—than other nations. As an example, there is the case of the new automobile manufacturing plant built by Volkswagen in Chattanooga, Tennessee, in 2011. The starting wage for assembly workers was $14.50 per hour, less than half of the salary for unionized workers at Ford or GM. More telling, however, was the comparison with automobile manufacturing facilities in Europe. With benefits, the Chattanooga workers received $27, but in Germany employees received $67 per hour from Volkswagen.[54] In other words, the German company opened up a plant in the United States to save money on employee costs.

Other studies suggest that the foreign country advantages related to employment costs in the United States are no longer present, given restructured U.S. wages.[55] To the extent that U.S. corporations are creating new jobs at home, they have done so by paying lower wages and benefits to ensure their profit margins. These jobs hardly represent any victory for the American worker.

Along with low salary schedules, the share of temporary workers in the United States is on the rise. One study shows that 25 percent of the workforce was temporary in 2013, up sharply from 17 percent in 2009.[56] Companies appreciate this arrangement because they can adjust their payrolls with little interference as a way of maintaining profit structures. And with a high number of unemployed people, they know that if a temporary worker quits, there will be many others lining up to take his or her place. Working under such circumstances leaves the temporary employee with little security while enduring an artificially low salary. Once again, the economy may show signs of recovery and even robust growth, but the employee has been left behind.

Diminished Employee Benefits

Members of the 21st-century workforce have fewer benefits today than in the past, causing hardship and straining wallets. Despite record profits, corporations have cut back on retirement plans, sometimes replacing them with less predictable 401(k) programs, and sometimes eliminating retirement plans altogether. With respect to healthcare, the changing landscape created by the Patient Protection and Affordable Care Act in 2010 has provided a path for some companies to reduce the number of work hours. Under the act, workers are considered full-time if they work 30 hours per week or more. By making more workers part-time, employers can avoid participation as health insurance providers. Together, these changes have reduced the quality of life for millions of American workers.

Retirement

When millions of Americans retire from their employment, they do so with the expectation that they will have enough financial resources to live the rest of their lives with some level of comfort. Much of their income will come from company pensions, or so they think. But retirees may not have the financial cushion they expected while working because of corporate neglect and indifference.

Despite sound financial management and generally good, and often record, profits over the past few years, many companies have not contributed enough to their pension programs to keep them fully funded for their future retirees. The funding hole is massive. A study by J.P. Morgan Asset Management in 2013 found a cumulative corporate pension funding deficit of $386 billion that missed the mark by nearly 20 percent. In simple terms, the gap means that for every $100 promised in retirement funds, companies collectively have set aside only $81.[57] That kind of math is not reassuring to the employee about to retire after working in a company for 25 or 30 years. Separate research by Bloomberg shows several leading American companies in deep trouble with pension obligations.

Among those with the most underfunded pension programs were United Technologies, 62 percent; GE, 53 percent; Pfizer, 48 percent; and Dow Chemical, 47 percent.[58] Once again, we find a painful, yet revealing irony: some of the most successful American corporations have not followed through with providing sufficiently for their future retirees.

Another element of the pension debacle focuses on the shift from defined benefit programs to defined contribution programs. With defined benefit programs, corporations commit to providing retirees with formula-based, guaranteed annuities for the rest of their lives. The formulas are typically based on years of service and income. Given this planned commitment, the retiree has a good sense of what to expect every month. The idea stems from the earliest days when corporations and employees displayed loyalty to one another.

With defined contribution programs, corporations typically set aside smaller amounts in the form of matching funds for 401(k) programs, allowing the employee to invest in the plan of his or her choice. With this approach the employer no longer guarantees an income for the retiree. Clearly, corporations save money with 401(k) programs. A survey of the Fortune 100 companies by Workforce in 2012 found 11 percent offering defined benefits packages to new employees, down from nearly 90 percent in 1985.[59] With respect to the workforce, between 1980 and 2008, the proportion of private sector employees with defined benefit plans fell from 38 percent to 20 percent.[60]

There is a cost to the future retiree and a benefit to the corporation from this funding shift. According to a study conducted at the National Bureau of Economic Research, incomes from defined benefits will be considerably more predictable than incomes from defined contributions because of the uncertain nature of investment returns from 401(k) programs and the fact that people are living longer lives today than 20 years ago.[61] With defined benefits, retirement funds flow until the end of life, and that has become an unnecessary corporate cost. With defined contributions, retirement funds flow until the investments run out. After that, the retiree has to worry about replacing a dried-up income stream, and that's pretty difficult, considering that he or she is not the best candidate to return to the workplace. Tellingly, retrenchment in retirement benefits has become a corporate benefit.

Insecure futures after employment have led millions of Americans to reconsider their retirement schedules. A recent study by the Conference Board, a global independent business research organization, found that in 2012, 62 percent of Americans in the workforce planned to delay their retirements. When asked the same question in 2010, only 42 percent planned to postpone their retirements. Among the reasons for deferment, 17 percent—one of every six—specifically cited salary and benefits reductions.[62] Defined contributions may help corporations save money, but they certainly don't serve the needs of their employees.

Healthcare

Healthcare has long been part of the employment benefits mix at major corporations. As of 2011, 52 percent of all businesses with 50 or more employees offered healthcare plans to their employees. The percentage slipped from 59 percent in 2001, no doubt due in part to the upswing of temporary employees who almost always don't qualify for employer-provided healthcare insurance. Employer insurance premiums have skyrocketed over the past few years. Annual premiums more than doubled by 2011 to $5,081 from $2,490 in 2001. During the same period, the average family premium soared even more to $14,447 from $6,415.[63]

The declining number of businesses providing healthcare insurance and growing costs contributed to the demand for the Patient Protection and Affordable Care Act. Under the terms of this legislation, businesses with 50 or more employees will be required to provide health insurance for employees working 30 hours or more per week and their families, and fined if they fail to do so. In addition to availing the health insurance, companies are required to pay a $63 per insured person fee. This has led some large companies to scream "foul," given their current commitments to healthcare costs. Boeing, for example, estimated an additional $25 million in fee-related costs in addition to the $25 billion in health insurance the company already pays for 405,000 employees and dependents, a figure that amounts to an additional one-tenth of 1 percent.[64] Yet, given that Boeing paid no federal taxes between 2002 and 2011 on profits of $35 billion, the concern hardly seemed credible. Clearly, American corporations will not go bankrupt from healthcare cost changes.

Nevertheless, seeking to avoid healthcare costs, some employers are searching for ways to pare down 30-hour weeks for their employees. One study has projected that as many as 2.3 million workers across the nation face the harmful prospect of losing hours as employers adapt to the new healthcare requirements in 2015.[65] Early indications point to fewer hours in low-pay fields such as restaurant workers, grounds keepers, and security guards so that companies can avoid providing health insurance that limits the employee contributions to no more than 9.5 percent.[66] How pervasive this effort will become remains to be seen.

A Bigger Pie with Different Size Slices

Let's put these pieces of the employment puzzle together. For several years, American manufacturers have been earning enormous profits. Much of their success stems from productivity in the manufacturing sector, which increased by 34 percent between 2002 and 2012.[67] That productivity, in turn, stems from fewer employees who get more done while working for less money. Translation: Higher corporate profits emerge from reduced labor costs. The economic pie may be larger today than in the past, but the slices are considerably larger for the corporate sector than those supporting it.

THE GREAT TAX ESCAPE

We turn now to another major reason for massive corporate profits—low taxes. Officially, the U.S. corporate income tax rate of 35 percent stands among the highest corporate tax schedules in the world, if not the highest. Indeed, in recent years, several countries have reduced their corporate tax rates to induce the presence of U.S. companies. But that's only part of the story. Even though the U.S. tax rate for large corporations stands at 35 percent, in fact, few American corporations pay anywhere near that percentage. With little effort, they stockpile most of their profits offshore or benefit from huge tax loopholes dedicated to specific industries. The result is an incredibly low actual tax rate for most, and in some cases, no taxes at all. All this occurs as the rest of us without corporate write-offs struggle to meet our tax obligations, which often are considerably higher in percentages than those of major corporations.

Offshore Storage of Profits

American corporations have become ingenious at storing vast amounts of profits offshore where they pay little or no taxes. In the process, they dramatically reduce their tax obligations at home. These are the same corporations that benefit from government-supported research and development programs, H1-B foreign worker benefits, and the full force of the U.S. government to weigh in when companies elsewhere are charged with intellectual property theft, benefiting from illegal foreign government subsidies, or other nefarious activities that bring potential harm to U.S. corporate well-being.

We're talking big bucks. A study by the Citizens for Tax Justice found that as of 2011, U.S.-based multinationals held more than $1.6 trillion in overseas locations, thereby preventing the collection of taxes on those incomes. The top 20 companies alone stockpiled $793 billion abroad in 2011, up from $648 billion in 2010 and $541 billion in 2009.[68] The Congressional Joint Committee on Taxation estimated that if those corporations with offshore holdings paid taxes on the profits from the previous year alone, $42 billion would be added to the U.S. Treasury.[69] That equals about half the federal spending dollars reduced by the sequester (automatic spending cuts) enacted by Congress in 2012 to reduce the size of the national budget deficit.

In recent years, corporate offshore funds have been so untouchable that companies have used the money for operations, buying back stock, or paying shareholder dividends. Sometimes they use the money for internal short-term loans, thereby avoiding the need to pay interest to an American lending institution.[70]

Because of their ability to store capital abroad, the typical average federal tax rate for multinational corporations in 2012 was 12.6 percent, far from the official 35 percent schedule that corporations scream about. Moreover, corporations have drastically reduced their portion of the tax load over the past few decades. Whereas they paid about 30 percent of the total national tax bill in 1950, U.S.-based corporations accounted for only 9 percent of the tax bill in 2012.[71] Some have paid much less. For example, because of its ability to shift most of its work to shell corporations abroad, Apple paid less than 2 percent in federal corporate taxes in 2012. During the same year, Facebook and Twitter paid zero.[72]

But perhaps the biggest effrontery has been found with the leadership of GE. In the decade between 2002 and 2011, GE averaged 1.8 percent federal taxes annually on profits of more than $81 billion over the period.[73] In the midst of preventing billions of dollars from going to the federal treasury, GE donated $1 million to the Committee for a Responsible Federal Budget, a group attempting to reduce federal spending because of annual deficits.[74] What would those deficits be if companies had paid anywhere near the

35 percent federal tax requirements for their sizes and profits? Regardless, given these data, corporate complaints about uncompetitive, overly high tax rates don't seem very sincere.

It's important to stress that all these corporate activities were legal, thanks to endless tax loopholes.[75] It's equally important to remember that not all companies avoid taxes; in fact, some pay close to the maximum. A 5-year study by Citizens of Tax Justice found that 288 of the Fortune 500 largest American corporations made profits every year between 2008 and 2012. Overall, they paid a federal tax rate of 19.4 percent. However, 26 corporations paid no taxes during the 5-year period; at the other end, 17 paid 34 percent or more during the same period.[76] Clearly, the system benefits some corporations—often the most wildly successful—more than others.

Repatriation

Some critics have suggested that the U.S. Congress should pass legislation that would temporarily reduce the tax obligations of the enormous accounts overseas in exchange for bringing the money home. Known as repatriation, this opportunity was afforded in 2004 with the American Jobs Creation Act. Under the terms of the legislation, corporations were allowed to retrieve funds from foreign subsidiaries at a one-time bargain tax rate of 5.25 percent, with the stipulation that the money brought home would be used only for job growth and not for corporate dividends or executive compensation. Upon signature by President George W. Bush, 843 U.S. corporations brought back $265 billion in offshore profits, which provided $18 billion in additional U.S. taxes. Corporate representatives were ecstatic with the opportunity to pay taxes at a 5.25 percent rate, rather than the obligatory 35 percent.

While repatriation was a boon for large American corporations, it was a bust for the American economy, and even more so for the American labor force. Sponsors of the bill predicted that the infusion of capital would create 500,000 jobs. No such employment wave transpired. An independent study by the Congressional Research Service in 2011 concluded that "much of the repatriated earnings were used for cash-flow purposes and little evidence exists that new investment was spurred."[77] Corporations did, however, stray far from the intended use of the funds. A separate study by economists at the National Bureau of Economic Research in 2009 found that for every repatriated dollar, 92 cents went to shareholder benefits—a use forbidden in the legislation.[78] Repatriation did not work as the bill's sponsors intended, much to the glee of the country's biggest and most powerful corporations.

Friendly Rules

How do they do it? How do so many corporations pay so little when many of the rest of us pay much higher percentages? The most common method of reducing tax obligation is for a corporation to transfer substantial parts of the company to wholly owned foreign affiliates housed in countries with little or no corporate taxes. For example, Intel has mastered the tax obligation game by intentionally setting up factories in more than 30 countries known for low taxes.[79] Their products are sold in the host countries and the earnings are kept in the host countries. To the extent that Intel and other corporations pay any taxes abroad, federal law allows corporations to deduct those taxes from what little they owe here.

There are other rules that benefit corporations as well. For instance, government subsidies may allow corporations to offset their tax obligations by the funds they receive from the federal government. Boeing benefited from $5 billion in government subsidies to develop the 787 Dreamliner, which it then used to offset corporate tax liabilities. A corporation can also deduct tax obligations because of the stock options it gives to its employees, a model used by Facebook and Twitter.

The hundreds of corporate tax loopholes have been built into the U.S. tax code over decades, jealously guarded by their sponsors. But every once in a while, fiscal conditions become so tense that reformers attempt to root out corporate tax breaks as a means of generating badly needed revenues. Such an effort was last made in 2013, when the House Ways and Means Committee and the Senate Finance Committee scheduled preliminary hearings after President Barack Obama called for "bipartisan, comprehensive reform." After much fanfare and testimony from companies paying little or no federal taxes, the committee shelved any reform proposals.

Corporations have made lobbying an art, so much so that they may actually spend more resources on lobbying for favorable conditions than paying federal income taxes. In one instance, an examination of 30 of the largest U.S. corporations by the nonpartisan group Public Campaign between 2008 and 2010 found that during that period, they paid $476 million in lobbying, a worthwhile activity given that 29 of the 30 paid no federal income taxes during the period. This effort has given return on investment an entirely new and successful meaning in the 21st century.[80]

Ironically, for some time there has been (and still is) nearly universal agreement on simplifying the unwieldy and often confusing tax code. Beyond that, most potentially affected groups hunkered down in defensive postures to defend their turfs. In 2013, more than 440 corporations and business groups spent tens of millions of dollars petitioning the tax committees through the efforts of 125 Washington lobbying and law firms. Corporate political action committees (PACs) contributed millions of dollars to the campaign war chests of key committee members. The committee principals issued a joint statement that said in part, "The political contributions do not affect policy decisions and don't make an ounce of difference" compared to the interests of their constituents and the American public.[81] Maybe so, but the year came and went without a single change in the tax code.

States Get into the Act

Not to be outdone by federal tax breaks, state governments have become active in providing tax breaks as incentive for corporate facilities. The examples vary, but the dollars lost to these governments add up into the billions. In 2013, New Jersey awarded $93 million in tax credits to five companies that agreed to hire 1,925 employees, making the commitment almost $51,000 per employee.[82] ESPN has greatly enlarged its headquarters in Connecticut since 2000, and for good reason. Between 2000 and 2012, the company received $260 million in tax breaks and credits, which amounts to a bargain of $65,000 for each of its 4,000 employees. But the biggest prize goes to Boeing, which in 2013 asked states for subsidy and tax break bids in exchange for production of its 777X jet, scheduled for service in 2020. Twelve states offered various enticement plans. Washington State won the bidding war, with the promise of $8.7 billion in tax breaks, credits, and exemptions over 16 years for employment of between 2,700 and 8,500 personnel. Even using the high number, that amounts to $1,023,529 per employee in reduced taxes.[83]

These financial commitments by governments to the private sector add up to incredible numbers. One 2012 study by the *New York Times* determined that the tax breaks to corporations provided by states, counties, and cities totaled a staggering $80 billion per year.[84] That's $80 billion not available for public education, job training, social welfare programs, transportation, and other infrastructure needs. Or, looking at the issue another way, that's $80 billion in badly needed government revenues that must be made up by somebody else who, in all likelihood, does not have the same resources or financial capabilities as wealthy corporate recipients. Once again, we return to the fairness issue.

Still, the fundamental question remains: Are state governments getting their money's worth for these investments, particularly since so much of the time the companies receiving the benefits are already profitable without any financial assistance? The myth notwithstanding, academic studies show that, for the most part, there is no correlation between tax breaks and a state economy's performance.[85] Simply put, governments are needlessly padding corporate profits as they reduce commitments to under-funded programs.

Happy Corporations, Neglected Society

American corporations are doing just fine, thank you, and that's good for their shareholders and good for some segments of the economy. Corporations have flourished in a friendly tax environment that has allowed for enormous profits and the ability to park much of those profits in untouchable offshore locations. Yet, as they have thrived, many corporations have done little to share the benefits of their successes with American workers, choosing instead to build their empires with the cheapest labor and parts wherever they are available, irrespective of their impact on the workforce or society. In addition, huge loopholes in federal law have allowed them to avoid paying their fair share of taxes, leaving individuals with far fewer resources to pay more than their share.

Rather than contributing to the greater good, corporations have promoted and taken advantage of laws that allow them to avoid responsibility, with society paying the price for their "accomplishments." But if society is the "sleeping giant" when it comes to corporate responsibility, the public may be awakening. In a Gallup Poll conducted in 2013, 66 percent of the respondents agreed that corporations paid "too little" taxes.[86] Whether that sentiment is enough to stimulate real reform remains to be seen, but clearly public antipathy toward corporate behavior is alive and well, and that's not good for the nation's well-being.

ON THE OUTSIDE LOOKING IN

In 21st-century America, some parts of society are doing much better than others. That in itself is no surprise; after all, there have always been differences among us for a variety of reasons.

But there is a distinction that separates today's socioeconomic environment from other eras. Many American corporations today are American in name only. They take advantage of opportunities that help their bottom lines, yet they minimize responsibilities to their workers and nation if those obligations carry virtually any significant cost. Because of their callous abandonment of their responsibilities at home, corporations have surrendered their American citizenship.

American society is the ultimate victim of the now international corporation stitched largely out of American cloth. The economic differences between those at the top and those at the bottom are the largest in the nation's history, due in large part to the self-promoting successes of the 21st-century American enterprise.

Corporations are not entirely at fault for this development. Congress has in many ways been the patron of corporate greed through the many loopholes that have appeared as legislation. Most of the time, screams of abuse from various public reports have not captured the public's attention, leaving Congress to carry the water of corporate lobbyists supposedly in the name of the public good. Shame on these elected officials for such protectionist legislation. Shame on them for not acknowledging the large role that their loopholes have played in causing budget revenue gaps for decades.

The public has its share of blame to bear as well. Many have sat back and passively accepted a declining role of the American worker without so much as questioning corporate priorities and the government's assistance to attain them. Rather than take a stand against greed and selfish opportunism, Americans have watched passively, choosing to wallow in self-pity. No voice means no respect. Many have also refused to alter their life course with retraining for jobs that might be easier to find, even if they pay less than they once did. In this respect, many in the workforce have been as narrow-minded as the corporations who have left them behind.

The status quo no longer works in American society. Some have figured out this truism and improved their lot, in spite of obstacles and long odds.

Most of us have been stuck in an "Ozzie and Harriet" time warp built on conditions that are a half century out of date. It's time for all of society to wake up and begin anew.

ENDNOTES

1. John Kenneth Galbraith, *The New Industrial State*, Boston, MA: Houghton Mifflin, 1967, p. 83.
2. Charles Perrow, *Organizing America: Wealth, Power and the Origins of Corporate Capitalism*, Princeton, NJ: Princeton University Press, 2002, pp. 40–41.
3. Galbraith, op. cit., pp. 243–244.
4. Robert Kuttner, *The Squandering of America: How the Failure of Our Politics Undermines Our Prosperity*, New York: Alfred A. Knopf, 2002, p. 192.
5. "Share of the Work Force in a Union Falls to a 97-Year Low, 11.3%," *New York Times*, January 24, 2013, pp. 1, 2.
6. "MaClatchy-Marist Poll: American Dream Seen as Out of Reach," February 13, 2014, http://www.mcclatchydc.com/2014/02/13/218026/mcclatchy-marist-poll-american. html.
7. "Recovery in U.S. Lifting Profits, Not Adding Jobs," *New York Times*, March 14, 2013, pp. A1, A3.
8. James K. Jackson, "U.S. Direct Investment Abroad: Trends and Current Issues," RS21118, Congressional Research Service, Washington, DC, December 11, 2013, p. 1.
9. Ibid.
10. "Economic News Release," Department of Labor Statistics, U.S. Department of Labor, Washington, DC, February 7, 2014, http://www.bls.gov/news.release/ empsit.a.htm.
11. "U.S. Companies, Hiring Abroad," *New York Times*, April 18, 2012, http://economix. blogs.nytimes.com/2012/04/18/u-s-companies-hiring-abroad/.
12. Quoted in "Report: American Corporations Are Adding More Jobs Overseas Than They Are at Home," *Think Progress*, April 27, 2012, http://thinkprogress.org/ economy/2012/04/27/472577/report-american-corporations-are-adding-more-jobs-overseas-than-they-are-at-home/.
13. "Recovery in U.S. Lifting Profits, Not Adding Jobs," op. cit.
14. "Not Made in China," *Wall Street Journal*, May 1, 2013, pp. B1, B2.
15. "More U.S. Companies Opening High-Tech Factories in Mexico," *Los Angeles Times*, November 29, 3013, http://articles.latimes.com/2013/nov/29/business/la-fi-overseas-manufacturing-20131130.
16. "Fast and Flawed Inspections of Factories Abroad," *New York Times*, September 2, 2013, pp. A1, B6.
17. "Factory Owners in Bangladesh Fear Apparel Firms Will Leave," *New York Times*, May 3, 2013, pp. B1, B4.
18. "How U.S. Lost Out on iPhone Work," *New York Times*, January 22, 2012, pp. 1, 22.
19. "Apple Profits Up but Net Profits Down in Fourth Quarter," *Macworld*, October 28, 2013, http://www.macworld.com/article/2058332/apple-revenues-up-but-net-profits-down-in-fourth-quarter.html.

20. "U.S. Firms Add Jobs Overseas," Associated Press, December 29, 2010, http://www.newsobserver.com/2010/12/29/886366/us-firms-add-jobs-overseas.html.
21. "As Drug Making Goes Global, Oversight Is Found Lacking," *USA Today*, October 21, 2012, http://www.usatoday.com/story/news/2012/10/21/global-drug-manufacturing-oversight/1646487/.
22. See "FDA Inspection of Foreign Drug Companies," *U.S. Pharmacist*, 33(6), 53–37, 2008, http://www.uspharmacist.com/content/c/9789/?t=men%27s_health,fda.
23. "As Drug Making Goes Global," op. cit.
24. Marcia Crosse, "Drug Safety: FDA Faces Challenges Overseeing the Foreign Drug Manufacturers Supply Chain," testimony before the Committee on Health, Education, Labor, and Pensions, U.S. Senate, September 14, 2011, U.S. Government Accounting Office, Report GAO-11-936T.
25. "After Heparin: Protecting Consumers of Substandard and Counterfeit Drugs," Pew Charitable Trust, Washington, DC, July 12, 2011, pp. 26–27.
26. "Drug Recalls Surge," CNN Money, August 16, 2010, http://money.cnn.com/2010/08/16/news/companies/drug_recall_surge/index.htm.
27. Ibid.
28. "Cholesterol Drug Recalled over Glass Concerns," CNN Health, November 26, 2012, http://www.cnn.com/2012/11/25/health/statin-recall/index.html.
29. "Fresenius Kabi USA Issues Voluntary Recall Because of Benztropine Mesylate Injection, USP 2 mg/2mL (1 mg/mL) in 2 mL Single Dose Vials," U.S. Food and Drug Administration, Washington, DC, June 30, 2013, http://www.fda.gov/Safety/Recalls/ucm359299.htm.
30. "Medicines Made in India Set Off Safety Worries," *New York Times*, February 15, 2014, pp. A1, A6.
31. "Defense Industrial Base Assessment: Counterfeit Electronics," U.S. Department of Commerce, Washington, DC, January 2010, p.13.
32. "Counterfeit Parts Infiltrate the Automobile Repair Industry," The Car Connection, February 28, 2011, http://www.thecarconnection.com/news/1055960_counterfeit-parts-infiltrate-the-auto-repair-industry.
33. "Fake Parts Reportedly Cost Ford $1 Billion," CNN Money, January 22, 2007, http://money.cnn.com/2007/01/22/news/companies/ford_counterfeit_parts/.
34. "General Motors Assists in Seizing 50,000 Counterfeit Parts in Saudi Arabia," March 13, 2013, http://gmauthority.com/blog/2013/03/general-motors-assists-in-seizing-50000-counterfeit-parts-in-saudi-arabia/.
35. "Three Automotive Parts Suppliers Charged in Manhattan Federal Court with Selling Counterfeit Replacement Parts," U.S. Attorney's Office, Southern District of New York, February 13, 2013, http://www.justice.gov/usao/nys/pressreleases/February13/MKDIndictmentsPR.php.
36. "Putting the Pedal to the Metal: Subsidies to China's Auto-Parts Industry from 2002 to 2011," EPI Briefing Paper 316, Economic Policy Institute, Washington, DC, January 31, 2012, p. 13.
37. "Feds Warn of Counterfeit Airbags Being Installed as Replacements," CNN, October 10, 2012, http://www.cnn.com/2012/10/10/us/counterfeit-airbags/index.html.
38. "To Cut Costs, Airlines Send Repairs Abroad," NPR, October 19, 2009, http://www.npr.org/templates/story/story.php?storyId=113877784.
39. "U.S. Airlines Outsource Majority of Repairs," NBC News, April 15, 2008, http://www.nbcnews.com/id/24068455/ns/business-us_business/t/us-airlines-outsource-majority-repairs/#.Uv_k5IWhOZE.

40. "Aircraft Maintenance in America: Who Is Fixing My Plane?" *Aviation Online Magazine*, March 21, 2011, http://avstop.com/march_2011/aircraft_maintenance_in_america_who_is_fixing_my_plane.htm.

41. Ibid.

42. See "Review of Air Carriers' Use of Aircraft Repair Stations," Report AV-2003-047, Office of the Inspector General, U.S. Department of Transportation, July 8, 2003.

43. "FAA Continues to Face Challenges in Implementing a Risk-Based Approach for Repair Station Oversight," Report AV-2013-073, Office of the Inspector General, U.S. Department of Transportation, May 1, 2013, pp. 3, 5, 6.

44. Lawrence Mishel, Josh Bivens, Elise Gould, and Heidi Shierholz, *The State of Working America*, 12th ed., Ithaca, NY: Cornell University press, 2012, p. 329.

45. Steven Rattner, "The Myth of Industrial Rebound," *New York Times*, January 26, 2014, pp. SR1, SR8.

46. "Reshoring and the Resurgence of U.S. High-Tech Manufacturing," *Today's Engineer*, January 2013, http://www.todaysengineer.org/2013/jan/reshoring.asp.

47. See "The U.S. Gains Factory Jobs, but Workers Give Ground on Wages," *New York Times*, December 30, 2011, pp. B1, B2, and "U.S. Manufacturing and the Troubled Promise of Reshoring," *The Guardian*, July 24, 2013, http://www.theguardian.com/business/2013/jul/24/us-manufacturing-troubled-promise-reshoring.

48. "Caterpillar Expands to China," Zacks Equity Research, March 12, 2012, http://www.zacks.com/stock/news/71806/caterpillar-expands-in-china.

49. "'Symbolic' Reshoring Will Not Lead to Jobs Boom, Survey Suggests," *The Globe and Mail*, May 10, 2013, http://www.theglobeandmail.com/report-on-business/economy/jobs/survey-says-reshoring-symbolic-and-will-not-lead-to-jobs-boom/article11855864/.

50. "Textile Plants Humming, but Not with Workers," *New York Times*, September 20, 2013, pp. A1, A20.

51. "Skilled Work, without the Worker," *New York Times*, August 18, 2012, http://www.nytimes.com/2012/08/19/business/new-wave-of-adept-robots-is-changing-global-industry.html?pagewanted=all&_r=0&pagewanted=print.

52. "Made in the USA," *Time*, April 22, 2013, pp. 23–29.

53. Quoted in "The U.S. Gains Factory Jobs, but Workers Give Ground on Wages," *New York Times*, December 30, 2011, pp. B1, B2.

54. Steven Rattner, "The Myth of Industrial Rebound," *New York Times*, January 26, 2014, pp. SR1, SR8.

55. For example, see "2011 U.S. Manufacturing-Outsourcing Index: What We Think," AlixPartners, December 2011.

56. "Efficient and Exhausted," *Los Angeles Times*, April 7, 2013, pp, A1, A14.

57. "Why the Pension Gap Is Soaring," *Wall Street Journal*, February 26, 2013, pp., B1, B8.

58. "Largest Corporate Pensions Are about 76% Funded," MarketWatch, *Wall Street Journal*, May 30, 2013, http://blogs.marketwatch.com/thetell/2013/05/30/largest-corporate-pensions-are-about-76-funded/tab/print/.

59. "Fewer Employers Offering Defined Benefit Pension Plans to New Salaried Employees," *Workforce*, October 3, 2012, http://www.workforce.com/articles/fewer-employers-offering-defined-benefit-pension-plans-to-new-salaried-employees.

60. Barbara A. Butrica, Howard M. Iams, Karen E. Smith, and Eric J. Toder, "The Disappearing Defined Benefit Pension and Its Potential Impact on the Retirement Incomes of Baby Boomers," *Social Security Bulletin*, 69(3), 1, 2009.

61. James Poterba, Steven Venti, and David Wise, "The Shift from Benefit Pensions to 401(k) Plans and the Pension Assets of the Baby Boom Cohort," *Proceedings of the National Academy of Sciences*, 10(33), 4, 2007, http://www.pnas.org/content/104/33/13238.full.

62. "Trapped on the Worker Treadmill?" Report 393, The Conference Board, New York, January 2013, p. 4.

63. "Fewer Businesses Provide Health Insurance," CNN Money, April 15, 2013, http://money.cnn.com/2013/04/15/smallbusiness/health-insurance/index.html.

64. "Employers Blast Fees from New Health Law," *Wall Street Journal*, March 113, 2013, pp. A1, A2.

65. "Health Law's Nasty Side Effect," *Los Angeles Times*, May 2, 2013, pp. A1, A9.

66. "The Shift to Part-Time," *Wall Street Journal*, July 15, 2013, pp. B1, B5.

67. "Flat U.S. Wages Help Fuel Rebound in Manufacturing," *Wall Street Journal*, May 29, 2012, pp. A1, A10.

68. "Fortune 500 Corporations Holding $1.6 Trillion in Profits Offshore," Citizens for Tax Justice, Washington, DC, December 13, 2012.

69. "For U.S. Companies, Money 'Offshore' Means Manhattan," *New York Times*, May 21, 2013, http://www.nytimes.com/2013/05/22/business/for-us-companies-money-offshore-means-manhattan.html?_r=0.

70. "How Firms Tap Overseas Cash," *Wall Street Journal*, March 29, 2013, pp. B1, B4.

71. "Big Companies Paid a Fraction of Corporate Tax Rate," *New York Times*, July 2, 2013, p. A3.

72. "Twitter and Other Tech Firms Poised to Shelter $11 Billion in Profits Using Stock Option Tax Loophole," Citizens for Tax Justice, November 5, 2013, http://ctj.org/ctjreports/2013/11/twitter_and_other_tech_firms_poised_to_shelter_11_billion_in_profits_using_stock_option_tax_loophole.php.

73. "General Electric Tax Rate 1.8 Percent over Decade, Report Finds," *Huffington Post*, February 18, 2004, http://www.huffingtonpost.com/2012/02/27/general-electric-tax-rate_n_1305196.html.

74. Lee Fang, "GE Gave $1 Million to Fix the Debt," *The Nation*, August 21, 2013, http://www.thenation.com/blog/175854/ge-gave-1-million-fix-debt.

75. "Offshore Profit Shifting and the U.S. Tax Code—Part 2 (Apple Inc.)," General Accounting Office, Washington, DC, May 21, 2013, p. 40.

76. See Robert S. McIntyre, Matthew Gardner, and Richard Phillips, "The Sorry State of Corporate Taxes: What Fortune 500 Firms Pay (or Don't Pay) in the USA and What They Pay Abroad—2008 to 2012," Citizens for Tax Justice, Washington, DC, February 2014.

77. Donald J. Marples and Jane G. Gravelle, "Tax Cuts on Reparation Earnings as Economic Stimulus: An Economic Analysis," R40178, Congressional Research Service, December 20, 2011, p. 6.

78. Dhammika Dharmapala, C. Fritz Foley, and Kristin J. Forbes, "Watch What I Do, Not What I Say: The Unintended Consequences of the Homeland Investment Act," Working Paper 15023, National Bureau of Economic Research, June 9, 2009, p. 26.

79. Robert Kuttner, *The Squandering of America*, New York: Alfred A. Knopf, 2007, pp. 200–201.

80. "30 Major U.S. Corporations Paid More to Lobby Congress than Income Taxes, 2008–2010," *International Business Times*, December 9, 2011, http://www.ibtimes.com/30-major-us-corporations-paid-more-lobby-congress-income-taxes-2008-2010-380982.

81. "As Momentum Builds toward Tax Reform, Lobbyists Prepare for a Fight," *Washington Post*, March 9, 2013, http://www.washingtonpost.com/politics/as-momentum-builds-toward-tax-reform-lobbyists-prepare-for-a-fight/2013/03/09/e46c0b3a-6ad9-11e2-af53-7b2b2a7510a8_story.html.
82. "Tax Break as a Not-So-Secret Weapon," *New York Times*, January 7, 2014, https://search.yahoo.com/search;_ylt=AuxsUN8icWyKdC6N7ej4ZjGbvZx4?p=tax+break+as+a+not-so-secret+weapon.&toggle=1&cop=mss&ei=UTF-8&fr=yfp-t-901.
83. "Boeing Holds a Bake-Off for Biggest Tax Breaks," *New York Times*, December 10, 2013, pp. B1, B2.
84. "As Companies Seek Tax Deals, Governments Pay High Price," *New York Times*, December 1, 2012, http://www.nytimes.com/2012/12/02/us/how-local-taxpayers-bankroll-corporations.html?hp&pagewanted=print.
85. See Richard Florida, "The Uselessness of Economic Development Incentives," *The Atlantic Cities*, December 7, 2012, A1NNRTMzOV8x/SIG=13va9qjmn/EXP=1393126493/**http%3a//www.theatlanticcities.com/jobs-and-economy/2012/12/uselessness-economic-development-incentives/4081/.
86. http://www.gallup.com/poll/1714/Taxes.aspx#1.

Section IV

Repair and Renewal

9

Policies for Making Citizenship Meaningful Again

Citizenship is a term filled with many dimensions. At its root, it confers special standing for someone who resides in a geopolitical setting defined by fixed boundaries. Often, that standing is automatic, simply as a result of birth or history. For an immigrant, sometimes citizenship may be acquired after an individual fulfills certain legal requirements over time and promises loyalty to his or her adopted country. Regardless, under this definition, citizenship provides a guarantee for an individual to reside and work in a specified jurisdiction with the knowledge that he or she belongs there.

In addition to the idea of a home or place of residence, citizenship includes rights, obligations, rules, and various cultural traits that connect each person with others and his or her nation. Some of these linkages arise as the result of shared social, political, and religious values, while others emerge as imperatives codified by government leaders. In a representative democracy, those leaders are placed in power by the governed. Upon their election, leaders swear allegiance to the rules guiding the country—commonly a constitution or similar document, along with the nation's attendant laws and regulations. For their part, citizens may retain or replace most of their policy makers at periodic elections, a right that has the potential to keep citizens engaged in the system while holding policy makers accountable to them.

Beyond these fairly straightforward concepts of citizenship, the term in a democratic society carries an even deeper, more fundamental essence. Inasmuch as democracy depends upon the exercise of free will by the people, that determination can be expressed with meaning only if all citizens have the same opportunities to state their case. The connection between opportunity and democracy takes us to the imperative of equality, which is the guarantee that all citizens may share the same basic opportunities to thrive and succeed in life. Without opportunity, society is vulnerable to a variety of corrupting and disrupting forces that jeopardize the legitimacy of government and the well-being of its citizens. Thus, Derek Heater concludes, "Discrimination, abuse of power, grossly unjust distribution of wealth and resources corrode equality and destroy any atmosphere of fairness, with the result that the virtues of citizenship are soured into apathy and alienation."[1] Such conditions also portend the potential for mass disengagement, a precursor for political implosion and questionable legitimacy of the governing process.

For many Americans, Heater's concerns describe their political, social, and economic circumstances. In previous pages, we have chronicled an American society far different from the expectations we read about or are taught. We see a society where people of color and women lack the same opportunities as others; where the education system produces terribly uneven results, largely because of preconditions that virtually ensure rigged outcomes; where some citizens are routinely disfranchised through discriminatory rules and practices, and therefore denied the right to exercise their citizenship; where corporate sovereignty has neglected responsibilities to the collective good; and where the economic differences between the "haves" and "have-nots" have grown demonstrably over time.

We have structural concerns as well. Ours has become a society where government institutions no longer live up to their responsibilities, leaving a poorly educated population and a decaying infrastructure as the consequence for failure of our leaders to act. And ours has become a society where the same rules are bent or ignored for those of means, while fiercely enforced for those with few resources to defend themselves. Combined, these conditions have denied many Americans a meaningful place at the starting gate of life, while others have shot through the course with little hindrance. Moreover, rather than observe differences flatten out over time, we find that they have become more exaggerated today than at any point in recent American history.

There is a consequence from these conditions. To the extent that Americans are left behind, they have little hope of economic success and little interest in participating in the political process. The reason seems clear enough: the political, economic, and psychological obstacles are just too difficult for too many to overcome and, given the long odds of attaining achievement, not worth the futile effort.

As a result of a system rigged against them, large numbers of Americans no longer feel connected to their country. They have lost their tether to the American dream, which William Hudson notes promised "the potential for material success and social mobility" for all.[2] Additionally, the more these adverse conditions persist from one generation to the next, the more the numbers of the disillusioned will grow. Under these circumstances, it's only a matter of time before the very legitimacy of American government will be at stake. That is the by-product of disengagement, a bleak future that may impact a few initially, but sure to impose its weight on most of us in the end.

What to do about the growing malaise? There are no simple answers to these complex problems. If there were, they would have been successfully addressed years ago. But there are some action steps than can provide relief, perhaps even solutions. The difficulty for some will be that the remedies will extract such a long overdue price from some sectors of society that they may be unwilling to pay, given their comfort relative to others. Still, if we do not make the necessary adjustments to citizen disengagement soon, the problems for American society will worsen over time, with the undoing of the polity as we know it a very real possibility.

The following pages contain a set of policy recommendations for reviving American engagement and restoring national community. They include a serious overhaul of American public education, restored citizenship rights, and comprehensive reform of the federal income and corporate tax systems. Together, these changes represent first steps in the civic reengagement of Americans.

I am not so arrogant or naïve as to define these recommendations as the only or best answers to solving citizen disengagement. Perhaps there are other approaches that will put American society back on track. That said, whatever else, these proposals represent a starting point for healthy discussions that have been ignored for too long, particularly by those in power—public and private—who can do something about America's malaise. No longer can we paper over our problems with empty slogans. Rather, we must commit to substantive, long-term action.

BOLSTERED PUBLIC EDUCATION

Education stands as a fundamental foundation for the well-being of any society. As John Dewey penned a century ago, "Without formal education it is not possible to transmit all the resources and achievements of a complex society."[3] One can't underscore this point enough in the 21st century. More than ever, education has emerged as the multifaceted stepping stone for individual growth, opportunity, and happiness, allowing us access to opportunities we otherwise would not have. Yet, contemporary American public education is in crisis. We noted in Chapter 1 that American education has fallen from its lofty preeminent position of the past. No longer do American students perform well on international tests; sizable percentages drop out long before the completion of their high school classes, all but ending any options for future success. Even large percentages of those who attain education milestones lack the conceptual rigor found among students in many other countries.

Those who are uneducated or undereducated have even fewer resources to succeed in life; early on, they are separated from others and left with limited options most likely lasting the rest of their lives. Moreover, their lack of success takes a toll on society in ways beyond formal learning. Education expert Diane Ravitch laments that "our abysmal public schools threaten not only the performance of our economy but our national security, our very survival as a nation."[4] People can't defend democratic norms and values if they don't understand and experience them. Education fosters political participation and the greater sense of belonging in society. As Sidney Verba and his colleagues have found in their seminal study on political behavior, education relates to interest, efficacy, and information,[5] ingredients that are conducive to civic engagement, key underpinnings of citizen engagement. Simply put, a comprehensive education helps an individual understand how he or she is part of the system, rather than feeling on the outside helplessly looking in.

But our education problems, while particularly harmful to those who drop out or who are virtually pushed out, extend to most of America's young. Simply put, they are not prepared enough to compete with better-educated people elsewhere, and that takes a psychological toll on individuals as well as society. Even American students sense their educational inadequacy. In research by the Organization for Economic Cooperation and Development (OECD) that asked high school students in 34 countries about their satisfaction with their education, U.S. students ranked 25th.[6] Something must be done.

Five changes can go a long way for better preparing Americans to play more substantive roles in the world: longer days and longer school years, second language instruction, meaningful English immersion programs for immigrants, meaningful job training programs, and inculcation of universal American values.

Longer School Days, Longer School Years

We begin with the basics. American students are not spending enough time in school. For decades, most American school years have included about 175–180 days in the classroom. But what once may have been enough is no longer so. Other countries are setting aside time (and money) for longer school years with better-performing students as a result. Some examples drive home the point. In 2012 international comparisons, Singapore, Japan, and Germany kept students in school for between 240 and 280 days per year. All scored higher in the science, math, and reading areas than their American counterparts who spent considerably less time in school.[7]

Studies show dramatic differences when additional time is introduced as an independent variable for student learning. Having a longer student day and year allows students to absorb more material and perform better on test scores. Research in Massachusetts compared schools that provided 25 percent more instructional time with those that did not with predictable results: when compared with state achievement test results, students in the schools with longer days scored 11 percent higher on English, 7 percent higher on math, and 5 percent higher on science.[8] More time equals more attention, which in turn equals better performance.

Attention in recent years has focused on technical education areas, including science, technology, engineering, and math, otherwise known as STEM. These are some of the brightest employment opportunities in the 21st century world over. Still, our students are unprepared to work in these fields. As of 2013, only 44 percent of U.S. high school graduates were ready for university math; only 36 percent were prepared for university-level science. Twenty-two percent of white students studied advanced high school algebra, a high percentage when compared to 9 percent of Latinos and 10 percent of African Americans. Statistics show even worse performances for students in the fourth and eighth grade benchmark years. Poor K–12 education programs set the table for future academic failures. Among those students who begin college majoring in a STEM subject area, only 38 percent graduate in that field.[9] In the 2012 Programme for International Student Assessment (PISA) examinations, the United States scored below the mean for the OECD nations.

It should not be surprising that our lack of K–12 preparedness extends to university shortcomings. Between 2000 and 2008, STEM-related degrees awarded in U.S. 4-year colleges and universities increased by 24 percent to 496,000. Over the same period, STEM-related degrees in China increased by 218 percent to 1,143,000.[10] Those numbers from China and elsewhere turn into American jobs because the United States isn't producing enough graduates to fill the need.

There are consequences from these patterns. With students in other countries performing at higher levels and in greater numbers, we can understand why American corporations are tempted to either shift production to the talent or bring that talent to the United States via H1-B visas. The issue has been addressed in Congress again and again, only to be caught in struggles over immigration, education, healthcare policies, and of course, funding.

Much of the comparative contemporary data demonstrating poor performance by U.S. students comes from recent PISA reports, which in 2012 reviewed education performances of 510,000 students in 65 countries.[11] Not everyone agrees with the PISA findings, which are unflattering to U.S. student performances. Economists Martin Carnoy and Richard Rothstein reject international comparisons on the basis that the composition of American students is more diverse than high-scoring countries that cater to high achievers, and as such includes many low-scoring students.[12] Unwittingly, perhaps, Carnoy and Rothstein make the point: American jobs and positions of good standing must be available to the broad spectrum of society.

That the United States is so diverse compels greater investment to address the wide swath of the American student population. To do otherwise leaves out large portions of the population, which exacerbates the differences between those likely to succeed because of their access to private resources and those who will be left behind. If Americans expect our kids to compete, we need to give them the opportunity to learn, and that begins with spending more time in the education environment.

Spending more time in school provides countless benefits beyond test scores. In fact, one research effort has found that "the effect of additional instructional days is quite similar to that of increasing teacher quality and reducing class size." In addition, longer school years tend to reduce dropout rates, thereby giving students the opportunity to succeed with more skills in future years.[13] The education environment can be a powerful tool for offsetting some of society's biggest shortcomings that hit the poor and minorities particularly hard. We must improve it.

Second Languages for All

Instruction time alone will not answer the call for improving our kids' ability to compete in the international arena. They must be given 21st-century tools to successfully communicate in an international context. Nowhere is this more important than providing students with a second language.

In the United States, less than one-fifth (18 percent) of K–12 students study a foreign language.[14] That percentage has remained relatively constant for more than a decade, despite the growing impact of globalization on communication. In fact, public schools have reduced their commitment to foreign language instruction. Between 1997 and 2008, foreign language classes in elementary schools dropped to 15 percent from 24 percent, while middle school instruction offerings dropped to 58 percent from 75 percent.[15] True, foreign language instruction increased at the university level, but the number of participants to those attending higher education is low compared to the size of the workforce. Overall, Americans have stepped away from foreign language at a time when increasingly employment opportunities demand it.

The number of American students taking a foreign language pales in comparison to the number of foreign language students in other parts of the world. One study finds that while 9.3 percent of all Americans speak a language other than English very well, almost all are immigrants. In fact, the same study shows that only 1.4 percent of native-born Americans fluently speak and write a foreign language well.[16]

The data are much more compelling elsewhere. For example, in the European Union, 60 percent of all students study a foreign language, including 93 percent in Sweden and 91 percent in France.[17] Some of this makes sense because of the proximity of European nations to one another, but foreign languages for students have become important in other countries too. China has required the study of English for all students, beginning at age 8, since 2000. Today approximately 35 percent of the population has participated in English learning, with 10 percent fluent in English.[18] In Japan, since 2002 English has been a required subject for all students beginning in the fifth grade, although 75 percent of all schools introduce English activities in the first grade. Japan adopted a comprehensive approach because numerous political and business leaders argued that the country was "not preparing Japan to fully compete in international business and technological innovation."[19] Thus, while the United States has deemphasized the importance of foreign languages, other countries have moved in the opposite direction.

Learning a foreign language has become an imperative for Americans who want to succeed in the global marketplace. As one business expert notes, Spanish is important for call centers, Arabic and Japanese make sense in finance and sales, and Mandarin "can be particularly useful especially in fields such as manufacturing."[20] Nelson Mandela once said, "If you talk to a man in a language he understands, that goes to his head. If you talk to him in his own language, that goes to his heart." It's not enough that some Americans in affluent school districts or private schools are given foreign language opportunities. The point is *all* Americans must be given access to these tools so that they can succeed.

The idea of American students learning a second language dovetails well with the need of immigrants to master English. With more than 45 million immigrants, the United States has more foreign-born residents than any other country—by far.[21] Except for those with technical or academic backgrounds, most immigrants come to the United States with little or no ability to manage the English language. Those in the workforce have little choice but to find their own, but their children are another matter. Without a firm foundation in English, they will be doomed to limited employment options and left on the periphery of American society.

Studies show that meaningful dual-language immersion programs provide incredible benefits. From the earliest ages on, children who are exposed to two languages show more developed ways to think, process, and problem solve than those who grow up with only a single language. Advantages of bilingualism extend to nonverbal activities as well as physical attributes. One scholar even cites research that shows less likelihood for dementia among those people who develop bilingual skills.[22] On a social level, students who learn foreign languages are more positive about people from other cultures; stereotypes break down and tolerance grows.[23] There also significant psychological benefits for all parties. English learners with their own language can become a source of information for native English speakers learning their second language. This kind of equality raises the status and efficacy of the immigrants and provides a source of bonding between various cultures.[24]

Some of this discussion connects with the immigration reform issue. For years, this country has dithered this question, moving neither forward nor backward, and leaving management of the question to temporary and often contradictory quick fixes. For example, at the same time that President Barack Obama was pushing for a comprehensive overhaul that included a path to citizenship for 11 million illegal immigrants, his administration was deporting illegal immigrants in record numbers. Whatever the outcome of the debate, surely the children of illegal immigrants should not pay the price for the political stalemate. Many are likely to be here the rest of their lives. If they expect to be productive while in the United States, they must have the tools to succeed without the threat of deportation hanging over them, and those tools begin with the ability to understand and manage the English language.

Admittedly, the second language proposal runs against the dominant American social value that has favored English as *the* language for U.S. students to master above and beyond anything else, as well as *the* language that others around the world should learn. Such thinking seems shortsighted, arrogant, and almost defensive, given both globalization and the changing makeup of American society. To regain our place in the world, we must understand the world on others' terms and in their voices. The simultaneous acquisition of another language by native-born English speakers and mastery of English by immigrants seems like a long-overdue win-win for all.

Meaningful Job Training Programs

Not every child is meant to or wants to gain higher education, irrespective of the socioeconomic environment in which he or she grows up. In addition, we know that disproportionate numbers of young adults not attending higher education come from communities populated by minorities and the poor. As we have documented earlier in this volume, their opportunities evaporate early in life. Whether by choice or discriminatory practices, these people need opportunities to excel. We can give them the tools to engage as contributors to society through meaningful training programs designed for high school graduates. Such programs can also be a safety net alternative for those students who dropped out of high school and want to find meaningful employment. Unlike many technology and engineering positions, many of these jobs can't be outsourced abroad. In other words, they can become stable career opportunities.

The irony is that blue-collar jobs are plentiful and are only waiting for those people who obtain the necessary skills through what has come to be known as career and technical education programs. Construction journeymen, skilled manufacturing operators, health technicians, pile driver operators, and dental hygienists are among the many vocations that require little training after high school, and in some cases even without a high school diploma. According to a 2011 study, more than 3.7 million such jobs are unfilled in these and similar employment fields.[25] Many of these areas have critical shortages and are desperate for workers. So, why aren't these jobs filled? Because people aren't trained. We spend so much time thinking about getting high school graduates into and through college that we overlook a huge segment of society capable of making meaningful contributions.

Rather than provide more job training for those in need, Congress has minimized the opportunities. In fact, between 2010 and 2013, Congress reduced appropriations for the 21 Department of Labor job training programs by 14 percent[26]—this as unemployment for high school graduates ages 17–20 not attending colleges hovered between 29 and 35 percent.[27] One can only imagine the unemployment rate for high school dropouts. These people have been left behind. Yet, with employment opportunities, they can wean themselves from the trappings of the welfare state, or perhaps, the life-changing penalty of incarceration. It's just common sense that the costs of government training programs are a drop in the bucket compared to the costs of the alternatives.

In 2014, President Barack Obama took a step toward addressing this problem when he proposed that Congress dedicate $1.1 billion to reauthorize the Carl Perkins Career and Technical Education Act, the primary government funding source for career and technical education. The proposal was exceedingly modest, given that it was $140 million below the 2010 funding level.[28] Congress failed to act on Obama's request, demonstrating once again the disregard for those who need help the most. The United States will never be able to help the unemployed become part of the labor force by providing fewer funds for those with the greatest needs. Worse yet, the more that these people remain outside the labor force, the more reason that they have to remain unengaged citizens.

Inculcation of Universal American Values

Schools teach us many things in addition to knowledge-based subject matter that students cram into their heads. Schools are also institutions that instill and reinforce basic collective values distributed among society in both historical and contemporary terms. Within this framework, tolerance, respect, cooperation, civility, and order are among the many concepts that students absorb en route to becoming functional and productive members of society. Combined, these values, along with others, become the foundation of our political culture, defined in one classic study as "the patterns in political orientation of a population in the political system."[29] The traits outlined above provide the foundation for civic engagement in a democratic polity. John Patrick connects these important dots when he notes: "Concepts and principles on the substance of democracy are prerequisites to the development and maintenance of an active and responsible community of self-governing citizens."[30] Civic knowledge about the value of maintaining democracy combined with the skill sets for participating as stakeholders in the democracy can connect students with their roles as members of society.

Instilling participation in students is not easy or terribly efficient from the standpoint of time management. It's not easy because education has become a means to an end in a structured environment that compels students to consume voluminous amounts of information in the forms of facts, figures, and formulas. It's not terribly efficient time-wise because getting students to participate in the discussion of issues is a process that requires nurturing, encouragement, and thoughtful debate. The point is that education is more than preparing students for adulthood or even a job. Education should prepare students to think, to engage, and to assume involvement in their society as they grow into adulthood.

Civic learning has its critics. Upon considering the concept, some will counter, "That's nice, but we don't have time for this fuzzy stuff; we need to prepare our kids for jobs and careers." Yet, that's the problem. Preparing students for jobs without helping them to understand the importance of their role in society as citizens is the unintended first step to minimizing an individual's connectedness and political efficacy, while allowing apathy and alienation to frame his or her limited role in society. These characteristics, in turn, have profound consequences for democracy and the political system. Upon examining the disinterest of contemporary American youth in politics, Stephen Earl Bennett concludes, "Unless we find some means to overcome young Americans' detachment from and dislike of politics, America's experiment with popular government will be at risk."[31] And let's not forget, detached young people become detached adults in a few short years. For the United States to continue as the world's exemplary democracy, its citizens must feel part of the system. The mandatory inclusion of civic learning in the schools will help to give Americans that precious opportunity.

The idea of learning how to think has applications beyond the understanding of one's self and place in society. There are concrete benefits that extend into the 21st-century workplace. An examination of the new global economy finds that young people aspiring to be part of it "must have a broad array of skills that enable them to learn in a rapidly changing technological environment, to deal with and conceptualize the abstract, to understand complex problem-solving, and to interact effectively in a non-hierarchical structure."[32] These skills come from thoughtful interaction, not memorization and fact storage.

One approach to bridging the gap between passive learning and citizen engagement has emerged with the concept of service learning. This pedagogical tool brings students into the political process by making participation a cornerstone of that process. In class, students settle on a societal issue of concern, do the research on how that concern can be addressed, identify those in the policy-making arena who can address that concern, and reach out to those people with the hope of finding resolution. Service learning can be utilized at almost any age. Elementary school students may focus on a leaky water fountain or cracked sidewalk; high school students may consider more involved issues, such as school violence or the quality of cafeteria food, or even more significant problems, such as police brutality or gang behavior. The point is that they become active participants in the political process as engaged members of society, and they embed that sense of efficacy into their adult personalities. Along the way, they learn tolerance, respect, cooperation, and the importance of engagement as a two-way process between the citizen and society.[33]

Service learning promotes civic knowledge, awareness, and coping skills. Most of all, it can integrate citizens and their issues into the body politic, regardless of background. Pointing to the dearth of student knowledge about the tenets of democracy, Robert Putnam writes: "Civics education in school should be part of our [citizenship] strategy—not just 'how a bill becomes a law,' but 'How can I participate publicly in the public life of my community?'"[34] Hands-on participation becomes a means of inclusion.

There's more. Civic education helps young people find a sense of meaning in their lives that they might not experience otherwise. Their sense of self-worth and belonging produces significant spillover effects. For example, studies show that poor, minority, urban, or rural students who participate in civic learning "perform considerably higher than their counterparts, demonstrating the possibility of civic learning to fulfill the ideal of civic equality."[35] While the inculcation of values and participation doesn't necessarily solve society's problems, these tools will help people develop skills that will enable them to close social and economic gaps.

Let's remember the central theme of this book: ours has become a society where large numbers of people feel left out of the political process and suffer dearly from their despair. The opportunities to respond to and overcome much of that loss begin in the earliest years, and can be nurtured in the educational setting. From there, empowered individuals can practice efficacious participation in the polity the rest of their lives and feel that their roles have meaning.

Paying More to Get More

Two other changes in American culture must come with education reform. If we want better-educated students, we must have 21st-century teachers. That means encouraging educators to obtain master's degrees and other specialized training for use in the classroom. In turn, for their efforts, teachers must be rewarded financially much more than they are paid today, and society needs to recognize their value for basically year-round teaching and learning. We know that low pay and poor working conditions such as overcrowded classrooms and poor support are the biggest reasons why nearly half of all teachers leave the profession within the first 5 years of employment.[36] Moreover, data show that U.S. teachers are compensated with salaries considerably less than their counterparts in other industrialized countries.[37] These conditions must change.

But there's another side to this dynamic cultural shift: ensuring excellent classroom performance by the educator. Expectations for teachers must be made clear (and reasonable), and they must be given every opportunity to excel through mentoring programs. If teachers fail to keep up with their fields, others who are better prepared and willing should be brought in their place to carry out the important tasks associated with this vocation. Teachers' unions may cringe at the thought of rigorous performance standards as an intrusion into long-standing conditions such as tenure and autonomy. But these changes do not have to be adversarial; they can be collaborative. That said, strict accountability of educators has to be part of the new respect and compensation for these individuals.

RESTORED CITIZENSHIP RIGHTS
AND NEW OBLIGATIONS

One critical element of citizenship lies with the ability of individuals to express themselves to government officials and fellow citizens on issues that affect their lives. Political participation comes in many shapes and forms, ranging from personal exchanges of ideas and values to organized events like strikes and email blasts to meetings with public officials. Whatever the form, this behavior is a crucial underpinning of American liberty. But there is another side to citizenship, one less obvious to many Americans. In addition to voluntary activities, citizen participation also takes place through the agreement of individuals to accept fundamental obligations required by society's collective needs. Such participation helps maintain the quality of our society. All this underscores the point that the relationship between the individual and society is not just a two-way political street, but one that is constant, thriving, and dynamic. Two elements crucial to citizenship are the ability to vote and the call to national service.

The Franchise

Of the many forms of voluntary political participation, none is more essential than the opportunity to vote in elections without hindrance or delay. These experiences determine who will serve and make policies for the people. For many, voting is regarded "as the most fundamental right of citizenship since it potentially leads to the expansion of social, civil, and even economic rights."[38] In terms of involvement, voting stands as our closest collective connection to being part of the governmental process; on matters of policy, it is the most direct connection between the governors and the governed. Who votes and who does not vote can have serious consequences for the composition of actions of those in government. In the words of E.E. Schattschneider, "The number of people involved in any conflict determines what happens; every change in the number of participants, every increase or reduction in the number of participants affects the result."[39] Given that voting is a very direct way through which Americans assert their stake in the process, availing that opportunity to as many as possible reinforces the legitimacy of that process.

The issue here is not whether people choose to vote; rather, the issue is whether people who intend to vote and are otherwise qualified are denied this precious right because those in power don't want them to participate. Such discrimination imposed on qualified voters by government representatives produces two outrageous outcomes: abuse of the tools of government and illegitimacy of government itself. American history is full of such miscarriages of justice, particularly with respect to African Americans and Latinos. More significantly, these denials continue to occur in the present day.

Until recently, the Voting Rights Act of 1965 served as the clear basis of guaranteeing the right to vote in the United States. That this act was even necessary signified the failure of the 15th Amendment, which declares in Section 1 that "the right of citizens of the United States to vote shall not be denied or abridged by the United States or by any State on account of race, color, or previous condition of servitude." Nevertheless, those rights were denied.

The Voting Rights Act came about because of persistent and widespread instances of organized white resistance, particularly against African American voters largely in the South, although sometimes in other areas as well. Subsequently supported by an activist Department of Justice and a litany of U.S. Supreme Court decisions relying upon the 15th Amendment as well as other constitutional guarantees, the 1965 legislation responded to the repeated disfranchisement perpetrated by state and local government leaders. In a clear and forthright manner, the new legislation paved the way for all eligible citizens to register and participate in the electoral process. Of particular importance was Section 5, which required nine southern states and dozens of cities and counties throughout the nation to obtain approval, or preclearance, from the U.S. Department of Justice before making any changes in voting rules or procedures.

Conditions changed dramatically in 2013 when the U.S. Supreme Court ruled by a slim 5–4 margin that Section 5 no longer reflected current conditions of racial discrimination. The majority made its decision because of its determination that Section 4, which set the criteria for preclearance states and localities, was demographically out of date. Writing for the majority, Chief Justice John Roberts Jr. declared that the Voting Rights Act was "based on 40-year-old facts that have no logical relationship to the present day,"[40] this even though Congress had reauthorized the legislation in 2006 by an overwhelming vote.

Left to their own devices, several states and cities immediately enacted legislation changing the conditions of voting as well as registration requirements for would-be voters. Within months of the ruling, nine states, including the four southern states of Arkansas, Tennessee, North Carolina, and Virginia, passed more restrictive laws that reduced the number of early voting days. North Carolina and Virginia also passed laws that increased the difficulty of voter registration along with Ohio, Kansas, and Arizona. These states focused on identification documents such as birth certificates, even though many older voters had long lost sight of such materials.

In all of these states, Republican-dominated legislatures passed the new laws and presented them as efforts to eliminate voter fraud despite the lack of any widespread evidence. In fact, once the inflammatory claims are examined, it turns out that voter fraud is extremely rare.[41] Nevertheless, the new laws have discouraged registration and voter turnout, particularly among African Americans.

Consider the uneven impact of North Carolina's Voter Information Verification Act, enacted shortly after the *Shelby* decision. The major components of the legislation eased registration for those over 70 (predominantly whites), reduced the early voting period (affecting those predominantly African American), and eliminated early registration of 16- and 17-years-olds (also predominantly African Americans). As a result, political scientists Daniel C. Heron and Michael Smith conclude that the new state law "will have disparate effects on black voters in North Carolina."[42] Clearly, those Americans already on the periphery of engagement now have yet another challenge to their imperiled citizenship.

The problems posed by the *Shelby* case can be corrected by congressional legislation, which, the U.S. Supreme Court majority wrote, would be acceptable assuming the use of more recent demographic data and updated criteria. Of course, given the tremendous partisan polarization that has beset the Congress in recent years, such action is highly unlikely. Still, if African Americans and other minorities in America are to have the same opportunities as others, Congress must act. Without equal opportunities to vote or participate in any other forms of political expression, excluded voters are marginalized, and that has to affect their feelings toward citizen engagement. Absent legislative action, congressional obstructionists must bear the responsibility for minimizing the citizenship value of fellow Americans, who, because of their color or ethnicity, remain second-class citizens. There is no room for such exclusion in 21st-century America.

Mandatory National Service

Along with rights, citizenship includes responsibilities to one's country and fellow citizens. Obeying the laws, paying our taxes, and waiting our turn in line are obvious everyday examples of citizenship. Yet, there is more. In his description of what it means to be a citizen, Peter Block writes: "A citizen is one who is willing to be accountable for and committed to the well-being of the whole."[43] The sense of belonging comes as a result of what we gain from as well as what we contribute to society, a compelling social synergy of sorts. To the extent that we share the benefits of citizenship, it follows that we should share support of protecting our citizenship.

No foundation for society is more imperative than mandatory national service, a commitment to the public good by all citizens. With national service, everyone has a part in contributing to the benefit of society. Such commitments could take place in a variety of venues and circumstances, including the military, forest protection, teaching assistance, medical support, and policing assistance, to name a few categories. Given the high levels of alienation and unequal treatment that exist in the United States, universal service can go a long way toward leveling the nation's terribly skewed playing field. On this topic, Adam Garfinkle writes, "We need to recreate a culture of national service that will have long-lasting benefits for civic participation that will frontload some equity for those young Americans who don't experience equality of opportunity, and that, above all, will refurbish our country's depleted stock of social capital."[44] Assuming participation by virtually everyone, this activity would provide a shared bond for all Americans as well as a welcome act of patriotism.

The concept of universal service as American public policy has emerged in various forms from time to time, but usually in a diluted, half-hearted fashion. When Bill Clinton pursued the presidency in 1992, he proposed a program where students could borrow money from the federal government and pay back their loans through community service for a year or two. After Clinton's election, Congress passed legislation that emerged as AmeriCorps, a program where individuals could work in nonprofits and other community organizations and then receive education stipends.[45] Approximately 80,000 young Americans ages 18–24 participate in the 11-month program each year. Peace Corps, an earlier iteration of national service originally proposed by President John F. Kennedy in 1960, enrolls 7,200 people annually to serve for 27 months in other countries on projects ranging from agricultural assistance to community health programs to classroom teaching in the language of the native country's students.

AmeriCorps and Peace Corps provide the basis of a contributory framework, but their successes are far from the expanse of mandatory national service. Building on the male military conscription programs of the past, a mandatory program would include required service for everyone right out of high school or of high school graduation age for those who do not complete high school. University students could obtain deferments until graduation or such time they completed their education, when they too would be required to participate in serving their country. Program enrollees would receive a modest stipend during their service designed to provide them with enough compensation for room and board. At the end of the service period, they would be given an additional lump sum. The money could be directed in whatever capacity they wished, whether it be for university tuition, new 21st-century job training skills, creation of a business, savings for a down payment on a home, or any other use. Plain and simple, the idea behind mandatory national service is for everyone to contribute to the well-being of their nation, regardless of their social, economic, or political standing.

National service works for participants and society as a powerful bonding agent. Upon their return from service, participants are much more engaged with society than their counterparts. Studies show that they are more likely to pursue jobs in the public sector, more committed to community involvement, and more likely to go on to obtain university educations.[46] In short, these people are energized with the tools to be more involved in and part of society. They are civically engaged.

National service is already the law of the land in many countries, although the forms of participation, circumstances, and conditions vary greatly. For example, Israel requires compulsory service to military conscription irrespective of gender. Nigeria obliges university students to serve in schools for a period after graduation. Mexico mandates newly trained physicians to provide services in disadvantaged communities. These and other examples are all good first steps, but they don't go far enough. We need a program that incorporates all Americans rather than self-selected

Americans in certain fields. With universal service, everyone would play a role in improving American society.

To be sure, the idea of universal national service has its detractors. Arguments against the concept tend to focus on philosophical differences and expense. Those philosophically opposed resent the idea of compulsory participation. People shouldn't have to do what they don't want to do, the argument goes, especially in a free society. Yet the fact remains that we already have a litany of compulsory participation in America, ranging from the requirement to placing a stamp on an envelope to stopping at a red light to paying income taxes and various other assessments. No one can opt out of those requirements without suffering a penalty. For most of the 20th century and until fairly recently, we had the draft, an obligation that all males sign up for and participate in military service. Other than conscientious objectors, no one could say, "I'll pass." And even those who qualified as conscientious objectors were assigned to alternative forms of public service to fulfill their national obligation. With so many different opportunities and venues to serve, participants could tailor their service to potential careers downstream, simultaneously providing value for themselves and society. Given America's needs and the wealth of talent available, mandatory national service is a collective experience and opportunity long overdue. Rather than cause damage to the meaning of a free society, mandatory national service preserves the free society by citizens making badly needed contributions to important areas of need.

With respect to cost, universal service would become a national budget item. On the surface, the cost seems high. For example, one 2003 study estimates the support expense at between $20,000 and $30,000 per participant, or about $120 billion per year.[47] Allowing for inflation, that cost in 2015 might be in the neighborhood of $180 billion. That may seem substantial, given that it would amount to 5 percent of the national budget. Nevertheless, the return on investment would be incalculable in terms of benefits provided to society and the individual pride accrued from serving one's country. It would also provide a useful job training framework leading to future employment.

In recent years, increasing numbers of public schools have added community service programs as integral components of the education curriculum. Known as experiential education, these programs connect students with community needs. Through these programs, students see firsthand the value and benefits of their contributions to society, whether picking up litter or setting up food collection programs for the poor in the community, or studying issues and recommending changes to policy makers. For some, this activity seems intrusive. Yet, when parents sued a school district on the grounds that experiential education constituted "involuntary servitude," the U.S. Supreme Court ultimately decided that schools have the right to include these requirements as part of their curricula.[48] The stage is set for the next step. Mandatory national service is a concept whose time has come.

SUBSTANTIVE TAX REFORM

The U.S. tax system is a fiscal nightmare fraught with more prospects for avoiding taxes than for paying taxes. In 2013, the cost of all tax breaks amounted to $1.18 trillion, easily exceeding the deficit of $702 billion. Tax breaks are anything but even in terms of their beneficiaries. Those individuals with wealth benefit from various write-offs and deductions that allow them to avoid paying the tax percentages originally attached to their income levels prior to their perks. Likewise, corporations are allowed to profit from countless deductions and exemptions, while storing vast amounts of cash overseas as a means of escaping their true liabilities at home. While most of these advantages accrue to the few and powerful, the middle class of individual income earners pays its share and more as the national government struggles to accrue revenues.

Revenue Objectives

Every tax reform proposal is predicated upon objectives. In recent years, most proposals have focused on either reducing overall revenues as a means to reducing the size of the federal government or making changes "revenue neutral," so that increases in some categories would be offset by decreases in others. We need to be clear here. The proposals below are not intended to reduce the size of government or leave overall budgets the way they are. Rather, they are intended to increase the size of government to carry out important, yet underfunded policies such as funding our decaying infrastructure, providing first-class education, repairing a weak social welfare safety net, and creating well-paying 21st-century employment opportunities.

This relates to our second objective: redistribution of resources. As chronicled elsewhere in this volume, the differences between those at the bottom and those at the top have increased dramatically over the past few decades. The well-to-do have done very well, thank you, showing little interest in taking their workers with them, whether through eliminated pensions, salaries that have not kept up with inflation, or an increasing sense of job insecurity. In addition to providing desperately needed government revenues, the proposals below are intended to redistribute resources to those in the middle class and poor who have been left behind.

We must bear in mind that the United States has been operating at a deficit for the past 15 years, as well as most of the past 100 years. The president's proposed budget for fiscal year 2015 narrows that deficit to the lowest amount since the onset of and recovery from the Great Recession. It estimates revenues of $3.34 trillion and expenditures of $3.90 trillion.[49] That's a deficit of $560 billion. The changes proposed below will vastly reduce that deficit, allowing the government to greatly reduce interest payments on the annual deficit, estimated at $194 billion in 2014.[50] Between added revenues and reduced interest, the federal government would have more funds to meet the needs discussed above.

Personal Income Taxes

On the surface, the United States operates with a graduated personal income tax. Under this taxation system, the more one earns, the higher percentage he or she pays, up to 39.6 percent of his or her adjusted gross annual income. Of course, exactly what types of income are adjusted and how are problematic issues. We know this much: whatever is adjusted is adjusted down because of numerous exemption categories that apply disproportionately to the wealthy. Therefore, we need to examine the elimination of the major loopholes that provide tremendous benefits for the very few at the expense of the many.

Some exemptions, such as the exclusion of employer-paid health insurance, home mortgage interest, and child care credits, help a wide swath of society, but other exemptions are almost exclusively tailored for those with the greatest assets.[51] Below we focus on the elimination of three major tax loopholes for the ultra-rich: artificially low tax rates for income from stocks, disproportionately low tax rates, and partially applied estate taxes. By changing the rates on three taxes, the U.S. government would collect about $300 billion annually in additional revenue, with virtually no harm to the wealthy taxpayers footing the bill.

Capital Gains

Capital gains from the sale of stock investments accrue almost exclusively to the wealthy; in fact, the top 1 percent of all wage earners command two-thirds of long-term capital gains income.[52] That makes sense, given that those with more discretionary income have the means to invest it. According to the Center on Budget and Policy Priorities, the richest 1 percent of Americans receive 71 percent of all capital gains.[53] As of 2013, the tax is no more than 20 percent, regardless of one's income tax bracket. It wasn't always that way. In fact, in 1986, President Ronald Reagan signed legislation that established capital gains tax at the same tax rate of other earned income. Subsequently, the tax was reduced over the next two decades to as low as 15 percent under President George W. Bush along with across-the-board income tax cuts passed in 2001 and 2003.

In 2012, President Obama and Congress agreed to modest budget reforms, which included raising the capital gains tax to the current 20 percent maximum level. But that's nowhere close to what it needs to be, given the vast wealth of those who pay it. According to a 2013 report by the Congressional Budget Office, simply taxing capital gains income at the rate of ordinary income would bring in an additional $161 billion to the U.S. Treasury each year.[54] This effort would go a long way toward rectifying undertaxed incomes.

Income Tax Rates

Over the past half century, individual federal income tax rates have changed dramatically, particularly with respect to the ultra-rich. In 1960, the tax rate for the top 0.01 percent of income earners was 91 percent. By 2004, the rate was 35 percent, largely due to the Bush tax cuts. Meanwhile, the share of annual earnings enjoyed by this very small group soared from 2.5 percent of the total U.S. income pie in the 1960s to more than 9 percent by 2000.[55] As of 2010, the top 1 percent of Americans had 17 percent of all income.[56] The differences seem to grow with every year and every generation.

The Obama administration and Congress put a small dent in the chasm with the passage of the American Taxpayer Relief Act on January 2, 2013.

Under the terms of this legislation, the Bush tax cuts of 2001 and 2003, which cost the government $1.8 trillion in revenue over the next decade, were maintained for all but the wealthiest taxpayers. Those earning $400,000 (or $450,000 for married couples) would see their maximum tax rates rise to 39.6 percent from 35 percent. Only 2 percent of all Americans fall into this income category. The net gain from these changes is expected to bring in an additional $600 billion over the next decade, offsetting only one-third of the revenue loss sustained from the Bush tax cuts.

Clearly, the Taxpayer Relief Act lives up to its promise; that is, it allows Americans, particularly wealthy Americans, to enjoy relief from paying taxes befitting of their incomes. Some Americans want to break this cycle, rather than massage it. In 2013, Democratic Representative Jan Schakowsky introduced legislation that faced the inequality issue head on. She proposed a 45 percent tax rate for people with annual incomes between $1 million and $10 million, 46 percent for those earning between $10 million and $100 million, 48 percent for those with annual incomes between $100 million and $1 billion, and 49 percent for those earning more than $1 billion. Her office estimated that this change would add about $80 billion annually to the treasury over a 10-year period. While the percentages are higher than the highest percentages today, the dollar amounts of income are substantial. Nevertheless, Congress hasn't moved on this approach.

Estate Taxes

The federal estate tax is a levy attached to the estate of a deceased person. The tax has two components: an exemption, the amount that is forgiven by the government before the estate tax kicks in, and a percentage of the value of the estate. These two elements have been consistently readjusted by Congress over the past two decades, with exemption amounts as low as $675,000 and tax rates as high as 55 percent. The last change occurred with the Taxpayer Relief Act, which set the exemption at $5 million, with annual inflation adjustments, and a tax of 40 percent after the first $5 million. As of 2014, the exemption is $5,340,000. Given the high exemption rate, few Americans pay any federal estate tax. In fact, one study estimates that only 0.14 percent of Americans pay any federal tax; that means 99.86 percent do not.[57]

President Obama reignited discussion of the estate tax in his FY 2015 federal budget proposal by recommending that the estate tax revert to the

248 • *Reviving Citizen Engagement*

2009 rules that were part of the Bush tax cuts. These changes would set the exemption at $3.5 million and a tax rate of 45 percent, with no inflation index. In addition, the proposal would include a 10 percent surtax on estates valued at more than $500 million. As with other tax increase recommendations, the estate tax changes would affect only the richest Americans. Back in 2009, only 0.3 percent of all deaths were impacted by this tax liability. A slightly higher number of individuals would be affected by the lower exemption bar, but the benefits would be worth the change. The Department of the Treasury estimates that the Obama proposal would bring in an additional $13 billion annually over the next decade.

Corporate Taxes

As noted in Chapter 8, with the benefits of loopholes, write-offs and shelters, the official corporate tax maximum rate of 35 percent means little in 21st-century America. Add to these schemes the ability to store trillions off-shore and most corporations pay nowhere near the maximum. Perhaps this explains how, according to one recent study, more than half of all U.S. corporations paid no corporate taxes between 2004 and 2010.[58] It also explains that while the effective tax rates of corporation are at a 40-year low,[59] corporate profits are at a 50-year high.[60]

It's time to call the bluff of corporations whose leaders complain about excessively high tax rates that force them to keep incomes offshore. The corporate tax rate should be lowered. In turn, the most egregious loopholes must be eliminated. In the end, the results should be tailored so that corporations finally pay their fair share. If corporations and their employees enjoy the benefits of American society in the forms of public education, public safety, and all the elements of infrastructure, they need to pony up to pay for them just like the rest of us. The recommendations below include ending accelerated depreciation and ending the ability of corporations to defer taxes on overseas profits.

Accelerated Depreciation

Corporations are able to reduce their profits by accelerating the depreciation of expenses such as the purchase of equipment, supplies, or buildings. This, in turn, reduces the effective tax rate. The idea behind this tactic is that assets are depreciated long before they wear out, thereby artificially lowering the tax rate by 4 to 15 percent, depending upon the type of purchase. It also frees businesses to turn around and purchase new equipment, starting the accelerated depreciation process again.

Accelerated depreciation comes at a massive cost in the form of lost government revenucs. In 2012, for example, the Office of the Management of the Budget estimated that accelerated depreciation cost the treasury $70 billion, and projected additional costs of $274 billion between 2012 and 2017, or an average of $55 billion annually. Removing this benefit will help reduce the deficit and provide more funds for badly needed domestic projects.

Deferred U.S. Taxes on Offshore Profits

Many American companies have established subsidiaries abroad for conducting business. That's because under current U.S. law, American corporations are permitted to defer taxes on the profits from their subsidiaries outside the United States until they bring their gains back to the United States. This corporate gimmick affects more than tax avoidance. When companies move their operations abroad, they hire employees there, denying economic growth at home. The organization of overseas subsidiaries is based on the myth that U.S. corporations pay exorbitantly high tax rates at home, which we know is not the case. It's just that they can make even more abroad by paying lower taxes. Between 1965 and 2009, corporate profits stemming from overseas revenues soared from 7 percent to 38 percent, thanks to their exceedingly low taxes.

As of 2013, U.S. corporations had nearly $2 trillion in profits stored in other countries, an amount double that of 2008.[61] As a result of corporations parking profits abroad, the U.S. government loses nearly $60 billion annually in taxes because of artificial conditions.[62] This problem can be solved by taxing U.S. corporations on their profits wherever they occur. Likewise, losses abroad should be permitted as well. It's simply a matter of providing an even playing field in an era of globalization.

Recently, American corporations have adopted a new strategy for avoiding U.S. tax obligations. Some have resorted to merging with foreign companies that do business in the same sector. Once under the merged corporate roof, the new multinational moves its headquarters to the country of the subsidiary. The process, known as inversion, places the company under the tax rules of its new host country, and allows the company to permanently shield tax obligations from the United States.[63] Unfortunately, this end-around play is developing momentum. Between 2008 and 2013, about two dozen major U.S. corporations used the merger process to shift their home to countries with lower taxes, about the same number as the previous quarter century. Inversion can be stopped if the U.S. government taxes once American companies as American companies, regardless of where they shift their headquarters.

Even so, inversion was controlled in part due to a 2004 federal rule that required the foreign partner to be worth at least 20 percent of the overall merged value. But the inversion frenzy has soared nonetheless in the name of U.S. companies saving taxes by relocating their headquarters abroad. Mergers with foreign partners in low-tax countries between 2011 and 2014 represented $800 billion worth of business and the long-term losses of billions of dollars in federal taxes annually.[64] In one stellar example, the consolidation of Medtronic, an American company, with Covidien, an Irish company, saved Medtronic $20 billion in what would have been U.S. taxable income.[65] With the exit floodgates apparently unencumbered, one analyst noted that the only question was "what the U.S. government is going to do about this, and how quickly they're going to shut the loophole down."[66] He had little to worry about. In 2014, several congressional bills proposed increasing the foreign value to at least 50 percent, leading some to wonder whether the new corporate tax escape would be shut down. As with just about everything else substantive that year, the proposed legislation died.

The lesson here is clear: much of the successes for American corporations occur simply from their ability to avoid taxes by storing profits abroad or relocating headquarters in other countries. These unpatriotic antics must be stopped. If Congress decides to tax all corporate profits regardless of wherever they are accrued, the U.S. Treasury will receive an additional $60 billion annually.

Corporate Taxes and Jobs

Through their lobbyists and other spokespersons, American corporations have insisted that high taxation rates keep them from hiring more employees. Here we must remind ourselves of the huge differences between official tax rates and effective tax rates; the average corporate tax bite is about one-third of the official rate. In fact, evidence seems to suggest findings to the contrary.

A study of 60 large and profitable U.S. Fortune 500 corporations between 2008 and 2012 found that 22 of the 30 corporations with the highest tax percentages created almost 200,000 jobs during the 4-year period. Meanwhile, of the 30 corporations with the lowest taxes, half added jobs, while half shed jobs. Collectively, however, these businesses dropped more than 50,000 jobs during the same period.[67] In fact, there is no correlation between tax rates and the ability to add new jobs.

Targeted Changes

Combined, the recommendations above would add an average of approximately $530 billion annually to the U.S. Treasury over the next decade. That amounts to less than half of all the tax loopholes and exemptions currently in place. These changes alone would virtually wipe out the 2015 national budget deficit. Many other personal and corporate income changes could be made, but the idea is not to rid the rich and successful corporations of their wealth; rather, these proposals are designed to temper the most extreme examples of wealth and tax loophole beneficiaries without causing any lifestyle changes of those who have gained such accomplishments. As such, these added revenues can go a long way toward strengthening the tattered social fabric that has left so many people outside the system helplessly looking in.

A Boost for the Economy, Not a Penalty

Some will resent the effort to garner additional taxes as an attempt to move the United States to a system closer to the high-tax environments of European countries. A nudge maybe, but that's about it. Let's remember that in terms of overall revenues, American taxes are much lower than those in European nations. The same goes for spending practices, and given the severe discontinuities in American society, it's clear that the present combination of low taxes and low expenditures benefits the few to the harm of the many.

Increased revenues will allow the nation to reinvest in infrastructure, particularly labor-intensive capital projects like dams, bridges, roads, schools, power grids, and public hospitals. Additional revenues can also be dedicated to job training and research and development, thereby allowing both the economy to employ more people and the United States to return to its leadership role in innovation. And with more people back at work, fewer people will be dependent on welfare programs. Redistribution can do a lot of good for American society.

There's another point: American consumers represent 70 percent of the U.S. economy. Without purchasing power for Americans, U.S. corporate success will fail in the long term. It's a stretch to believe that the loss in purchasing power here will be made up by the rest of the world, given the growing global differences between the haves and the have-nots. Therefore, it's in the strategic interest of big business to go along with some added revenue.

POLICIES REPOSITIONED MORE FOR THE WHOLE THAN THE PARTS

Contemporary American society is out of balance. From the earliest days of a child's life to adulthood, the political, social, and economic environments separate the few from the many. Segregated communities and different roads to education are early indicators of the future. Workplace opportunities are skewed, with the best-educated and nonminority white males having the best opportunities of rising to the top.

Increasing numbers of minorities relative to whites have left the dominant class trying to protect the status quo with little choice other than to rig the voting system by finding ways to dilute their quantities. And rather than respect their obligations to train their workers, compensate their employees with fair wages, and pay their fair share of taxes, American corporations have become sovereign entities. It's not a pretty picture, but it's the picture of a modern America where the few take care of themselves and the rest are left to their own devices.

Governments haven't helped. Rather than confront some of our thorniest problems, national and state elected officials have looked away. They have found it easier to abide by the status quo than ruffle feathers. The actions and inactions of public leaders may pave the way for short-term gains, but massive long-term losses for society loom.

Some have viewed these developments as the result of individual choice, rather than treatment meted out by an unfair system. Thus, in his *Coming Apart*, Charles Murray writes that success and happiness have always depended on four core values: marriage, industriousness, honesty, and religiosity. He argues that Americans who adhere to these values will do just fine, thank you. By not so doing, society falls apart.[68] In other words, it's the individual who has control of his or her life chances and destiny.

The data discussed throughout this volume prove otherwise. Opportunities to succeed vary dramatically among Americans. There are an awful lot of hardworking, industrious people whose futures are limited because of lousy educations, questioned social values, and institutional discrimination. Moreover, differences have grown over time and now are spinning out of control. No wonder so many feel removed from society and without loyalty to the political system; their opportunities are predetermined. No wonder America is adrift, slowly losing its place in the world forum. While other countries are increasing their social, economic, and infrastructure commitments to be more competitive in the future, we are coasting on our past successes. That's not a healthy long-term plan.

It's time to start back at square one. It's time to deal with the root causes of our disaggregated society. It's time to give all citizens, not just the privileged, reasons for being connected to our country. It's time for every American to take responsibility. Most of all, it's time for government institutions and the private sector to provide overdue actions along with words.

For people to be engaged citizens, they must feel that they have a real stake in society. That stake doesn't come from empty rhetoric; rather, it comes from substantive policies that restructure the system and offer opportunities to all. Only then will Americans once again appreciate the value and power of their citizenship.

ENDNOTES

1. Derek Heater, *What Is Citizenship?* Maldon, MA: Polity Press, 1999, p. 84.
2. William Hudson, *American Democracy in Peril: Eight Challenges to America's Future*, 7th ed., Thousand Oaks, CA: CQ Press, 2013, pp. 272–273.
3. John Dewey, *Democracy and Education*, Middlesex, England, 2007, p. 9, originally published in 1916 by Macmillan and Company, New York.
4. Diane Ravitch, *Reign of Terror*, New York: Alfred A Knopf, 2013, p. 3.
5. Sidney Verba, Kay Lehman Schlozman, and Henry E. Brady, *Voice and Equality: Civic Voluntarism in American Politics*, Cambridge, MA: Harvard University Press, 1995, p. 350.
6. "PISA 2012 Results in Focus: What 15-Year-Olds Know and What They Can Do with What They Know," p. 21, http://www.oecd.org/pisa/keyfindings/pisa-2012-results-overview.pdf.
7. See Programme for International Student Assessment, 2012 Results, p. 5, http://www.oecd.org/pisa/keyfindings/pisa-2012-results.htm and "Extended School Day and Year Are under Review across the Country," *Heartlander*, February 1, 2008, http://news.heartland.org/print/22698.
8. "Longer School Days Weighed; New Study Shows Tests Jump with More Learning Time," *Newbury News*, December 3, 2007, http://www.newburyportnews.com/local/x845833361/Longer-school-days-weighed-New-study-shows-test-scores-jump-with-more-learning-time.
9. "The STEM Crisis," National Science + Math Initiative, http://www.nms.org/Education/TheSTEMCrisis.aspx.

10. "The Competition That Really Matters," Center for American Progress, Washington, DC, 2012, p. 19.

11. http://www.oecd.org/pisa/.

12. See Martin Carnoy and Richard Rothstein, "What Do International Tests Really Show about U.S. Student Performance?" Economic Policy Institute, Washington, DC, January 28, 2013.

13. Dave E. Marcotte and Benjamin Hansen, "Time for School?" *EducationNext*, Winter 2010, vol. 10, no. 1, http://educationnext.org/time-for-school/.

14. "Are Students Prepared for a Global Society?" American Council on the Teaching of Foreign Languages, Washington, DC, p. 1, http://www.actfl.org/sites/default/files/pdfs/ReportSummary2011.pdf.

15. "America's Foreign Language Deficit," *Forbes*, August 27, 2012, http://www.forbes.com/sites/collegeprose/2012/08/27/americas-foreign-language-deficit/print/.

16. "Issue Briefing: Americans and Language," U.S. English Foundation, Washington, DC, 2007, p. 4, http://usefoundation.org/userdata/file/Publications/amlangpart3.pdf.

17. "Foreign Language Learning Statistics," September 2012, http://epp.eurostat.ec.europa.eu/statistics_explained/index.php/Foreign_language_learning_statistics.

18. Dominika Kmiecik-Micali, "What Languages Do the Chinese Speak? Language Education in China," July 27, 2013, http://foreignlanguagesreview.com/language-education-in-china/.

19. Satoshi Hasimoto, "Foreign Language Education in Japan: A Japanese Perspective," paper presented at Policy Forum: Global Approaches to Plurillingual Education, June 28–29, 2004, Council of Europe, Strasburg, France.

20. Ruth Mantell, "Tongue Tied," *MarketWatch*, September 16, 2007, http://www.marketwatch.com/story/learning-a-second-language-can-boost-your-career-but-its-costly.

21. "24/7 Wall Street: Countries with the Most Immigrants," *USA Today*, September 28, 2013, http://www.usatoday.com/story/money/business/2013/09/28/countries-with-most-immigrants/2886783/.

22. See Ellen Bialystok, "Reshaping the Mind: The Benefits of Bilingualism," *Canadian Journal of Experimental Psychology*, 65(4), 232, 2011.

23. JoeyLynn Selling, "The Social and Academic Benefits of Second-Language Learning at the Elementary Education Level," master's thesis, Northern Michigan University, November 27, 2011, p. 34.

24. April Linton, "Learning in Two Languages: Spanish-English Immersion in U.S. Public Schools," Working Paper 106, Center for Comparative Immigration Studies, University of California, San Diego, November 2004, p. 66.

25. See Tamar Jacoby, "Vocational Education 2.0: Employers Hold the Key to Better Career Training," Civic Report 83, Manhattan Institute for Policy Research, November 2013, p. 2.

26. "Fiscal Year (Fy) 2014 Appropriations for Job Training and Education," National Skills Coalition, http://www.nationalskillscoalition.org/federal-policies/federal-funding/federal-funding-documents/2013_01_16-fy-2014-approps.pdf.

27. See "Class of 2013: Young Graduates Still Face Grim Job Prospects," Economic Policy Institute, Washington, DC, April 10, 2013, http://www.epi.org/publication/class-of-2013-graduates-job-prospects/.

28. "Obama's 2015 Budget: More Early Education Funds, New Race to the Top," *U.S. News*, March 14, 2014, http://www.usnews.com/news/articles/2014/03/04/obamas-2015-budget-more-early-education-funds-new-race-to-the-top.

29. See Gabriel A. Almond and Sidney, *Civic Culture*, Boston: Little, Brown and Company, 1965, p. 32.

30. John J. Patrick, "Introduction to Education for Civic Engagement in Democracy," in *Education for Civic Engagement in Democracy: Service Learning and Other Promising Practices*, edited by Sheilah Mann and John J. Patrick, St. Paul, MN: Education Resources Information Center, 2000, p. 3.

31. Stephen Earl Bennett, "Political Apathy and Avoidance of News Media among Generations X and Y: America's Continuing Problem," in *Education for Civic Engagement in Democracy*, ibid., p. 23.

32. Peter A. Benoliel, "Education to What End—Vocation or Virtue"? in *Civic Education and the Future of American Citizenship*, edited by Elizabeth Kaufer Busch and Jonathan W. White, Lantham, MD: Lexington Books, 2013, p. 131.

33. For more on civic learning, see my *Public Policymaking in a Democratic Society: A Guide to Civic Engagement*, 2nd ed., Armonk, NY: M.E. Sharpe Publisher, pp. 179–187.

34. Robert D. Putnam, *Bowling Alone*, New York: Simon & Schuster, 2000, p. 405.

35. Jonathan Gould, ed., "Guardian of Democracy: The Civic Mission of Schools," Leonore Annenberg Institute for Civics, University of Pennsylvania, Philadelphia, 2013, p. 6.

36. See "Eight Questions on Teacher Recruitment and Retention," Education Commission of the States, Denver, CO, September 2005.

37. Joydeep Roy, "Compared to Other Countries, U.S. Flunks in Teacher Pay," Economic Policy Institute, April 1, 2008, http://www.epi.org/publication/webfeatures_snapshots_20080402/.

38. Eduardo Bonilla-Silva and Sarah Montoya, "On (Not) Belonging," in *State of White Supremacy: Racism, Governance and the United States*, edited by Moon-Kie Jung, Joao H. Costa Vargas, and Eduardo Bonilla-Silva, Stanford, CA: Stanford University Press, 2011, p. 87.

39. E.E. Schattschneider, *The Semi-Sovereign People*, New York: Holt, Reinhart, and Winston, 1960, p. 2.

40. "Justices Void Oversight of States, Issue at Heart of Voting Rights Act," *New York Times*, June 26, 2013, pp. A1, A16. The case was *Shelby County v. Holder*.

41. For a summary, see Ed Kilgore, "Behind the Myth of Voter Fraud," *Washington Monthly*, July 3, 2012, http://www.washingtonmonthly.com/political-animal-a/2012_07/behind_the_myth_of_voter_fraud038321.php.

42. Daniel C. Heron and Michael Smith, "Race, Shelby County, and the Voter Information Verification Act in North Carolina," unpublished paper, February 14, 2014, p. 44.

43. Peter Block, *Community: The Structure of Belonging*, San Francisco, CA: Barrett-Koehler Publishers, 2008, p. 63.

44. Adam Garfinkle, "Bonds of Citizenship," *Washington Monthly Magazine*, May/June 2013, http://www.washingtonmonthly.com/magazine/may_june_2013/ten_miles_square/bonds_of_citizenship044509.php.

45. For discussion of the Clinton proposal, see Craig A. Rimmerman, *The New Citizenship*, 3rd ed., Boulder, CO: Westview Press, 2005, pp. 124–129.

46. See "Americorps: Changing Lives, Changing America," Corporation for National Community Service, Washington, DC, 2007, http://www.nationalservice.gov/sites/default/files/documents/07_0515_ac_memberimpact.pdf.

47. Bruce Chapman, "A Bad Idea Whose Time Has Passed," in *United We Serve: National Service and the Future of Citizenship*, edited by E.J. Dionne, Kayla Meltzer Drogosz, and Robert E. Litan, Washington, DC: Brookings Institution Press, 2003, pp. 112–113.

48. See Donald J. Eberly and Reuven Gal, *Service without Guns*, lulu.com, 2006, p. 68.

49. For more details see "Fiscal Tear 2015: Budget of the U.S. Government," Executive Office of the President of the United States, Washington, DC, March 4, 2014, http://www.whitehouse.gov/sites/default/files/omb/budget/fy2015/assets/budget.pdf.

50. "Interest Expense on the Debt Outstanding," U.S. Department of the Treasury, Washington, DC, http://treasurydirect.gov/govt/reports/ir/ir_expense.htm.

51. "Tax Breaks Exceed $1 Trillion: Report," *Wall Street Journal*, March 24–25, 2012, p. A2.

52. "Ending the Capital Gains Tax Preference Would Improve Fairness, Raise Revenue, and Simply the Tax Code," Citizens for Tax Justice, September 20, 2013, http://www.ctj.org/pdf/cgdiv2012.pdf.

53. "Chart Book: 10 Things You Need to Know about the Capital Gains Tax," Center on Budget and Policy Priorities, Washington, DC, September 20, 2012, http://www.cbpp.org/cms/?fa=view&id=3798.

54. "CBO Study Shows Tax Breaks Favor the Rich," *The Daily Kos*, May 30, 2013, http://www.dailykos.com/story/2013/05/30/1212662/-CBO-study-shows-tax-breaks-favor-the-rich.

55. Thomas Piketty and Emmanuel Saez, "How Progressive Is the U.S. Federal Tax System? A Historical and International Perspective," *Journal of Economic Perspectives*, 21(1), 13–14, 2007.

56. Lawrence Mishel, Josh Bivens, Elise Gould, and Heidi Shierholz, *The State of Working America*, 12th ed., Ithaca, NY: Cornell University Press, 2012, p. 379.

57. "Myths and Realities about the Estate Tax," Center on Budget and Policy Priorities, Washington, DC, August 29, 2013, http://www.cbpp.org/files/estatetaxmyths.pdf.

58. "U.S. Business Has High Tax Rates but Pays Less," *New York Times*, May 2, 2011, http://www.nytimes.com/2011/05/03/business/economy/03rates.html?_r=0&pagewanted=print.

59. "Reality Check: Effective U.S. Corporate Tax Rate Much Lower than Most Other Developed Nations," *Think Progress*, March 30, 2012, http://thinkprogress.org/economy/2012/03/30/456005/reminder-corporate-taxes-very-low/.

60. Scott Klinger and Katherine McFate, "The Corporate Tax Debate," Center for Effective Government, Washington, DC, December 2013, p. 11.

61. "U.S. Firms Pack Up for Tax Benefits," *Wall Street Journal*, May 12, 2012, pp. B1, B8.

62. "Working Paper on Tax Reform Options," Citizens for Tax Justice, February 4, 2013, http://ctj.org/pdf/workingpapertaxreform.pdf.

63. "U.S. Firms Pack Up for Tax Benefits," op. cit., p. B1.

64. "A Double Punch for Tax 'Inversion Deals," *Wall Street Journal*, August 6, 2014, pp. B1, B7.

65. "Inverse Logic," *The Economist*, June 21, 2014, pp. 62–63.

66. "Inversion Frenzy Rocks Drug Sector," *The Wall Street Journal*, August 21–22, 2014, pp. B1, B4.

67. Scott Klinger and Katherine McFate, op. cit., p. 1.

68. Charles Murray, *Coming Apart*, New York: Cox and Murray Publishers, 2012.

Index